C-1503   CAREER EXAMINATION SERIES

*This is your
PASSBOOK for...*

Supervising Court Officer

*Test Preparation Study Guide
Questions & Answers*

COPYRIGHT NOTICE

This book is SOLELY intended for, is sold ONLY to, and its use is RESTRICTED to individual, bona fide applicants or candidates who qualify by virtue of having seriously filed applications for appropriate license, certificate, professional and/or promotional advancement, higher school matriculation, scholarship, or other legitimate requirements of education and/or governmental authorities.

This book is NOT intended for use, class instruction, tutoring, training, duplication, copying, reprinting, excerption, or adaptation, etc., by:

1) Other publishers
2) Proprietors and/or Instructors of "Coaching" and/or Preparatory Courses
3) Personnel and/or Training Divisions of commercial, industrial, and governmental organizations
4) Schools, colleges, or universities and/or their departments and staffs, including teachers and other personnel
5) Testing Agencies or Bureaus
6) Study groups which seek by the purchase of a single volume to copy and/or duplicate and/or adapt this material for use by the group as a whole without having purchased individual volumes for each of the members of the group
7) Et al.

Such persons would be in violation of appropriate Federal and State statutes.

PROVISION OF LICENSING AGREEMENTS – Recognized educational, commercial, industrial, and governmental institutions and organizations, and others legitimately engaged in educational pursuits, including training, testing, and measurement activities, may address request for a licensing agreement to the copyright owners, who will determine whether, and under what conditions, including fees and charges, the materials in this book may be used them. In other words, a licensing facility exists for the legitimate use of the material in this book on other than an individual basis. However, it is asseverated and affirmed here that the material in this book CANNOT be used without the receipt of the express permission of such a licensing agreement from the Publishers. Inquiries re licensing should be addressed to the company, attention rights and permissions department.

All rights reserved, including the right of reproduction in whole or in part, in any form or by any means, electronic or mechanical, including photocopying, recording, or by any information storage and retrieval system, without permission in writing from the Publisher.

Copyright © 2025 by
National Learning Corporation

212 Michael Drive, Syosset, NY 11791
(516) 921-8888 • www.passbooks.com
E-mail: info@passbooks.com

PASSBOOK® SERIES

THE *PASSBOOK® SERIES* has been created to prepare applicants and candidates for the ultimate academic battlefield – the examination room.

At some time in our lives, each and every one of us may be required to take an examination – for validation, matriculation, admission, qualification, registration, certification, or licensure.

Based on the assumption that every applicant or candidate has met the basic formal educational standards, has taken the required number of courses, and read the necessary texts, the *PASSBOOK® SERIES* furnishes the one special preparation which may assure passing with confidence, instead of failing with insecurity. Examination questions – together with answers – are furnished as the basic vehicle for study so that the mysteries of the examination and its compounding difficulties may be eliminated or diminished by a sure method.

This book is meant to help you pass your examination provided that you qualify and are serious in your objective.

The entire field is reviewed through the huge store of content information which is succinctly presented through a provocative and challenging approach – the question-and-answer method.

A climate of success is established by furnishing the correct answers at the end of each test.

You soon learn to recognize types of questions, forms of questions, and patterns of questioning. You may even begin to anticipate expected outcomes.

You perceive that many questions are repeated or adapted so that you can gain acute insights, which may enable you to score many sure points.

You learn how to confront new questions, or types of questions, and to attack them confidently and work out the correct answers.

You note objectives and emphases, and recognize pitfalls and dangers, so that you may make positive educational adjustments.

Moreover, you are kept fully informed in relation to new concepts, methods, practices, and directions in the field.

You discover that you are actually taking the examination all the time: you are preparing for the examination by "taking" an examination, not by reading extraneous and/or supererogatory textbooks.

In short, this PASSBOOK®, used directedly, should be an important factor in helping you to pass your test.

SUPERVISING COURT OFFICER

DUTIES
Supervising Court Officers are responsible for maintaining order and providing security in court buildings and courtrooms. They work under the direct supervision of court clerks. Supervising Court Officers are peace officers, required to wear uniforms, and may be authorized to carry firearms. Supervising Court Officers execute warrants and make arrests and may coordinate the activities of other court security personnel.

EXAMPLES OF TYPICAL TASKS
Provides security by standing in the courtroom and patrolling the courthouse; guards felons and persons accused of felonies, and may guard individuals accused of lesser crimes while they are in the courtroom and escorts them to and from detention pens; physically restrains unruly individuals; uses established search procedures to assure that no weapons or electronic or photographic equipment are brought into the courtroom; escorts judges, juries, witnesses and prisoners to and from the courtroom; escorts, guards and delivers material to sequestered juries; provides general information to visitors on court premises; checks to ensure that all necessary documents are available prior to court sessions; displays and safeguards exhibits in the courtroom; provides assistance in emergency situations; maintains and updates court records and prepares incident reports; distributes and posts appropriate documents and court records; arrests individuals according to established procedures.

SCOPE OF THE EXAMINATION
The written test will cover knowledge, skills and/or abilities in such areas as:

1. Reading, understanding and interpreting written material;
2. Remembering facts and information;
3. Applying facts and information to given situations;
4. Peace officer knowledge; and
5. Supervision.

HOW TO TAKE A TEST

I. YOU MUST PASS AN EXAMINATION

A. *WHAT EVERY CANDIDATE SHOULD KNOW*

Examination applicants often ask us for help in preparing for the written test. What can I study in advance? What kinds of questions will be asked? How will the test be given? How will the papers be graded?

As an applicant for a civil service examination, you may be wondering about some of these things. Our purpose here is to suggest effective methods of advance study and to describe civil service examinations.

Your chances for success on this examination can be increased if you know how to prepare. Those "pre-examination jitters" can be reduced if you know what to expect. You can even experience an adventure in good citizenship if you know why civil service exams are given.

B. *WHY ARE CIVIL SERVICE EXAMINATIONS GIVEN?*

Civil service examinations are important to you in two ways. As a citizen, you want public jobs filled by employees who know how to do their work. As a job seeker, you want a fair chance to compete for that job on an equal footing with other candidates. The best-known means of accomplishing this two-fold goal is the competitive examination.

Exams are widely publicized throughout the nation. They may be administered for jobs in federal, state, city, municipal, town or village governments or agencies.

Any citizen may apply, with some limitations, such as the age or residence of applicants. Your experience and education may be reviewed to see whether you meet the requirements for the particular examination. When these requirements exist, they are reasonable and applied consistently to all applicants. Thus, a competitive examination may cause you some uneasiness now, but it is your privilege and safeguard.

C. *HOW ARE CIVIL SERVICE EXAMS DEVELOPED?*

Examinations are carefully written by trained technicians who are specialists in the field known as "psychological measurement," in consultation with recognized authorities in the field of work that the test will cover. These experts recommend the subject matter areas or skills to be tested; only those knowledges or skills important to your success on the job are included. The most reliable books and source materials available are used as references. Together, the experts and technicians judge the difficulty level of the questions.

Test technicians know how to phrase questions so that the problem is clearly stated. Their ethics do not permit "trick" or "catch" questions. Questions may have been tried out on sample groups, or subjected to statistical analysis, to determine their usefulness.

Written tests are often used in combination with performance tests, ratings of training and experience, and oral interviews. All of these measures combine to form the best-known means of finding the right person for the right job.

II. HOW TO PASS THE WRITTEN TEST

A. NATURE OF THE EXAMINATION

To prepare intelligently for civil service examinations, you should know how they differ from school examinations you have taken. In school you were assigned certain definite pages to read or subjects to cover. The examination questions were quite detailed and usually emphasized memory. Civil service exams, on the other hand, try to discover your present ability to perform the duties of a position, plus your potentiality to learn these duties. In other words, a civil service exam attempts to predict how successful you will be. Questions cover such a broad area that they cannot be as minute and detailed as school exam questions.

In the public service similar kinds of work, or positions, are grouped together in one "class." This process is known as *position-classification*. All the positions in a class are paid according to the salary range for that class. One class title covers all of these positions, and they are all tested by the same examination.

B. FOUR BASIC STEPS

1) Study the announcement

How, then, can you know what subjects to study? Our best answer is: "Learn as much as possible about the class of positions for which you've applied." The exam will test the knowledge, skills and abilities needed to do the work.

Your most valuable source of information about the position you want is the official exam announcement. This announcement lists the training and experience qualifications. Check these standards and apply only if you come reasonably close to meeting them.

The brief description of the position in the examination announcement offers some clues to the subjects which will be tested. Think about the job itself. Review the duties in your mind. Can you perform them, or are there some in which you are rusty? Fill in the blank spots in your preparation.

Many jurisdictions preview the written test in the exam announcement by including a section called "Knowledge and Abilities Required," "Scope of the Examination," or some similar heading. Here you will find out specifically what fields will be tested.

2) Review your own background

Once you learn in general what the position is all about, and what you need to know to do the work, ask yourself which subjects you already know fairly well and which need improvement. You may wonder whether to concentrate on improving your strong areas or on building some background in your fields of weakness. When the announcement has specified "some knowledge" or "considerable knowledge," or has used adjectives like "beginning principles of..." or "advanced ... methods," you can get a clue as to the number and difficulty of questions to be asked in any given field. More questions, and hence broader coverage, would be included for those subjects which are more important in the work. Now weigh your strengths and weaknesses against the job requirements and prepare accordingly.

3) Determine the level of the position

Another way to tell how intensively you should prepare is to understand the level of the job for which you are applying. Is it the entering level? In other words, is this the position in which beginners in a field of work are hired? Or is it an intermediate or advanced level? Sometimes this is indicated by such words as "Junior" or "Senior" in the class title. Other jurisdictions use Roman numerals to designate the level – Clerk I, Clerk II, for example. The word "Supervisor" sometimes appears in the title. If the level is not indicated by the title, check the description of duties. Will you be working under very close supervision, or will you have responsibility for independent decisions in this work?

4) Choose appropriate study materials

Now that you know the subjects to be examined and the relative amount of each subject to be covered, you can choose suitable study materials. For beginning level jobs, or even advanced ones, if you have a pronounced weakness in some aspect of your training, read a modern, standard textbook in that field. Be sure it is up to date and has general coverage. Such books are normally available at your library, and the librarian will be glad to help you locate one. For entry-level positions, questions of appropriate difficulty are chosen – neither highly advanced questions, nor those too simple. Such questions require careful thought but not advanced training.

If the position for which you are applying is technical or advanced, you will read more advanced, specialized material. If you are already familiar with the basic principles of your field, elementary textbooks would waste your time. Concentrate on advanced textbooks and technical periodicals. Think through the concepts and review difficult problems in your field.

These are all general sources. You can get more ideas on your own initiative, following these leads. For example, training manuals and publications of the government agency which employs workers in your field can be useful, particularly for technical and professional positions. A letter or visit to the government department involved may result in more specific study suggestions, and certainly will provide you with a more definite idea of the exact nature of the position you are seeking.

III. KINDS OF TESTS

Tests are used for purposes other than measuring knowledge and ability to perform specified duties. For some positions, it is equally important to test ability to make adjustments to new situations or to profit from training. In others, basic mental abilities not dependent on information are essential. Questions which test these things may not appear as pertinent to the duties of the position as those which test for knowledge and information. Yet they are often highly important parts of a fair examination. For very general questions, it is almost impossible to help you direct your study efforts. What we can do is to point out some of the more common of these general abilities needed in public service positions and describe some typical questions.

1) General information

Broad, general information has been found useful for predicting job success in some kinds of work. This is tested in a variety of ways, from vocabulary lists to questions about current events. Basic background in some field of work, such as sociology or economics, may be sampled in a group of questions. Often these are principles which have become familiar to most persons through exposure rather than through formal training. It is difficult to advise you how to study for these questions; being alert to the world around you is our best suggestion.

2) Verbal ability

An example of an ability needed in many positions is verbal or language ability. Verbal ability is, in brief, the ability to use and understand words. Vocabulary and grammar tests are typical measures of this ability. Reading comprehension or paragraph interpretation questions are common in many kinds of civil service tests. You are given a paragraph of written material and asked to find its central meaning.

3) Numerical ability

Number skills can be tested by the familiar arithmetic problem, by checking paired lists of numbers to see which are alike and which are different, or by interpreting charts and graphs. In the latter test, a graph may be printed in the test booklet which you are asked to use as the basis for answering questions.

4) Observation

A popular test for law-enforcement positions is the observation test. A picture is shown to you for several minutes, then taken away. Questions about the picture test your ability to observe both details and larger elements.

5) Following directions

In many positions in the public service, the employee must be able to carry out written instructions dependably and accurately. You may be given a chart with several columns, each column listing a variety of information. The questions require you to carry out directions involving the information given in the chart.

6) Skills and aptitudes

Performance tests effectively measure some manual skills and aptitudes. When the skill is one in which you are trained, such as typing or shorthand, you can practice. These tests are often very much like those given in business school or high school courses. For many of the other skills and aptitudes, however, no short-time preparation can be made. Skills and abilities natural to you or that you have developed throughout your lifetime are being tested.

Many of the general questions just described provide all the data needed to answer the questions and ask you to use your reasoning ability to find the answers. Your best preparation for these tests, as well as for tests of facts and ideas, is to be at your physical and mental best. You, no doubt, have your own methods of getting into an exam-taking mood and keeping "in shape." The next section lists some ideas on this subject.

IV. KINDS OF QUESTIONS

Only rarely is the "essay" question, which you answer in narrative form, used in civil service tests. Civil service tests are usually of the short-answer type. Full instructions for answering these questions will be given to you at the examination. But in case this is your first experience with short-answer questions and separate answer sheets, here is what you need to know:

1) Multiple-choice Questions

Most popular of the short-answer questions is the "multiple choice" or "best answer" question. It can be used, for example, to test for factual knowledge, ability to solve problems or judgment in meeting situations found at work.

A multiple-choice question is normally one of three types—
- It can begin with an incomplete statement followed by several possible endings. You are to find the one ending which *best* completes the statement, although some of the others may not be entirely wrong.
- It can also be a complete statement in the form of a question which is answered by choosing one of the statements listed.

- It can be in the form of a problem – again you select the best answer.

Here is an example of a multiple-choice question with a discussion which should give you some clues as to the method for choosing the right answer:

When an employee has a complaint about his assignment, the action which will *best* help him overcome his difficulty is to
  A. discuss his difficulty with his coworkers
  B. take the problem to the head of the organization
  C. take the problem to the person who gave him the assignment
  D. say nothing to anyone about his complaint

In answering this question, you should study each of the choices to find which is best. Consider choice "A" – Certainly an employee may discuss his complaint with fellow employees, but no change or improvement can result, and the complaint remains unresolved. Choice "B" is a poor choice since the head of the organization probably does not know what assignment you have been given, and taking your problem to him is known as "going over the head" of the supervisor. The supervisor, or person who made the assignment, is the person who can clarify it or correct any injustice. Choice "C" is, therefore, correct. To say nothing, as in choice "D," is unwise. Supervisors have and interest in knowing the problems employees are facing, and the employee is seeking a solution to his problem.

2) True/False Questions

The "true/false" or "right/wrong" form of question is sometimes used. Here a complete statement is given. Your job is to decide whether the statement is right or wrong.

SAMPLE: A roaming cell-phone call to a nearby city costs less than a non-roaming call to a distant city.

This statement is wrong, or false, since roaming calls are more expensive.

This is not a complete list of all possible question forms, although most of the others are variations of these common types. You will always get complete directions for answering questions. Be sure you understand *how* to mark your answers – ask questions until you do.

V. RECORDING YOUR ANSWERS

Computer terminals are used more and more today for many different kinds of exams.

For an examination with very few applicants, you may be told to record your answers in the test booklet itself. Separate answer sheets are much more common. If this separate answer sheet is to be scored by machine – and this is often the case – it is highly important that you mark your answers correctly in order to get credit.

An electronic scoring machine is often used in civil service offices because of the speed with which papers can be scored. Machine-scored answer sheets must be marked with a pencil, which will be given to you. This pencil has a high graphite content which responds to the electronic scoring machine. As a matter of fact, stray dots may register as answers, so do not let your pencil rest on the answer sheet while you are pondering the correct answer. Also, if your pencil lead breaks or is otherwise defective, ask for another.

Since the answer sheet will be dropped in a slot in the scoring machine, be careful not to bend the corners or get the paper crumpled.

The answer sheet normally has five vertical columns of numbers, with 30 numbers to a column. These numbers correspond to the question numbers in your test booklet. After each number, going across the page are four or five pairs of dotted lines. These short dotted lines have small letters or numbers above them. The first two pairs may also have a "T" or "F" above the letters. This indicates that the first two pairs only are to be used if the questions are of the true-false type. If the questions are multiple choice, disregard the "T" and "F" and pay attention only to the small letters or numbers.

Answer your questions in the manner of the sample that follows:

32. The largest city in the United States is
    A. Washington, D.C.
    B. New York City
    C. Chicago
    D. Detroit
    E. San Francisco

1) Choose the answer you think is best. (New York City is the largest, so "B" is correct.)
2) Find the row of dotted lines numbered the same as the question you are answering. (Find row number 32)
3) Find the pair of dotted lines corresponding to the answer. (Find the pair of lines under the mark "B.")
4) Make a solid black mark between the dotted lines.

VI. BEFORE THE TEST

Common sense will help you find procedures to follow to get ready for an examination. Too many of us, however, overlook these sensible measures. Indeed, nervousness and fatigue have been found to be the most serious reasons why applicants fail to do their best on civil service tests. Here is a list of reminders:

- Begin your preparation early – Don't wait until the last minute to go scurrying around for books and materials or to find out what the position is all about.
- Prepare continuously – An hour a night for a week is better than an all-night cram session. This has been definitely established. What is more, a night a week for a month will return better dividends than crowding your study into a shorter period of time.
- Locate the place of the exam – You have been sent a notice telling you when and where to report for the examination. If the location is in a different town or otherwise unfamiliar to you, it would be well to inquire the best route and learn something about the building.
- Relax the night before the test – Allow your mind to rest. Do not study at all that night. Plan some mild recreation or diversion; then go to bed early and get a good night's sleep.
- Get up early enough to make a leisurely trip to the place for the test – This way unforeseen events, traffic snarls, unfamiliar buildings, etc. will not upset you.
- Dress comfortably – A written test is not a fashion show. You will be known by number and not by name, so wear something comfortable.

- Leave excess paraphernalia at home – Shopping bags and odd bundles will get in your way. You need bring only the items mentioned in the official notice you received; usually everything you need is provided. Do not bring reference books to the exam. They will only confuse those last minutes and be taken away from you when in the test room.
- Arrive somewhat ahead of time – If because of transportation schedules you must get there very early, bring a newspaper or magazine to take your mind off yourself while waiting.
- Locate the examination room – When you have found the proper room, you will be directed to the seat or part of the room where you will sit. Sometimes you are given a sheet of instructions to read while you are waiting. Do not fill out any forms until you are told to do so; just read them and be prepared.
- Relax and prepare to listen to the instructions
- If you have any physical problem that may keep you from doing your best, be sure to tell the test administrator. If you are sick or in poor health, you really cannot do your best on the exam. You can come back and take the test some other time.

VII. AT THE TEST

The day of the test is here and you have the test booklet in your hand. The temptation to get going is very strong. Caution! There is more to success than knowing the right answers. You must know how to identify your papers and understand variations in the type of short-answer question used in this particular examination. Follow these suggestions for maximum results from your efforts:

1) Cooperate with the monitor

The test administrator has a duty to create a situation in which you can be as much at ease as possible. He will give instructions, tell you when to begin, check to see that you are marking your answer sheet correctly, and so on. He is not there to guard you, although he will see that your competitors do not take unfair advantage. He wants to help you do your best.

2) Listen to all instructions

Don't jump the gun! Wait until you understand all directions. In most civil service tests you get more time than you need to answer the questions. So don't be in a hurry. Read each word of instructions until you clearly understand the meaning. Study the examples, listen to all announcements and follow directions. Ask questions if you do not understand what to do.

3) Identify your papers

Civil service exams are usually identified by number only. You will be assigned a number; you must not put your name on your test papers. Be sure to copy your number correctly. Since more than one exam may be given, copy your exact examination title.

4) Plan your time

Unless you are told that a test is a "speed" or "rate of work" test, speed itself is usually not important. Time enough to answer all the questions will be provided, but this does not mean that you have all day. An overall time limit has been set. Divide the total time (in minutes) by the number of questions to determine the approximate time you have for each question.

5) Do not linger over difficult questions

If you come across a difficult question, mark it with a paper clip (useful to have along) and come back to it when you have been through the booklet. One caution if you do this – be sure to skip a number on your answer sheet as well. Check often to be sure that you have not lost your place and that you are marking in the row numbered the same as the question you are answering.

6) Read the questions

Be sure you know what the question asks! Many capable people are unsuccessful because they failed to *read* the questions correctly.

7) Answer all questions

Unless you have been instructed that a penalty will be deducted for incorrect answers, it is better to guess than to omit a question.

8) Speed tests

It is often better NOT to guess on speed tests. It has been found that on timed tests people are tempted to spend the last few seconds before time is called in marking answers at random – without even reading them – in the hope of picking up a few extra points. To discourage this practice, the instructions may warn you that your score will be "corrected" for guessing. That is, a penalty will be applied. The incorrect answers will be deducted from the correct ones, or some other penalty formula will be used.

9) Review your answers

If you finish before time is called, go back to the questions you guessed or omitted to give them further thought. Review other answers if you have time.

10) Return your test materials

If you are ready to leave before others have finished or time is called, take ALL your materials to the monitor and leave quietly. Never take any test material with you. The monitor can discover whose papers are not complete, and taking a test booklet may be grounds for disqualification.

VIII. EXAMINATION TECHNIQUES

1) Read the general instructions carefully. These are usually printed on the first page of the exam booklet. As a rule, these instructions refer to the timing of the examination; the fact that you should not start work until the signal and must stop work at a signal, etc. If there are any *special* instructions, such as a choice of questions to be answered, make sure that you note this instruction carefully.

2) When you are ready to start work on the examination, that is as soon as the signal has been given, read the instructions to each question booklet, underline any key words or phrases, such as *least, best, outline, describe* and the like. In this way you will tend to answer as requested rather than discover on reviewing your paper that you *listed without describing*, that you selected the *worst* choice rather than the *best* choice, etc.

3) If the examination is of the objective or multiple-choice type – that is, each question will also give a series of possible answers: A, B, C or D, and you are called upon to select the best answer and write the letter next to that answer on your answer paper – it is advisable to start answering each question in turn. There may be anywhere from 50 to 100 such questions in the three or four hours allotted and you can see how much time would be taken if you read through all the questions before beginning to answer any. Furthermore, if you come across a question or group of questions which you know would be difficult to answer, it would undoubtedly affect your handling of all the other questions.

4) If the examination is of the essay type and contains but a few questions, it is a moot point as to whether you should read all the questions before starting to answer any one. Of course, if you are given a choice – say five out of seven and the like – then it is essential to read all the questions so you can eliminate the two that are most difficult. If, however, you are asked to answer all the questions, there may be danger in trying to answer the easiest one first because you may find that you will spend too much time on it. The best technique is to answer the first question, then proceed to the second, etc.

5) Time your answers. Before the exam begins, write down the time it started, then add the time allowed for the examination and write down the time it must be completed, then divide the time available somewhat as follows:
   - If 3-1/2 hours are allowed, that would be 210 minutes. If you have 80 objective-type questions, that would be an average of 2-1/2 minutes per question. Allow yourself no more than 2 minutes per question, or a total of 160 minutes, which will permit about 50 minutes to review.
   - If for the time allotment of 210 minutes there are 7 essay questions to answer, that would average about 30 minutes a question. Give yourself only 25 minutes per question so that you have about 35 minutes to review.

6) The most important instruction is to *read each question* and make sure you know what is wanted. The second most important instruction is to *time yourself properly* so that you answer every question. The third most important instruction is to *answer every question*. Guess if you have to but include something for each question. Remember that you will receive no credit for a blank and will probably receive some credit if you write something in answer to an essay question. If you guess a letter – say "B" for a multiple-choice question – you may have guessed right. If you leave a blank as an answer to a multiple-choice question, the examiners may respect your feelings but it will not add a point to your score. Some exams may penalize you for wrong answers, so in such cases *only*, you may not want to guess unless you have some basis for your answer.

7) Suggestions
   a. Objective-type questions
      1. Examine the question booklet for proper sequence of pages and questions
      2. Read all instructions carefully
      3. Skip any question which seems too difficult; return to it after all other questions have been answered
      4. Apportion your time properly; do not spend too much time on any single question or group of questions

5. Note and underline key words – *all, most, fewest, least, best, worst, same, opposite,* etc.
6. Pay particular attention to negatives
7. Note unusual option, e.g., unduly long, short, complex, different or similar in content to the body of the question
8. Observe the use of "hedging" words – *probably, may, most likely,* etc.
9. Make sure that your answer is put next to the same number as the question
10. Do not second-guess unless you have good reason to believe the second answer is definitely more correct
11. Cross out original answer if you decide another answer is more accurate; do not erase until you are ready to hand your paper in
12. Answer all questions; guess unless instructed otherwise
13. Leave time for review

b. Essay questions
1. Read each question carefully
2. Determine exactly what is wanted. Underline key words or phrases.
3. Decide on outline or paragraph answer
4. Include many different points and elements unless asked to develop any one or two points or elements
5. Show impartiality by giving pros and cons unless directed to select one side only
6. Make and write down any assumptions you find necessary to answer the questions
7. Watch your English, grammar, punctuation and choice of words
8. Time your answers; don't crowd material

8) Answering the essay question

Most essay questions can be answered by framing the specific response around several key words or ideas. Here are a few such key words or ideas:

M's: manpower, materials, methods, money, management
P's: purpose, program, policy, plan, procedure, practice, problems, pitfalls, personnel, public relations

a. Six basic steps in handling problems:
1. Preliminary plan and background development
2. Collect information, data and facts
3. Analyze and interpret information, data and facts
4. Analyze and develop solutions as well as make recommendations
5. Prepare report and sell recommendations
6. Install recommendations and follow up effectiveness

b. Pitfalls to avoid
1. *Taking things for granted* – A statement of the situation does not necessarily imply that each of the elements is necessarily true; for example, a complaint may be invalid and biased so that all that can be taken for granted is that a complaint has been registered

2. *Considering only one side of a situation* – Wherever possible, indicate several alternatives and then point out the reasons you selected the best one
3. *Failing to indicate follow up* – Whenever your answer indicates action on your part, make certain that you will take proper follow-up action to see how successful your recommendations, procedures or actions turn out to be
4. *Taking too long in answering any single question* – Remember to time your answers properly

IX. AFTER THE TEST

Scoring procedures differ in detail among civil service jurisdictions although the general principles are the same. Whether the papers are hand-scored or graded by machine we have described, they are nearly always graded by number. That is, the person who marks the paper knows only the number – never the name – of the applicant. Not until all the papers have been graded will they be matched with names. If other tests, such as training and experience or oral interview ratings have been given, scores will be combined. Different parts of the examination usually have different weights. For example, the written test might count 60 percent of the final grade, and a rating of training and experience 40 percent. In many jurisdictions, veterans will have a certain number of points added to their grades.

After the final grade has been determined, the names are placed in grade order and an eligible list is established. There are various methods for resolving ties between those who get the same final grade – probably the most common is to place first the name of the person whose application was received first. Job offers are made from the eligible list in the order the names appear on it. You will be notified of your grade and your rank as soon as all these computations have been made. This will be done as rapidly as possible.

People who are found to meet the requirements in the announcement are called "eligibles." Their names are put on a list of eligible candidates. An eligible's chances of getting a job depend on how high he stands on this list and how fast agencies are filling jobs from the list.

When a job is to be filled from a list of eligibles, the agency asks for the names of people on the list of eligibles for that job. When the civil service commission receives this request, it sends to the agency the names of the three people highest on this list. Or, if the job to be filled has specialized requirements, the office sends the agency the names of the top three persons who meet these requirements from the general list.

The appointing officer makes a choice from among the three people whose names were sent to him. If the selected person accepts the appointment, the names of the others are put back on the list to be considered for future openings.

That is the rule in hiring from all kinds of eligible lists, whether they are for typist, carpenter, chemist, or something else. For every vacancy, the appointing officer has his choice of any one of the top three eligibles on the list. This explains why the person whose name is on top of the list sometimes does not get an appointment when some of the persons lower on the list do. If the appointing officer chooses the second or third eligible, the No. 1 eligible does not get a job at once, but stays on the list until he is appointed or the list is terminated.

X. HOW TO PASS THE INTERVIEW TEST

The examination for which you applied requires an oral interview test. You have already taken the written test and you are now being called for the interview test – the final part of the formal examination.

You may think that it is not possible to prepare for an interview test and that there are no procedures to follow during an interview. Our purpose is to point out some things you can do in advance that will help you and some good rules to follow and pitfalls to avoid while you are being interviewed.

What is an interview supposed to test?

The written examination is designed to test the technical knowledge and competence of the candidate; the oral is designed to evaluate intangible qualities, not readily measured otherwise, and to establish a list showing the relative fitness of each candidate – as measured against his competitors – for the position sought. Scoring is not on the basis of "right" and "wrong," but on a sliding scale of values ranging from "not passable" to "outstanding." As a matter of fact, it is possible to achieve a relatively low score without a single "incorrect" answer because of evident weakness in the qualities being measured.

Occasionally, an examination may consist entirely of an oral test – either an individual or a group oral. In such cases, information is sought concerning the technical knowledges and abilities of the candidate, since there has been no written examination for this purpose. More commonly, however, an oral test is used to supplement a written examination.

Who conducts interviews?

The composition of oral boards varies among different jurisdictions. In nearly all, a representative of the personnel department serves as chairman. One of the members of the board may be a representative of the department in which the candidate would work. In some cases, "outside experts" are used, and, frequently, a businessman or some other representative of the general public is asked to serve. Labor and management or other special groups may be represented. The aim is to secure the services of experts in the appropriate field.

However the board is composed, it is a good idea (and not at all improper or unethical) to ascertain in advance of the interview who the members are and what groups they represent. When you are introduced to them, you will have some idea of their backgrounds and interests, and at least you will not stutter and stammer over their names.

What should be done before the interview?

While knowledge about the board members is useful and takes some of the surprise element out of the interview, there is other preparation which is more substantive. It *is* possible to prepare for an oral interview – in several ways:

1) Keep a copy of your application and review it carefully before the interview

This may be the only document before the oral board, and the starting point of the interview. Know what education and experience you have listed there, and the sequence and dates of all of it. Sometimes the board will ask you to review the highlights of your experience for them; you should not have to hem and haw doing it.

2) Study the class specification and the examination announcement

Usually, the oral board has one or both of these to guide them. The qualities, characteristics or knowledges required by the position sought are stated in these documents. They offer valuable clues as to the nature of the oral interview. For example, if the job involves supervisory responsibilities, the announcement will usually indicate that knowledge of modern supervisory methods and the qualifications of the candidate as a supervisor will be tested. If so, you can expect such questions, frequently in the form of a hypothetical situation which you are expected to solve. NEVER go into an oral without knowledge of the duties and responsibilities of the job you seek.

3) Think through each qualification required

Try to visualize the kind of questions you would ask if you were a board member. How well could you answer them? Try especially to appraise your own knowledge and background in each area, *measured against the job sought*, and identify any areas in which you are weak. Be critical and realistic – do not flatter yourself.

4) Do some general reading in areas in which you feel you may be weak

For example, if the job involves supervision and your past experience has NOT, some general reading in supervisory methods and practices, particularly in the field of human relations, might be useful. Do NOT study agency procedures or detailed manuals. The oral board will be testing your understanding and capacity, not your memory.

5) Get a good night's sleep and watch your general health and mental attitude

You will want a clear head at the interview. Take care of a cold or any other minor ailment, and of course, no hangovers.

What should be done on the day of the interview?

Now comes the day of the interview itself. Give yourself plenty of time to get there. Plan to arrive somewhat ahead of the scheduled time, particularly if your appointment is in the fore part of the day. If a previous candidate fails to appear, the board might be ready for you a bit early. By early afternoon an oral board is almost invariably behind schedule if there are many candidates, and you may have to wait. Take along a book or magazine to read, or your application to review, but leave any extraneous material in the waiting room when you go in for your interview. In any event, relax and compose yourself.

The matter of dress is important. The board is forming impressions about you – from your experience, your manners, your attitude, and your appearance. Give your personal appearance careful attention. Dress your best, but not your flashiest. Choose conservative, appropriate clothing, and be sure it is immaculate. This is a business interview, and your appearance should indicate that you regard it as such. Besides, being well groomed and properly dressed will help boost your confidence.

Sooner or later, someone will call your name and escort you into the interview room. *This is it*. From here on you are on your own. It is too late for any more preparation. But remember, you asked for this opportunity to prove your fitness, and you are here because your request was granted.

What happens when you go in?

The usual sequence of events will be as follows: The clerk (who is often the board stenographer) will introduce you to the chairman of the oral board, who will introduce you to the other members of the board. Acknowledge the introductions before you sit down. Do not be surprised if you find a microphone facing you or a stenotypist sitting by. Oral interviews are usually recorded in the event of an appeal or other review.

Usually the chairman of the board will open the interview by reviewing the highlights of your education and work experience from your application – primarily for the benefit of the other members of the board, as well as to get the material into the record. Do not interrupt or comment unless there is an error or significant misinterpretation; if that is the case, do not hesitate. But do not quibble about insignificant matters. Also, he will usually ask you some question about your education, experience or your present job – partly to get you to start talking and to establish the interviewing "rapport." He may start the actual questioning, or turn it over to one of the other members. Frequently, each member undertakes the questioning on a particular area, one in which he is perhaps most competent, so you can expect each member to participate in the examination. Because time is limited, you may also expect some rather abrupt switches in the direction the questioning takes, so do not be upset by it. Normally, a board member will not pursue a single line of questioning unless he discovers a particular strength or weakness.

After each member has participated, the chairman will usually ask whether any member has any further questions, then will ask you if you have anything you wish to add. Unless you are expecting this question, it may floor you. Worse, it may start you off on an extended, extemporaneous speech. The board is not usually seeking more information. The question is principally to offer you a last opportunity to present further qualifications or to indicate that you have nothing to add. So, if you feel that a significant qualification or characteristic has been overlooked, it is proper to point it out in a sentence or so. Do not compliment the board on the thoroughness of their examination – they have been sketchy, and you know it. If you wish, merely say, "No thank you, I have nothing further to add." This is a point where you can "talk yourself out" of a good impression or fail to present an important bit of information. Remember, *you close the interview yourself.*

The chairman will then say, "That is all, Mr. _____, thank you." Do not be startled; the interview is over, and quicker than you think. Thank him, gather your belongings and take your leave. Save your sigh of relief for the other side of the door.

How to put your best foot forward

Throughout this entire process, you may feel that the board individually and collectively is trying to pierce your defenses, seek out your hidden weaknesses and embarrass and confuse you. Actually, this is not true. They are obliged to make an appraisal of your qualifications for the job you are seeking, and they want to see you in your best light. Remember, they must interview all candidates and a non-cooperative candidate may become a failure in spite of their best efforts to bring out his qualifications. Here are 15 suggestions that will help you:

1) Be natural – Keep your attitude confident, not cocky

If you are not confident that you can do the job, do not expect the board to be. Do not apologize for your weaknesses, try to bring out your strong points. The board is interested in a positive, not negative, presentation. Cockiness will antagonize any board member and make him wonder if you are covering up a weakness by a false show of strength.

2) Get comfortable, but don't lounge or sprawl

Sit erectly but not stiffly. A careless posture may lead the board to conclude that you are careless in other things, or at least that you are not impressed by the importance of the occasion. Either conclusion is natural, even if incorrect. Do not fuss with your clothing, a pencil or an ashtray. Your hands may occasionally be useful to emphasize a point; do not let them become a point of distraction.

3) Do not wisecrack or make small talk

This is a serious situation, and your attitude should show that you consider it as such. Further, the time of the board is limited – they do not want to waste it, and neither should you.

4) Do not exaggerate your experience or abilities
In the first place, from information in the application or other interviews and sources, the board may know more about you than you think. Secondly, you probably will not get away with it. An experienced board is rather adept at spotting such a situation, so do not take the chance.

5) If you know a board member, do not make a point of it, yet do not hide it
Certainly you are not fooling him, and probably not the other members of the board. Do not try to take advantage of your acquaintanceship – it will probably do you little good.

6) Do not dominate the interview
Let the board do that. They will give you the clues – do not assume that you have to do all the talking. Realize that the board has a number of questions to ask you, and do not try to take up all the interview time by showing off your extensive knowledge of the answer to the first one.

7) Be attentive
You only have 20 minutes or so, and you should keep your attention at its sharpest throughout. When a member is addressing a problem or question to you, give him your undivided attention. Address your reply principally to him, but do not exclude the other board members.

8) Do not interrupt
A board member may be stating a problem for you to analyze. He will ask you a question when the time comes. Let him state the problem, and wait for the question.

9) Make sure you understand the question
Do not try to answer until you are sure what the question is. If it is not clear, restate it in your own words or ask the board member to clarify it for you. However, do not haggle about minor elements.

10) Reply promptly but not hastily
A common entry on oral board rating sheets is "candidate responded readily," or "candidate hesitated in replies." Respond as promptly and quickly as you can, but do not jump to a hasty, ill-considered answer.

11) Do not be peremptory in your answers
A brief answer is proper – but do not fire your answer back. That is a losing game from your point of view. The board member can probably ask questions much faster than you can answer them.

12) Do not try to create the answer you think the board member wants
He is interested in what kind of mind you have and how it works – not in playing games. Furthermore, he can usually spot this practice and will actually grade you down on it.

13) Do not switch sides in your reply merely to agree with a board member
Frequently, a member will take a contrary position merely to draw you out and to see if you are willing and able to defend your point of view. Do not start a debate, yet do not surrender a good position. If a position is worth taking, it is worth defending.

14) Do not be afraid to admit an error in judgment if you are shown to be wrong

The board knows that you are forced to reply without any opportunity for careful consideration. Your answer may be demonstrably wrong. If so, admit it and get on with the interview.

15) Do not dwell at length on your present job

The opening question may relate to your present assignment. Answer the question but do not go into an extended discussion. You are being examined for a *new* job, not your present one. As a matter of fact, try to phrase ALL your answers in terms of the job for which you are being examined.

Basis of Rating

Probably you will forget most of these "do's" and "don'ts" when you walk into the oral interview room. Even remembering them all will not ensure you a passing grade. Perhaps you did not have the qualifications in the first place. But remembering them will help you to put your best foot forward, without treading on the toes of the board members.

Rumor and popular opinion to the contrary notwithstanding, an oral board wants you to make the best appearance possible. They know you are under pressure – but they also want to see how you respond to it as a guide to what your reaction would be under the pressures of the job you seek. They will be influenced by the degree of poise you display, the personal traits you show and the manner in which you respond.

ABOUT THIS BOOK

This book contains tests divided into Examination Sections. Go through each test, answering every question in the margin. We have also attached a sample answer sheet at the back of the book that can be removed and used. At the end of each test look at the answer key and check your answers. On the ones you got wrong, look at the right answer choice and learn. Do not fill in the answers first. Do not memorize the questions and answers, but understand the answer and principles involved. On your test, the questions will likely be different from the samples. Questions are changed and new ones added. If you understand these past questions you should have success with any changes that arise. Tests may consist of several types of questions. We have additional books on each subject should more study be advisable or necessary for you. Finally, the more you study, the better prepared you will be. This book is intended to be the last thing you study before you walk into the examination room. Prior study of relevant texts is also recommended. NLC publishes some of these in our Fundamental Series. Knowledge and good sense are important factors in passing your exam. Good luck also helps. So now study this Passbook, absorb the material contained within and take that knowledge into the examination. Then do your best to pass that exam.

EXAMINATION SECTION

EXAMINATION SECTION
TEST 1

DIRECTIONS: Each question or incomplete statement is followed by several suggested answers or completions. Select the one that BEST answers the question or completes the statement. *PRINT THE LETTER OF THE CORRECT ANSWER IN THE SPACE AT THE RIGHT.*

Questions 1-3.

DIRECTIONS: Questions 1 through 3 are to be answered on the basis of the following paragraph.

    The Jingle-Dress dance is a popular competitive dance performed at intertribal powwows. The costume of the Jingle-Dress dancer is adorned with small metal cones. The cones are made from chewing tobacco lids, which are rolled into cylinders and sewn onto the dress. During the dance, these tin cones strike one another to produce a soft, rhythmic sound. The dancer blends complicated footwork with a series of gentle hops, causing the cones to jingle in time to the drumbeat.

1. The purpose of the cones in the Jingle-Dress dance is to　　　　　　　　　　　　　　1.____

    A. shine and sparkle during the dance
    B. produce a soft, rhythmic sound
    C. aid the dancer with the complicated footwork required by the dance
    D. make use of recycled tobacco can lids

2. The dancer causes the cones to make sounds by　　　　　　　　　　　　　　　　　　2.____

    A. making large cones to sew onto the dress
    B. sewing the cones as close to another as possible
    C. jumping up and down as quickly as possible
    D. combining footwork with gentle hops

3. The Jingle-Dress dance is performed as a　　　　　　　　　　　　　　　　　　　　3.____

    A. ceremonial dance at semi-annual powwows
    B. healing dance at intertribal powwows
    C. competitive dance at intertribal powwows
    D. costume dance at annual powwows

Questions 4-6.

DIRECTIONS: Questions 4 through 6 are to be answered on the basis of the following paragraph.

    Although volleyball is a unique sport, it shares one important similarity with other well-known sports. Like most sports, the ability to win doesn't just depend on a team's ability to score the most points, but on its ability to make the fewest number of errors. In volleyball, a team cannot score unless it is serving. Serving errors, therefore, are extremely costly since losing the serve also means granting your opponent a scoring opportunity.

1

4. To win a volleyball game, it is MOST important to make sure your team

    A. makes the fewest number of errors
    B. plays good defense
    C. grants scoring opportunities to your opponents
    D. serves first

5. What important similarity does volleyball share with other sports?

    A. It's exciting to watch.
    B. Winning depends on a powerful serve.
    C. A volleyball team cannot score unless it is serving.
    D. The winning team usually commits the fewest errors.

6. Serving errors are costly in a volleyball game because they

    A. count as an error against your team
    B. provide your opponent with a scoring opportunity
    C. place your team in a receiving position
    D. can result in a delay-of-game penalty

Questions 7-8.

DIRECTIONS: Questions 7 and 8 are to be answered on the basis of the following paragraph.

Throughout history, solar eclipses have sometimes caused great fear and anxiety. Some cultures believed eclipses predicted the end of the world. Many older cultures believed a dragon was swallowing the sun and, in order to save the sun, people made as much noise as possible to frighten the dragon away. When the sun returned, whole and bright, the noise-makers celebrated their success.

7. Why have eclipses caused such anxiety throughout history?

    A. People believed they signaled the end of the world
    B. No one knows what causes them
    C. Because people make so much noise when they appear
    D. Because watching one can harm the eyes

8. Why did ancient cultures often make noise during an eclipse?

    A. People were frightened in the darkness
    B. To celebrate the arrival of the eclipse
    C. To summon the dragon who would swallow the sun
    D. To chase away the dragon they thought had swallowed the sun

Questions 9-11.

DIRECTIONS: Questions 9 through 11 are to be answered on the basis of the following paragraph.

In the films of the 1940s, most American Indians appeared as enemies. They spoke broken English and blocked civilization's progress. During this same time, however, a group of Navajo Indians used their unique language to develop a code for the U.S. military which would become one of the most successful codes in military history. During World War II, this group, known as the Navajo Code Talkers, played a key role in many of the most crucial victories fought by the U.S. military in the Pacific.

9. What role did the Navajo Code Talkers play in World War II? 9._____
They

    A. appeared as enemies in many films
    B. spoke broken English and blocked civilization's progress
    C. developed a military code which helped win the war in the Pacific
    D. used their unique language to block civilization's progress

10. In films from the 1940s, American Indians were most often depicted as enemies by 10._____

    A. speaking broken English and blocking civilization's progress
    B. speaking only in their native Navajo tongue
    C. using their language to develop secret codes
    D. trying to block crucial American victories in the Pacific

11. The Navajo Code Talkers used their language to 11._____

    A. block civilization's progress
    B. fight Hollywood stereotypes
    C. defeat their enemies in other tribes
    D. develop one of the most effective U.S. military codes in history

Questions 12-13.

DIRECTIONS: Questions 12 and 13 are to be answered on the basis of the following paragraph.

In the last several years, judges throughout the country have attracted controversy by practicing *creative sentencing*. The term refers to the judges' tendency for offering defendants what they consider valid alternatives to jail sentences. For example, to qualify for probation, one defendant had to wear a tee shirt that announced his status as a criminal on probation. An abusive husband had to donate his car to a shelter for battered women. In one case, a judge gave a woman found guilty of child abuse a chance to avoid jail if she would voluntarily allow Norplant, a form of birth control, to be implanted in her arm.

12. What does the term *creative sentencing* refer to? 12._____

    A. Various judicial controversies
    B. Judges who offer defendants alternatives to jail sentences

C. Defendants who are forced to undergo humiliating punishments in addition to jail sentences
D. Judges who have the power to determine how much time a defendant spends in jail

13. Creative sentencing is considered controversial because the 13.___

    A. judges are overstepping the bounds of their power by forcing defendants to submit to these punishments
    B. defendants have no opportunity to defend themselves
    C. alternatives offered to defendants are often surprising and odd
    D. judges have been forced to these extreme measures because of prison overcrowding

Questions 14-16.

DIRECTIONS: Questions 14 through 16 are to be answered on the basis of the following paragraph.

When examined closely, Earth's position in the solar system is something of a miracle. If it were closer to the sun, the heat would be so intense that water would be vaporized. If it were farther away, water would be frozen. Of all the planets in the solar system, only Earth and Mars share the temperature band which allows water to exist in the three states which are necessary to produce and sustain life. But only Earth is surrounded by a protective ozone layer which aids water in making the transition between these three states.

14. Why is Earth's position in the solar system something of a miracle? 14.___

    A. If it were closer to the sun, water would vaporize.
    B. If it were farther from the sun, water would freeze.
    C. It exists in the narrow temperature band which allows water to exist in the three states necessary to sustain life.
    D. It exists in the narrow temperature band which allows a protective ozone layer to form around the planet.

15. What is the difference between Earth and Mars? 15.___

    A. Mars is surrounded by a protective ozone layer.
    B. Earth is surrounded by a protective ozone layer.
    C. Only Earth exists within the narrow temperature band which allows water to exist in the three states necessary to sustain life.
    D. Only Mars exists within the narrow temperature band which allows water to exist in the three states necessary to sustain life.

16. The ozone layer is important to the production and sustenance of life because it 16.___

    A. helps water make the transition between the three forms necessary to sustain life
    B. keeps water from being vaporized by the sun's harmful rays
    C. keeps water from being frozen when the sun sets
    D. keeps water from leaving the atmosphere

Questions 17-19.

DIRECTIONS: Questions 17 through 19 are to be answered on the basis of the following paragraph.

During the seventeenth century, sailors at sea often suffered from muscle weakness and unexplained bleeding. This disease often proved fatal until the discovery that sailors who ate oranges and lines either didn't get sick, or suffered a much milder form of the illness. As a result, the British navy required every ship to provide lemons and limes for the entire crew. By accident, it had discovered that the vitamin C contained in the citrus fruits prevented scurvy.

17. What disease did sailors at sea often suffer from?   17.____

    A. Malnourishment
    B. Overdoses of vitamin C
    C. Muscle weakness and unexplained bleeding
    D. Scurvy

18. How is the disease prevented?   18.____

    A. Consumption of vitamin C   B. Consumption of fresh water
    C. Hard work   D. Bed rest

19. The cure for scurvy was discovered   19.____

    A. as a result of careful testing in laboratories
    B. through the accidental discovery that sailors who consumed vitamin C didn't grow ill
    C. through the accidental discovery that sailors who consumed vitamin C often grew ill
    D. as a result of years of study and experimentation

Questions 20-22.

DIRECTIONS: Questions 20 through 22 are to be answered on the basis of the following paragraph.

Unlike dogs, cats are typically a solitary animal species who avoid social interaction, but they do display specific social responses to each other upon meeting. When two cats meet who are strangers, their first actions and gestures determine who the *dominant* cat will be. If a cat desires dominance or sees the other cat as a threat to its territory, it will stare directly at the intruder with a lowered tail. If the other cat responds with a similar gesture, or with the strong defensive posture of an arched back, laid-back ears, and raised tail, a fight or chase is likely if neither cat gives in. This is unlikely, however; before such a point of open hostility is reached, one of the cats will usually take the *submissive* position of crouching down while looking away from the other cat.

20. A cat signals its dominance over another cat by   20.____

    A. crouching down and looking away from the other cat
    B. arching its back and raising its tail
    C. staring directly at the other cat and lowering its tail
    D. chasing the other cat

21. Cats usually greet each other by 21.___

    A. displaying specific social responses
    B. staring directly at one another
    C. raising their tails
    D. arching their backs

22. Why is it unlikely for cats who are strangers to reach a point of open hostility with one another? 22.___

    A. Cats are solitary animals.
    B. One of the cats usually runs away.
    C. One of the cats usually takes a submissive position before they reach the point of open hostility.
    D. The two cats generally stare at each other with lowered tails until the hostility passes.

Questions 23-25.

DIRECTIONS: Questions 23 through 25 are to be answered on the basis of the following paragraph.

Between the nineteenth and twentieth centuries, the area in America known as the Great Plains underwent startling changes. At the beginning of the nineteenth century, there were few settlements. One could walk for miles without seeing a house. By the end of the century, settlements had sprung up all over. More and more people began to seek their fortunes in this area. In 1800, the Plains were covered by herds of buffalo. These huge animals were the natural cattle of the Plains. By 1900 the buffalo had almost disappeared, however, and the tribes who had roamed the Plains in pursuit of the buffalo had been forced to live on reservations.

23. When did these changes occur on the Great Plains? 23.___

    A. Between the 1700s and the 1800s
    B. Between the 1800s and the 1900s
    C. During the 1900s
    D. Between 1850 and 1950

24. What caused the sudden increase in the number of settlements on the Great Plains? 24.___

    A. The disappearance of the buffalo
    B. The disappearance of the Plains tribes
    C. An increased desire to hunt buffalo for sport
    D. An increased number of people seeking their fortunes in the area

25. What happened to the Plains tribes after the buffalo disappeared? 25.___
    They

    A. were forced to live on reservations
    B. were all killed
    C. died of starvation
    D. moved farther west, away from the settlers

Questions 26-28.

DIRECTIONS: Questions 26 through 28 are to be answered on the basis of the following paragraph.

One important line of thinking about stress focuses on the differences between Type A and Type B personalities. Type A individuals are extremely competitive, are very devoted to work, and have a strong sense of time urgency. They are likely to be aggressive, impatient, and very work-oriented. Type B individuals are less competitive, less devoted to work, and have a weaker sense of time urgency. These individuals are less likely to experience conflict with other people and more likely to have a balanced, relaxed approach to life.

26. Type B individuals are likely to display which of the following characteristics?   26.____

    A. A strong sense of time urgency
    B. Devotion to work
    C. A balanced approach to life
    D. Aggressiveness

27. Type A individuals are likely to display which of the following characteristics?   27.____

    A. A balanced approach to life
    B. Passivity
    C. Contentment
    D. A strong sense of time urgency

28. These personality types help researchers study which of the following problems?   28.____

    A. Stress   B. Apathy
    C. Criminal behavior D. Underachievement

Questions 29-36.

The paragraphs which follow contain blank spaces with numbers corresponding to the questions. Each of the corresponding questions contains one lettered choice whose meaning fits in the space. Place the letter of the correct choice in the answer space to the right of the question.

Most successful job interviews (29) three basic steps. Step 1 lasts about three minutes and (30) when you first introduce yourself. Those people who have a firm handshake, who maintain eye contact, smile, and seem friendly, are the (31) successful during this phase. Step 2 is the (32) phase. This is the point at which interviewees (33) their skills and work to *sell* themselves. Step 3 comes at the (34) of the interview and, like Step 1, lasts only a few minutes. After the employer says, *We'll call you,* successful interviewees are quick (35) respond, *I'll get in touch with you if I don't hear from you in a few days.* This final gesture conveys (36).

29.	A. lack C. follow			B. mimic D. end with				29.___
30.	A. begins	B. ends		C. stalls		D. fails		30.___
31.	A. least	B. mostly		C. more		D. most		31.___
32.	A. least challenging C. longest			B. most boring D. shortest				32.___
33.	A. brag about	B. explain		C. enunciate		D. lie about		33.___
34.	A. middle	B. outset		C. beginning		D. end		34.___
35.	A. to	B. at		C. with		D. for		35.___
36.	A. insistence C. enthusiasm			B. impatience D. hope				36.___

Questions 37-40.

The idea of duty is important to the followers of Hinduism, the major (37) in India. In fact, the many duties prescribed by Hinduism make it a way of life that (38) each day. From an early age, children learn that nothing is more important (39) doing one's duty. In fact doing (40) duty is, in itself, a form of worship.

37.	A. belief C. system			B. religion D. political institution				37.___
38.	A. organizes C. produces			B. disrupts D. destabilizes				38.___
39.	A. if	B. with		C. of		D. than		39.___
40.	A. your	B. his		C. one's		D. its		40.___

Questions 41-46.

Strong emotions are accompanied (41) physiological changes. When we are extremely fearful or angry, for example, (42) heartbeat speeds up, our pulse races, and our breathing rate tends to increase. The body's metabolism (43), burning up sugar in the bloodstream and fats in the tissues at a faster rate. The salivary glands become less active, making the mouth feel (44). The sweat glands may overreact, (45) a dripping forehead, clammy hands, and cold sweat. Finally, the pupils may (46), producing the wide-eyed look that is characteristic of both terror and rage.

41.	A. with	B. to	C. beside	D. by	41.___
42.	A. your	B. our	C. the	D. a	42.___

43.	A. accelerates	B. slows down	43.____
	C. works	D. stays the same	

44.	A. hot	B. cold	C. wet	D. dry	44.____
45.	A. with	B. showing	C. producing	D. fearing	45.____
46.	A. dilate	B. enlarge	C. blacken	D. disappear	46.____

Questions 47-52.

Increased numbers of women are (47) going to college and graduating with degrees in law and medicine. More women than ever before are (48) careers and earning as much as men. Many career women who are married have also achieved economic equality (49) their husbands. The number of women in elected office has also increased, and a large majority of Americans are now willing to vote for a qualified (50) for president. A growing number of women are entering the military, with the U.S. now having more female soldiers than any other (51). These are all signs that women have made significant headway toward (52) equality.

47.	A. now	B. then	C. yet	D. not	47.____
48.	A. leaving	B. changing	C. avoiding	D. pursuing	48.____
49.	A. to	B. with	C. at	D. for	49.____
50.	A. Republican	B. candidate	C. woman	D. man	50.____
51.	A. woman	B. country	C. man	D. branch	51.____
52.	A. racial	B. economic	C. religious	D. gender	52.____

Questions 53-56.

Understanding does not mean manipulating someone to agree (53) your point of view. Although a manipulative person views understanding as having someone else come around to his or her opinion, an understanding person conveys a sense of open-mindedness and (54). A communicator who is understanding does (55) insist upon agreement. He or she understands that, in order to be understood, you must also (56) others.

53.	A. to	B. at	C. with	D. for	53.____
54.	A. acceptance	B. exclusion	C. anger	D. elation	54.____
55.	A. always	B. not	C. sometimes	D. generally	55.____

56.	A. disagree with	B. judge	56.____
	C. love	D. understand	

Questions 57-62.

DIRECTIONS: Questions 57 through 62 are to be answered on the basis of the following facts.

Apollo Elementary School serves students in grades kindergarten through fifth. The school library is located in the center of the school. Classrooms surround the library, forming a large circle. Throughout the school day, teachers bring their classes into the library to conduct research and reading activities. There are usually several classes using the library at any one time.

The school librarian is Mrs. Samuels. She is a tall, middle-aged woman with brown hair and green eyes. Her part-time assistant is Velma Thomas. Velma is a student at the local community college, where she studies library science.

On the afternoon of Wednesday, April 11, Mrs. Simon brought her fourth-grade class to the library at approximately 1:50 P.M. Mrs. Samuels was already working with a third-grade class, so Velma began assisting the fourth grade students. A young girl from Mrs. Simon's class asked Velma how to find her book in the card catalog. As Velma guided the girl through the procedure, she noticed that one of the third graders had drifted away from his class and was attempting to reach a book by standing on one of the bookshelves.

Just as Velma called to the boy, he lost his footing and fell. Mrs. Samuels rushed to his side and checked him for injuries. The boy had a slight bruise on his wrist, but was otherwise uninjured.

57. Who checked the boy for injuries after his fall?

    A. Mrs. Samuels   B. Velma Thomas
    C. Mrs. Simon   D. The third grade teacher

58. Who is the school librarian?

    A. Mrs. Samuels
    B. Velma Thomas
    C. Mrs. Simon
    D. She is not named in this passage

59. On what day of the week did the incident occur?

    A. Monday   B. Tuesday   C. Wednesday   D. Friday

60. In what grade was the boy who fell from the shelf?

    A. Fifth   B. Fourth   C. Third   D. Second

61. What grade does Mrs. Simon teach?

    A. Fifth   B. Fourth   C. Third   D. Second

62. What grades does Apollo Elementary serve? 62._____

    A. First through fifth
    B. First through sixth
    C. Kindergarten through fourth
    D. Kindergarten through fifth

Questions 63-68.

DIRECTIONS: Questions 63 through 68 are to be answered on the basis of the following facts.

There is a small hot dog cart located in the outdoor plaza of the Smith County Courthouse. The cart sells Polish hot dogs, sausages, bratwurst, soft pretzels, and soda. In the mornings between 7:00 and 9:30, fresh coffee and danishes are also sold. Employees of the court and other nearby businesses often purchase their lunch there, and eat on the plaza benches and tables.

The cart opens at 7:00 A.M. and closes at 3:00 P.M. during weekdays. It does not operate on weekends. It is owned and operated by Luisa Gonzalez, who is a 21-year-old college student with brown hair and brown eyes. Her father is Martin Gonzalez, a retired police officer, and he often works with her. At approximately 12:00 P.M. on October 3, Court Officer Laura Innes stopped at the cart to buy her lunch. After paying Luisa, Laura moved to the condiment table, located just to the right of the cart. She noticed Martin Gonzalez struggling to pour a large tub of boiling water into the hot dog steamer. Before she could move to help him, however, Martin lost his grip and dropped the tub of water, splashing himself.

The Court Officer administered first aid, and Martin was taken to St. Luke's hospital. He had received second degree burns on his arms and feet and was not able to return to the hot dog cart for three weeks.

63. What hospital was Martin taken to? 63._____

    A. St. Mark's   B. St. Peter's
    C. St. Mary's   D. St. Luke's

64. What part of his body did Martin burn? 64._____
    His

    A. arms and feet   B. arms
    C. feet and ankles   D. arms and face

65. Who owns the hot dog cart? 65._____

    A. Martin Gonzalez   B. Luisa Gonzalez
    C. Laura Innes   D. Luke Martin

66. During what hours does the cart operate on weekends? 66._____

    A. 7:00 A.M. to 3:00 P.M.
    B. 9:30 A.M. to 3:00 P.M.
    C. 7:00 A.M. to 9:30 A.M.
    D. The cart does not operate on weekends

67. Where is the hot dog cart located?
    On the _____ of the courthouse.

    A. first floor
    B. roof
    C. outdoor plaza
    D. third floor

68. Who was first to administer first aid to Martin?

    A. Laura Innes
    B. Luisa Gonzalez
    C. Luke Martin
    D. Paramedics

Questions 69-74.

DIRECTIONS: Questions 69 through 74 are to be answered on the basis of the following facts.

The offices of Judge Anjelica Chen are located on the third floor of the Peak County Courthouse. The offices of Judge Benjamin Laurence are also located on the third floor of the courthouse, across a courtyard. The windows of these offices face one another.

Judge Chen keeps her pet parrot, Mabel, in her offices. Although Mabel has a cage, Judge Chen keeps the door open, allowing Mabel to perch on bookshelves and lamps while the Judge finishes paperwork late in the evenings. Judge Laurence has no pets, but he often feeds pigeons from his window, sprinkling breadcrumbs along his sill.

On the evening of Tuesday, May 2, Court Officer Roger Crawford heard a scream from Judge Chen's office. He arrived to find the judge searching frantically through her office for Mabel, who had apparently disappeared. The window to the judge's office was open. The court officer assisted the judge in her search. At approximately 7:30, nearly 45 minutes after he had arrived in Judge Chen's office, the court officer heard someone hollering from the other side of the building.

Officer Crawford rushed toward the noise and found Judge Laurence in his office, trying to fend off the bright parrot flying back and forth across his office. The court officer summoned Judge Chen, who calmed Mabel and led her back to her cage.

69. Where was Mabel found?

    A. In Judge Chen's office
    B. In Judge Laurence's office
    C. In the courtyard
    D. In her cage

70. What kind of bird is Mabel?

    A. Pigeon
    B. Canary
    C. Chickadee
    D. Parrot

71. Where is Judge Chen's office located?
    _____ Judge Laurence's office.

    A. Below
    B. Next to
    C. Across from
    D. Above

72. Why does Judge Laurence leave breadcrumbs on his window-sill? 72.____

    A. To feed pigeons
    B. To feed Mabel
    C. To feed squirrels
    D. To keep food litter out of his office

73. How long did Judge Chen and Officer Crawford look for Mabel before they heard Judge 73.____
    Laurence yelling in his office?
    _____ minutes.

    A. 30   B. 45   C. 60   D. 15

74. Why does Judge Chen leave Mabel's cage door open? 74.____

    A. To allow Mabel to escape
    B. To allow Mabel a clearer view of Judge Laurence's windowsill
    C. Judge Chen does not leave Mabel's cage door open
    D. To allow Mabel to perch on bookshelves and lamps while the Judge finishes her paperwork

Questions 75-80.

DIRECTIONS: Questions 75 through 80 are to be answered on the basis of the following facts.

The Hickory Ridge Courthouse is located just across the street from the Hickory Ridge Public Library. Employees begin arriving at the courthouse at approximately 7:00 A.M. each weekday morning. The library opens at 9:00 A.M. and closes at 5:00 P.M. each weekday. Both the courthouse and the library have bicycle stands in front of them. Bicyclists lock their bikes to the stands while they run their errands and conduct their business.

Court Officer Melinda Thompson eats her lunch each day at a small cafe next to the library. The cafe caters mainly to employees of the library and courthouse. It operates from 11:00 A.M. to 3:00 P.M. each day.

On the afternoon of August 11, the court officer observed a young man with a backpack lock his bike to a stand in front of the library. The young man had blond hair, green eyes, and long sideburns. Approximately 30 minutes after the young man entered the library, a dark-haired man emerged from the cafe where the court officer was eating her lunch. The man had a beard, and was of medium build. He walked to the bicycle stand and began jiggling a lock on one of the bikes.

The court officer recognized the bicycle as the same one the blond-haired young man had locked to the stand. By the time the court officer reached the bicycle stand, the second man had already broken the lock. Although she called for him to stop, he rode away on the young man's bicycle. Her excellent description, however, helped police locate the bicycle thief and the bicycle a short time later.

75. What time does the library open? 75.____

    A. 7:00 A.M.   B. 9:00 A.M.   C. 11:00 A.M.   D. 3:00 P.M.

76. Where is the cafe located?

    A. Next to the courthouse
    B. Across from the library
    C. Next to the library
    D. Between the library and the courthouse

77. Who stole the bicycle?

    A. The blond-haired man
    B. The dark-haired man
    C. The man with the backpack
    D. The man with the long sideburns

78. What hours is the cafe open?

    A. 11:00 A.M. to 3:00 P.M.
    B. 9:00 A.M. to 5:00 P.M.
    C. 7:00 A.M. to 5:00 P.M.
    D. 7:00 A.M. to 3:00 P.M.

79. When do employees begin arriving at the courthouse each day?

    A. 7:00 A.M.   B. 9:00 A.M.   C. 10:00 A.M.   D. 11:00 A.M.

80. What did the bicycle thief do when the court officer ordered him to stop?

    A. He stopped.
    B. He rode away.
    C. He threw down the bicycle and ran.
    D. He insisted the bicycle was his.

Questions 81-87.

DIRECTIONS: Questions 81 through 87 are to be answered on the basis of the following facts.

The Jade Market is located on the first floor of the Angel County Courthouse. The courthouse is located across the street from San Gabriel High School. Jade Market sells newspapers, magazines, sandwiches, beverages, and sodas. In the mornings, between 7:00 A.M. and 9:00 A.M., the market is frequented mostly by employees of the courthouse. In the afternoons, between 1:45 and 2:45, the small market is crowded with teenagers wearing cumbersome backpacks. Classes at San Gabriel High School end at 1:30 P.M.

Jade Market is operated by James Chang, who is 55 years old, with graying black hair and brown eyes. His wife, Lola, also helps at the market during the afternoon and evening hours.

On the afternoon of Thursday, September 1, Court Officer Mason Stewart stopped at Jade Market to buy a newspaper and some coffee. While he was talking with Lola Chang, twelve to fifteen high school students walked into the market. They moved noisily up and down the narrow aisles. They each carried a heavy backpack. As they walked through the store, their packs often knocked items from the shelves.

As the court officer watched the students, he noticed one young woman knock several magazines from the magazine stand located at the back of the store. Several other students walked past the magazine stand before the young woman was able to turn around and pick the magazines up. The young woman had blond hair and brown eyes, and she carried a red backpack. When she returned to the stand, Officer Stewart saw that she only replaced one magazine.

When the court officer approached the girl about the missing magazines, she insisted that she had not seen them. He asked her to wait at the front counter, which she did. Officer Stewart studied the magazine stand for a brief moment, and then bent down to peer beneath it. He saw the magazines lying there, where they had been accidentally kicked by the other passing students. The young woman helped gather the magazines, and then left the store after apologizing to Mr. and Mrs. Chang.

81. What hours is the market open?

    A. 7:00 A.M. to 2:45 P.M.
    B. 7:00 A.M. to 9:00 A.M.
    C. 7:00 A.M. to 1:30 P.M.
    D. The passage doesn't contain this information

82. Where were the missing magazines found?

    A. Inside the girl's backpack
    B. On the magazine stand
    C. Beneath the magazine stand
    D. They were never found

83. What did the girl do when Officer Stewart asked her about the missing magazines? She

    A. ran from the store
    B. denied stealing them
    C. confessed
    D. ran to the front counter

84. Where is the Jade Market located?

    A. On the first floor of the courthouse
    B. On the third floor of the courthouse
    C. Next to Angel High School
    D. In the plaza of Angel High School

85. When does Lola Chang work in the market?

    A. All day
    B. Afternoons
    C. Afternoons and evenings
    D. The passage doesn't contain this information

86. On what day of the week did the incident occur?

    A. Monday   B. Tuesday   C. Wednesday   D. Thursday

87. What time are students at San Gabriel High School dismissed from class? 87.___

    A. 1:30 P.M.
    B. 1:45 P.M.
    C. 2:45 P.M.
    D. The passage does not contain this information

Questions 88-89.

DIRECTIONS: Questions 88 and 89 are to be answered on the basis of the following facts.

Procedure: The Service Station at the Friendly Car Dealership has a policy which allows customers to drop off their cars the night before they are to be worked on. This allows customers the convenience of not having to take time off from work to have their cars serviced. Cars must be dropped off between 9 P.M. and 11 P.M. the night before. Keys must be labeled with the make and license plate number of the car to which they belong. They are then placed into envelopes and dropped into a locked drop box outside the service station office. Cars must be picked up by 9:00 P.M. on the day repairs are completed. If the car cannot be picked up on that day, other arrangements must be made with the service department by 3:00 P.M. of that day.

Situation: Sarah Stone drops her car off at 10:45 P.M. the night before it is to be serviced. She labels her key, places it in the envelope and leaves it in the drop box. Her car is repaired by 11:00 A.M. the next morning. Because Sarah has to catch up on a backlog of work, she is unable to pick her car up before 6:00 P.M. on the day after the repairs have been completed.

88. Based on the above procedure, which one of the following statements regarding Stone's 88.___
    actions is correct?
    Stone

    A. should have dropped her car off before 10:45 P.M. the night before it was to be serviced
    B. should have given her keys to someone in the service department instead of dropping them in a box
    C. should have notified the service department of her plans by 3:00 P.M. on the day the car was repaired
    D. did everything according to proper procedure

89. If Stone wishes to pick her car up at 8:00 P.M. the day the repairs are completed, which 89.___
    of the following things must she do?
    She

    A. must make special arrangements with the service department
    B. must wait until the following morning to pick up her car
    C. must make a special appointment to pick up her car after hours
    D. does not need to do anything

Questions 90-91.

DIRECTIONS: Questions 90 and 91 are to be answered on the basis of the following facts.

Procedure: Notification of absence due to illness must be made between 9:00 A.M. and 10:00 A.M. on the first day of illness. Illness which results in more than four days of consecutive absence must be confirmed by a doctor's note stating the nature of the illness and the approximate date of return to work.

Situation: Officer Janus Lee becomes sick on the night of June 25 while at home. At 10:15 on the morning of June 26, Lee notifies his office that he will not be in. On July 4, Lee submits a doctor's note confirming and identifying his illness and stating that Lee will return to work on July 5.

90. Based on the above procedure, which one of the following statements regarding Lee's actions is correct? 90.____
Officer Lee

    A. should have notified his office of his absence by 10:00 A.M. on the morning of June 26
    B. should have notified his office of his absence by 10:00 A.M. on the morning of June 25
    C. should have submitted the doctor's note on June 26
    D. followed the procedure correctly

91. Officer Lee's note from the doctor states that he will be absent from the office from June 26 through July 4. Which of the following notification procedures should he follow on those days? 91.____

    A. Officer Lee must notify his office of his absence on each morning between June 26 and July 4 by 10:00 A.M.
    B. Officer Lee's doctor must notify his office of Officer Lee's absence on each morning between June 26 and July 4 by 10:00 A.M.
    C. Officer Lee must contact his office periodically between June 26 and July 4 to notify them of his progress.
    D. Once he has submitted his doctor's note, Officer Lee does not need to notify his office any further so long as he returns to work on July 5.

Questions 92-93.

DIRECTIONS: Questions 92 and 93 are to be answered on the basis of the following facts.

Procedure: Court officers in Montgomery County who work overtime are awarded compensation time instead of overtime pay. Each hour of over-time is equal to one hour of compensation time. In order to use compensation time, court officers must submit a written vacation request two weeks in advance of the desired time off. The request must contain the beginning and ending dates of the requested vacation. It must be signed by the officer's supervisor before the officer may utilize the compensation time.

Situation: Officer Sabrina Hellman wishes to use compensation time for a vacation beginning October 1 and ending October 10. The vacation will require 7 days of compensation time. Officer Hellman submits her vacation request on September 24. The request contains the beginning and ending dates of her desired vacation.

92. Based on the above procedure, which of the following statements regarding Officer Hellman's actions is correct?
Officer Hellman

   A. should have submitted her vacation request by September 17
   B. should have submitted her vacation request by September 1
   C. should have submitted the beginning and ending dates of her vacation
   D. followed the procedures correctly

93. How many hours of overtime must Officer Hellman have in order to accumulate 100 hours of compensation time?

   A. 50   B. 75   C. 150   D. 100

Questions 94-95.

DIRECTIONS: Questions 94 and 95 are to be answered on the basis of the following facts.

Procedure: Court officers in Salinas County who work overtime are awarded compensation time instead of overtime pay. Each hour of overtime is equal to one hour of compensation time. At the end of each calendar year, compensation time which has not been used is automatically erased unless employees submit a written request to have their compensation time rolled over to the next year. Rollover requests must be submitted no later than November 1. They must contain the employee's name, social security, and the total number of compensation hours s/he wishes to rollover.

Situation: Officer Larry Bernstein accumulated 20 hours of compensation time during calendar year 2008. In addition to that, he has 40 hours of compensation time which was rolled over from 2007. On October 30, Officer Bernstein submits a written request asking that his remaining compensation time be rolled over to calendar year 2009.

94. Based on the above procedure, which of the following statements regarding Officer Bernstein's actions is correct? Officer Bernstein

   A. should have submitted his rollover request by November 1, 2008
   B. should have submitted his vacation request by October 1, 2008
   C. should have submitted the total number of hours he wanted to be rolled over
   D. followed the procedures correctly

95. Based on the above procedure and situation, how many hours of compensation time can Officer Bernstein expect to be rolled over to calendar year 2009?

   A. 20   B. 40   C. 60   D. 80

Questions 96-97.

DIRECTIONS: Questions 96 and 97 are to be answered on the basis of the following facts.

Procedure: Court officers in Salinas County who work overtime are awarded compensation time instead of overtime pay. Each hour of overtime is equal to one hour of compensation time. If a court officer is laid off or chooses to leave his or her employment as a court officer with the county, and he or she has compensation time remaining, then he or she can choose one of two options. The first option is for the employee to use the remaining compensation time as paid vacation time. This would allow the officer to cease his or her duties early, but still be paid until the end of his or her regular employment. In order to utilize this option, employees must submit a written request 30 days before the start of the paid vacation. The second option is for the employee to remain through the end of his or her regular employment, and receive a check for any remaining compensation time. In order to utilize this option, employees must submit a written request 90 days before the scheduled departure date.

Situation: Officer Glen Regan is due to retire at the end of calendar year 2008. Through the course of his career as a court officer, Glen has accumulated 200 hours of compensation time. This equals approximately 25 standard working days.

96. If Officer Regan decides that he would like to retire early, he should submit a written request by _____ 1, 2008.

    A. December   B. November   C. October   D. September

97. If Officer Regan decides to receive a check for his unused compensation time, he should submit a written request by _____ 1, 2008.

    A. December   B. November   C. October   D. September

Questions 98-100.

DIRECTIONS: Questions 98 through 100 are to be answered on the basis of the following facts.

Procedure: Court officers in James County are granted 10 paid sick days each year. Sick days are to be used only in the case of unforeseen illness. Employees are also granted 5 paid personal days. Officers who work overtime are also granted compensation time instead of overtime pay. Each hour of overtime is equal to one hour of compensation time. In order to use a sick day, employees must notify a supervisor by 10:00 A.M. on the day of their absence. In order to use a personal day, employees must notify a supervisor two working days in advance. In order to use a compensation-time day, employees must notify a supervisor two weeks in advance.

Situation: Court Officer Carla Lewis has a doctor and a dentist appointment on Monday, October 5.

98. In order to use a compensation day for these appointments, by what date must Carla notify her supervisor?

    A. Friday, September 4   B. Monday, September 14
    C. 10:00 A.M. October 5   D. Thursday, September 1

99. If Officer Carla Lewis wants to use a personal day for these appointments, by what date must she notify her supervisor?

    A. Friday, September 4   B. Monday, September 14
    C. 10:00 A.M. October 5   D. Thursday, October 1

100. If Officer Carla Lewis wants to use a sick day for these appointments, by what date must she notify her supervisor?

   A. 10:00 A.M. on October 5
   B. Monday, September 14
   C. She cannot use a sick day for these appointments
   D. She does not have to notify her supervisor until after she returns to work

KEY (CORRECT ANSWERS)

1.	B	21.	A	41.	D	61.	B	81.	D
2.	D	22.	C	42.	B	62.	D	82.	C
3.	C	23.	B	43.	A	63.	D	83.	B
4.	A	24.	D	44.	D	64.	A	84.	A
5.	D	25.	A	45.	C	65.	B	85.	C
6.	B	26.	C	46.	B	66.	D	86.	D
7.	A	27.	D	47.	A	67.	C	87.	A
8.	D	28.	A	48.	D	68.	A	88.	C
9.	C	29.	C	49.	B	69.	B	89.	D
10.	A	30.	A	50.	C	70.	D	90.	A
11.	D	31.	D	51.	B	71.	C	91.	D
12.	B	32.	C	52.	D	72.	A	92.	A
13.	C	33.	B	53.	C	73.	B	93.	D
14.	C	34.	D	54.	A	74.	D	94.	D
15.	B	35.	A	55.	B	75.	B	95.	C
16.	A	36.	C	56.	D	76.	C	96.	B
17.	D	37.	B	57.	A	77.	B	97.	C
18.	A	38.	A	58.	A	78.	A	98.	B
19.	B	39.	D	59.	C	79.	A	99.	D
20.	C	40.	C	60.	C	80.	B	100.	C

EXAMINATION SECTION

TEST 1

DIRECTIONS: Each question or incomplete statement is followed by several suggested answers or completions. Select the one that BEST answers the question or completes the statement. *PRINT THE LETTER OF THE CORRECT ANSWER IN THE SPACE AT THE RIGHT.*

Questions 1-4 are based solely on the information in the paragraph below:

A Court Officer shall give reasonable aid to a sick or injured person. He or she shall summon an ambulance, if necessary, by telephoning the Police Department, which shall notify the hospital. He or she shall wait in a place where the arriving ambulance can see him or her, if possible, so as to direct the ambulance attendant to the patient. If the ambulance does not arrive within a half-hour, the Court Officer should call a second time, telling the department that this is a second call. However, if the injured person is conscious, the Court Officer should ask whether such person is willing to go to a hospital before calling for an ambulance.

1. The Court Officer who wishes to summon an ambulance should telephone the
   A. nearest hospital
   B. Health and Hospitals Corporation
   C. Police Department
   D. nearest police precinct

   1._____

2. If an ambulance does not arrive within half an hour, the Court Officer should
   A. ask the person injured if he/she wants to go to the hospital in a cab
   B. call the Police Department
   C. call the nearest police precinct
   D. call the nearest hospital

   2._____

3. A Court Officer who is called to help a person who has fallen on the courthouse steps and apparently has a broken leg should
   A. put the leg in traction so the doctor will have no difficulty setting it
   B. ask the person, if he/she is conscious, whether he/she wishes to go to the hospital
   C. attempt to get the story behind the injury
   D. put in a call for an ambulance at once

   3._____

4. A Court Officer who is present when a witness becomes ill while waiting to testify should
   A. wait in front of the room until the ambulance arrives
   B. send a bystander to the courtroom to page a doctor
   C. ask the witness if he/she wishes to go to a hospital
   D. call the Court Clerk for instructions

   4._____

21

5. "Physical and mental health are essential to the Court Officer."
According to this statement, a peace officer must be
    A. wise as well as strong
    B. smarter than most people
    C. sound in mind and body
    D. smarter than the average criminal

6. "Teamwork is the basis of successful law enforcement."
The factor stressed by this statement is
    A. cooperation
    B. determination
    C. initiative
    D. pride

7. "A sufficient quantity of material supplied as evidence enables the laboratory expert to determine the true nature of the substance, whereas an extremely limited specimen may be an abnormal sample containing foreign matter not indicative of the true nature of the material."
On the basis of this statement alone, it may be concluded that a reason for giving an adequate sample of material for evidence to a laboratory expert is that
    A. a limited specimen spoils more quickly than a larger sample
    B. a small sample may not truly represent the evidence
    C. he or she cannot analyze a small sample correctly
    D. he or she must have enough material to keep a part of it untouched to show in court

8. "The Housing Authority not only faces every problem of the private developer, it must also assume responsibilities of which a private building is free. The authority must account to the community; it must conform to Federal regulations and it must overcome the prejudices of contractors, bankers and prospective tenants against public operations. These authorities are being watched for the first error of judgment or the first evidence of high costs that can be torn to bits before a congressional committee."
On the basis of this selection, which statement would be most correct?
    A. Private builders do not have the opposition of contractors, bankers and prospective tenants
    B. Congressional committees impede the progress of public housing by petty investigations
    C. A housing authority must deal with all the difficulties encountered by the private builder
    D. Housing authorities are not more immune to errors in judgment than private developers

9. Accident proneness is a subject that deserves much more objective and competent study than it has received to date. In discussing accident proneness, it is important to differentiate between the employee who is a "repeater" and one who is truly accident-prone. It is obvious that any person assigned to work without thorough training is liable to injury until he or she does learn the "how" of it. Few workers left to their own devices develop adequate safe practices, and therefore they must be trained. Only those who fail to respond to proper training should be regarded as accident-prone. The repeater whose accident record can be explained by a correctable physical defect, correctable plant or machine hazards, or by assignment to work for which he or she is not suited because of physical deficiencies or special abilities cannot be fairly called accident-prone.

According to the passage, people are considered accident-prone if
   A. they have accidents regardless of the fact that they have been properly trained
   B. they have many accidents
   C. it is possible for them to have accidents
   D. they work at a job where accidents are possible

Questions 10 through 12 are based on the following paragraph:

Discontent of some citizens with the practices and policies of local government leads to the creation of local civic associations. Completely outside of government, manned by a few devoted volunteers, understaffed, and with pitifully few dues-paying members, they attempt to arouse widespread public opinion on selected issues by presenting facts and ideas. The findings of these civic associations are widely trusted by the press and public, and amidst the records of rebuffs received are found more than enough achievements to justify what little their activities cost. Civic associations are politically non-partisan. Hence their vitality is drawn from true political independents who in most communities are a trifling minority. Except in a few large cities, civic associations are seldom affluent enough to maintain an office or to afford even a small paid staff.

10. The main reason for the formation of civic associations is to
    A. provide independent candidates for local public office with an opportunity to be heard
    B. bring about changes in the activities of local government
    C. allow persons who are politically non-partisan to express themselves on local public issues
    D. permit the small minority of true political independents to supply leadership for non-partisan causes

11. The statements that civic associations make on issues of general interest are
    A. accepted by large segments of the public
    B. taken at face value only by the few people who are true political independents
    C. questioned as to their accuracy by most newspapers
    D. expressed as a result of aroused widespread public opinion

12. It is most accurate to conclude that since 12._____
    A. they deal with many public issues, the cost of their efforts on each issue is small
    B. their attempts to attain their objectives often fail, little money is contributed to civic associations
    C. they spend little money in their efforts, they are ineffective when they become involved in major issues
    D. their achievements outweigh the small cost of their efforts, civic associations are considered worthwhile

13. "If you are in doubt as to whether any matter is properly mailable, you should ask the postmaster. Even though the post office has not expressly declared any matter to be nonmailable, the sender of such matter may be held fully liable for violation of law if he does actually send nonmailable matter through the mails." 13._____
    Of the following, the most accurate statement made concerning this selection is
    A. nonmailable matter is not always clearly defined
    B. ignorance of what constitutes nonmailable matter relieves the sender of all responsibility
    C. though doubt may exist about the mailability of any matter, the sender is fully liable for any law violation if such matter should be nonmailable
    D. the post office is not explicit in its position on the violation of the nonmailable matter law

Questions 14 through 16 are based on the following paragraph:

What is required is a program that will protect our citizens and their property from criminal and anti-social acts, will effectively restrain and reform juvenile delinquents, and will prevent the further development of anti-social behavior. Discipline and punishment of offenders must necessarily play an important part in any such program. Serious offenders cannot be mollycoddled merely because they are under 21. Restraint and punishment necessarily follow serious anti-social acts. But punishment, if it is to be effective, must be a planned part of a more comprehensive program of treating delinquency.

14. The one goal not included among those listed in the paragraph is to 14._____
    A. stop young people from defacing public property
    B. keep homes from being broken into
    C. develop an intra-city boys baseball league
    D. change juvenile delinquents into useful citizens

15. Punishment is 15._____
    A. not satisfactory in any program dealing with juvenile delinquents
    B. the most effective means by which young vandals and hooligans can be reformed
    C. not used sufficiently when dealing with serious offenders who are under 21
    D. of value in reducing juvenile delinquency only if it is part of a complete program

5 (#1)

16. With respect to serious offenders who are under 21 years of age, the paragraph suggests that they   16._____
    A. be mollycoddled
    B. be dealt with as part of a comprehensive program to punish mature criminals
    C. should be punished
    D. be prevented, by brute force if necessary, from performing anti-social acts

17. Statistics tell us that heart disease kills more people than any other illness, and the death rate continues to rise. People over 30 have a 50-50 chance of escaping, for heart disease is chiefly an illness of people in late middle age and advanced years. Since more people in this age group are living today than were some years ago, heart disease is able to find more victims.   17._____
    On the basis of this selection, the statement which is most nearly correct is that
    A. half the people over 30 years of age have heart disease today
    B. more people die of heart disease than of all other diseases combined
    C. older people are the chief victims of heart disease
    D. the rising birth rate has increased the possibility that the average person will die of heart disease

18. Assume that a Court Officer is allowed 25 cents a mile for the use of her automobile for the purpose of conducting defendants to and from court sessions. The first month she drove 416 miles; the second month 328 miles; the third month 2,012 miles; the fourth month 187 miles; the fifth month 713 miles; the sixth month 1,608 miles. Her expenditures for gasoline averaged $2.70 a gallon and her general average of miles per gallon was 16; she used 32 quarts of oil at $1.25 per quart and spent $351.20 on care and general upkeep of her car for the six months. Without considering the depreciation in value of her car, she would have received above her expenditures: 18._____
    A. $36.50
    B. $40
    C. $96.10
    D. $263.20

19. Assume that you borrowed $2,000 on Nov. 1, 1999, for the use of which you were required to pay simple interest semi-annually at seven percent a year. By May 1, 2005, you would have paid interest amounting to   19._____
    A. $140
    B. $280
    C. $700
    D. $770

20. A courtroom contains 72 persons, which is two-fifths of its capacity. The number of persons that the courtroom can hold is   20._____
    A. 28   B. 129   C. 180   D. 200-300

21. The total cost of 30 pencils at 18 cents a dozen, 12 paper pads at 27-1/2 cents each and eight boxes of paper clips at 5-1/4 cents a box is
    A. more than $10
    B. $1.50
    C. $4.17
    D. $1.52

    21._____

22. "A" worked five days on overhauling an old car. Then "B" worked four days to finish the job. After the sale of the car, the net profit was $243. They wanted to divide the profit on the basis of time spent by each. A's share of the profit was
    A. $108
    B. $135
    C. $127
    D. $143

    22._____

Questions 23-26

DIRECTIONS: Each of the following questions contains four sentences. Select the sentence in each question that is best with respect to grammar and good usage.

23. A. One of us have to make the reply before tomorrow.
    B. Making the reply before tomorrow will have to be done by one of us.
    C. One of us has to reply before tomorrow.
    D. Anyone has to reply before tomorrow.

    23._____

24. A. There is several ways to organize a good report.
    B. Several ways exist in organizing a good report.
    C. To organize a good report, several ways exist.
    D. There are several ways to organize a good report.

    24._____

25. A. All employees whose record of service ranged between 51 down to 40 years were retired.
    B. All employees who had served from 40 to 51 years were retired.
    C. All employees serving 40 to 51 years were retired.
    D. Those retired were employees serving 40 to 51 years.

    25._____

26. A. Of all the employees, he spends the most time at the office.
    B. He spends more time at the office than that of his employees.
    C. His working hours are longer than or equal to those of other employees.
    D. He devotes as much, if not more, time to his work than the rest of the employees.

    26._____

Question 27 is based on the following paragraph:

Certain inmate types are generally found in prisons. These types are called gorillas, toughs, hipsters and merchants. Gorillas deliberately use violence to intimidate fearful inmates into providing favors. Toughs are swift to explode into violence against prisoners, because of real or imagined insults. Exploitation of others is not their major goal. Hipsters are bullies who choose victims with caution in order to win acceptance among inmates by demonstrating physical bravery. Their bravery, however, is false. Merchants exploit other inmates through manipulation in sharp trading of goods stolen from prison supplies or in trickery in gambling.

27. Martins frequently beats up Smith and Brooks. Smith and Brooks provide Martins with extra cigarettes and coffee. Martins is a
    A. tough
    B. gorilla
    C. merchant
    D. hipster

27._____

Questions 28 through 30 are based on the following description of the duties of the Court Officer:

Throughout the session of the court, the officer must see that proper order and decorum are maintained in the courtroom. Above all else, silence must be constantly observed, and every possible distraction must be eliminated so as not to delay the most efficient functioning of the court.

The officer must carry out such duties as may be required by the court and clerk. Examples of such duties are directing witnesses to the witness stand and assisting the Court Clerk and counsel in the handling of exhibits. At times, the officer must act as a messenger in procuring any books from the court library that are required by the attorneys and ordered by the Court Clerk.

The enforcement of the rules of the court requires courteous behavior on the part of the Court Officer, although firmness and strictness are necessary when the occasion requires such an attitude.

28. Testimony has been given, the witnesses have been cross-examined and the attorneys have given their summations. Now the judge is charging the jury. A Court Officer has been stationed outside the courtroom door to prevent anyone from entering during the charge. The City Council President arrives, accompanied by a woman, and attempts to enter the courtroom. The Court Officer should
    A. apologize and explain why they cannot be permitted to enter
    B. permit the man to enter, since he is the City Council President, but exclude the woman
    C. permit them to enter because surely the judge would make an exception for such important people
    D. send a note to the judge to ask whether they may be permitted to enter

28._____

29. A witness who is waiting to be called to the stand appears to be very nervous. He wiggles and squirms, stands and stretches, looks over his shoulder at the courtroom door and waves to spectators. The officer should
    A. tell the witness to leave the courtroom at once
    B. handcuff the witness
    C. ask the witness to please sit still and try to restrain himself
    D. suggest to the judge that he call this witness next

29._____

30. During the course of cross-examination, a defendant frequently refers to a book that she claims has had a great influence on her life and that she claims justifies her behavior in the crime for which she is charged. In the jury box, two jurors begin a lively discussion of whether the defendant is quoting accurately. The best action for the Court Officer is to
    A. ask the Court Clerk for permission to go to the library to get the book
    B. send a messenger to get the book
    C. assure the jurors that the book is being accurately quoted and that only the interpretation is in question
    D. remind the jurors that they are not to converse in the courtroom

30._____

31. "Ideally, a correctional system should include several types of institutions to provide different degrees of custody."
    On the basis of this statement, one could most reasonably say that
    A. as the number of institutions in a correctional system increases, the efficiency of the system increases
    B. the difference in degree of custody for the inmate depends on the types of institutions in a correctional system
    C. the greater the variety of institutions, the stricter the degree of custody that can be maintained
    D. the same type of correctional institution is not desirable for the custody of all prisoners

31._____

32. "The enforced idleness of a large percentage of adult men and women in our prisons is one of the direct causes of the tensions that burst forth in riot and disorder."
    On the basis of this statement, a good reason why inmates should perform daily work of some kind is that
    A. better morale and discipline can be maintained when inmates are kept busy
    B. daily work is an effective way of punishing inmates for the crimes they have committed
    C. law-abiding citizens must work therefore labor should also be required of inmates
    D. products of inmates' labor will in part pay the cost of their maintenance

32._____

33. "With industry invading rural areas, the use of the automobile, and the speed of modern communications and transportation, the problems of neglect and delinquency are no longer peculiar to cities but are an established feature of everyday life."
This statement implies most directly that
- A. delinquents are moving from cities to rural areas
- B. delinquency and neglect are found in rural areas
- C. delinquency is not as much of a problem in rural areas as in cities
- D. rural areas now surpass cities in industry

34. "Young men from minority groups, if unable to find employment, become discouraged and hopeless because of their economic position and may finally resort to any means of supplying their wants."
The most reasonable of the following conclusions that may be drawn from this statement only is that
- A. discouragement sometimes leads to crime
- B. in general, young men from minority groups are criminals
- C. unemployment turns young men from crime
- D. young men from minority groups are seldom employed

35. "To prevent crime, we must deal with the possible criminals long before they reach the prison. Our aim should be not merely to reform the lawbreakers but to strike at the roots of crime: neglectful parents, bad companions, unsatisfactory homes, selfishness, disregard for the rights of others and bad social conditions."
The above statement recommends
- A. abolition of prisons
- B. better reformatories
- C. compulsory education
- D. general social reform

36. "There is evidence that shows that comic books which glorify the criminal and criminal acts have a distinct influence in producing young criminals."
According to this statement
- A. comic books affect the development of criminal careers
- B. comic books specialize in reporting criminal acts
- C. young criminals read comic books exclusively
- D. young criminals should not be permitted to read comic books

37. A study shows that juvenile delinquents are equal in intelligence to but three school grades behind juvenile nondelinquents. On the basis of this information only, it is most reasonable to say that
- A. a delinquent usually progresses to the educational limit set by intelligence
- B. educational achievement depends on intelligence only
- C. educational achievement is closely associated with delinquency
- D. lack of intelligence is closely associated with delinquency

38. "Prevention of crime is of greater value to the community than the punishment of crime."
If this statement is accepted as true, greatest emphasis should be placed on
   A. execution
   B. medication
   C. imprisonment
   D. rehabilitation

39. A Court Assistant being instructed in his duties was told by the Court Clerk, "experience is the best teacher."
The one of the following that most nearly expresses the meaning of this quotation is:
   A. A good teacher will make a hard job look easy
   B. Bad experience does more harm than good
   C. Lack of experience will make an easy job hard
   D. The best way to learn to do a thing is by doing it

40. "Once the purposes or goals of an organization have been determined, they must be communicated to subordinate levels of supervisory staff."
On the basis of this quotation, the most accurate statement is that
   A. supervisory personnel should participate in the formulation of the goals of an organization
   B. the structure of an organization should be considered in determining the organization's goals
   C. the goals that have been established for the different levels of an organization should be reviewed regularly
   D. information about the goals of an organization should be distributed to supervisory personnel

41. "Close examination of traffic accident statistics reveals that traffic accidents are frequently the result of violations of traffic laws—and usually the violations are the result of illegal and dangerous driving behavior, rather than the result of mechanical defects or poor road conditions."
According to this statement, the majority of dangerous traffic violations are cause by
   A. poor driving
   B. bad roads
   C. unsafe cars
   D. unwise traffic laws

Questions 42 through 44 are based on the following paragraph:

The supervisor gains the respect of his staff members and increases his influence over them by controlling his temper and avoiding criticizing anyone publicly. When a mistake is made, the good supervisor will talk it over with the employee quietly and privately. The supervisor listens to the employee's story, suggests a better way to do the job, and offers help so the mistake won't happen again. Before closing the discussion, the supervisor should try to find something good to say about other aspects of the employee's work. Some praise and appreciation, along with instruction, is likely to encourage an employee to improve in those areas where he is weakest.

42. A good title that would show the meaning of this entire paragraph would be:
    A. How to Correct Employee Errors
    B. How to Praise Employees
    C. Mistakes are Preventable
    D. The Weak Employee

43. According to the preceding paragraph, the work of an employee who has made a mistake is more likely to improve if the supervisor
    A. avoids criticizing him
    B. gives him a chance to suggest a better way of doing the work
    C. listens to the employee's excuses to see if he's right
    D. praises good work at the same time he corrects the mistake

44. When a supervisor needs to correct an employee's mistake, it is important that he
    A. allow some time to go by after the mistake has been made
    B. do so when other employees are not present
    C. show his influence by his tone of voice
    D. tell other employees to avoid the same mistake

45. "Determination of total, or even partial, guilt and responsibility as viewed by law cannot be made solely on the basis of a consideration of the external factors of the case, but rather should be made mainly in the light of the individual defendant's history and development."
    The above statement reflects a philosophy of law that requires that
    A. the punishment fit the crime
    B. the individual, rather than the crime, be considered first
    C. motivations behind a crime are relatively unimportant
    D. the individual's knowledge of right and wrong be the sole determinant of guilt

46. A traffic regulation says, "No driver shall enter an intersection unless there is sufficient unobstructed space beyond the intersection to accommodate the vehicle he or she is operating, not withstanding any traffic-control signal indication to the contrary."
This regulation means that:
   A. a driver should not go through an intersection if there are no parking spaces available on the next block
   B. a driver should not enter an intersection when the traffic light is red
   C. a driver should not enter an intersection if traffic ahead is so badly backed up that he or she would not be able to go ahead and would block the intersection
   D. a driver should ignore traffic signals completely whenever there are obstructions in the road ahead

46._____

Questions 47 through 51 are based on the following passage:

A large proportion of people behind bars are not convicted criminals, but people who have been arrested and are being held until their trial in court. Experts have often pointed out that this detention system does not operate fairly. For instance, a person who can afford to pay bail usually will not get locked up.

The theory of the bail system is that the person will make sure to show up in court when he or she is supposed to; otherwise, bail will be forfeited—the person will lose the money that was put up. Sometimes a person who can show that he or she is a stable citizen with a job and a family will be released on "personal recognizance" (without bail). The result is that the well-to-do, the employed and the family men can often avoid the detention system. The people who do wind up in detention tend to be the poor, the unemployed, the single and the young.

47. People who are put behind bars
   A. are almost always dangerous criminals
   B. include many innocent people who have been arrested by mistake
   C. are often people who have been arrested but have not yet come to trial
   D. are all poor people who tend to be young and single

47._____

48. The passage says that the detention system works unfairly against people who are
   A. rich
   B. old
   C. married
   D. unemployed

48._____

49. The passage uses the expression "bail will be forfeited." Even if you had not seen the word *forfeit* before, you could figure out from the way it is used that forfeiting probably means _____ something.
   A. losing track of
   B. finding
   C. giving up
   D. avoiding

49._____

50. When someone is released on personal recognizance, this means that
    A. the judge knows that the person is innocent
    B. he or she does not have to show up for a trial
    C. he or she has a record of previous convictions
    D. he or she does not have to pay bail

51. Suppose that two men were booked on the same charge at the same time and that the same bail was set for both of them. One man was able to put up bail and was released. The second man was not able to put up bail and was held in detention. The writer of the passage would most likely feel that this result is
    A. unfair, because it does not have any relationship to guilt or innocence
    B. unfair, because the first man deserves severe punishment
    C. fair, because the first man is obviously innocent
    D. fair, because the law should be tougher on the poor people than on the rich

Questions 52 through 55 are based on the following passage:

The Court Officer has important functions in connection with control of the jury. He or she must confirm that every juror has the proper place in the box and must be constantly on watch to prevent any juror from leaving the jury box while the trial is in progress. Should a juror decide to leave the box while the case is going on, the Court Officer must first inform the judge of the juror's desire to determine whether the judge will grant or refuse the juror's wish. If the judge approves, the trial is stopped and the Court Officer is instructed to accompany the juror while he or she is out of the jury box.

In order to prevent any stoppage or mistrial, the Court Officer must not allow the juror to get out of the range of sight or hearing. The officer must always bear in mind that the juror should be returned as quickly as possible, without any unnecessary delay. The juror must not enter into any conversation with anybody or read any matter that he or she may have or that may be given by another person.

The Court Officer must be particularly careful when placed in charge of a jury that has retired to deliberate. The Court Officer must conduct the jury to the jury room and see to it that no juror talks with anyone on the way. If a juror does talk with someone, the event may afford grounds for a mistrial.

52. A juror has requested and received permission to go to the men's room. As he approaches the door, he takes out a sports magazine he has brought from home as "bathroom literature." The Court Officer should
    A. permit the juror to read the magazine
    B. check the magazine for papers that might be hidden between the pages, then let the juror read it
    C. offer the juror something of his own to read, something that he knows will not influence the juror in any way
    D. tell the juror that reading in the men's room is not permitted

53. While leading a jury from the courtroom to the jury room, a Court Officer notices a person leaning against a corridor wall making active hand motions as a juror stares intently. The *first* thing for a Court Officer to do is
    A. tell the juror to look straight ahead and keep walking
    B. step between the juror and the person so as to interrupt the juror's line of vision
    C. ask the juror what he is looking at
    D. call a police officer to arrest the person with the active hands

54. If the Court Officer ascertains that a message has been transmitted by an outside person to a juror, it would be best for the Court Officer to
    A. keep this information secret
    B. ask the juror what the message was about
    C. deliver the juror to the jury room, then discuss the matter with the Court Clerk
    D. accompany the juror to the judge and tell the judge exactly what the Court Officer observed

55. During the course of testimony, a juror begins to cough uncontrollably. The coughing is loud and distressing. The Court Officer should
    A. summon a doctor at once
    B. lead the juror from the courtroom as quickly and quietly as possible
    C. bring the juror a glass of water
    D. ask the judge what to do

KEY (CORRECT ANSWERS)

1. C	11. A	21. C	31. D	41. A	51. A
2. B	12. D	22. B	32. A	42. A	52. D
3. B	13. C	23. C	33. B	43. D	53. A
4. C	14. C	24. D	34. A	44. B	54. B
5. C	15. D	25. B	35. D	45. B	55. B
6. A	16. C	26. A	36. A	46. C	
7. B	17. C	27. B	37. C	47. C	
8. C	18. A	28. A	38. D	48. D	
9. A	19. D	29. C	39. D	49. C	
10. A	20. C	30. D	40. D	50. D	

EXAMINATION SECTION
TEST 1

DIRECTIONS: Each question or incomplete statement is followed by several suggested answers or completions. Select the one that BEST answers the question or completes the statement. *PRINT THE LETTER OF THE CORRECT ANSWER IN THE SPACE AT THE RIGHT.*

1. Physical and mental health are essential to the officer. According to this statement, the officer MUST be

    A. as wise as he is strong
    B. smarter than most people
    C. sound in mind and body
    D. stronger than the average criminal

2. Teamwork is the basis of successful law enforcement. The factor stressed by this statement is

    A. cooperation
    C. initiative
    B. determination
    D. pride

3. Legal procedure is a means, not an end. Its function is merely to accomplish the enforcement of legal rights.
   A litigant has no vested interest in the observance of the rules of procedure as such. All that he should be entitled to demand is that he be given an opportunity for a fair and impartial trial of his case. He should not be permitted to invoke the aid of technical rules merely to embarrass his adversary.
   According to this paragraph, it is MOST correct to state that

    A. observance of the rules of procedure guarantees a fair trial
    B. embarrassment of an adversary through technical rules does not make a fair trial
    C. a litigant is not interested in the observance of rules of procedure
    D. technical rules must not be used in a trial

4. One theory states that all criminal behavior is taught by a process of communication within small intimate groups. An individual engages in criminal behavior if the number of criminal patterns which he has acquired exceed the number of non-criminal patterns. This statement indicates that criminal behavior is

    A. learned
    C. hereditary
    B. instinctive
    D. reprehensible

5. The law enforcement staff of today requires training and mental qualities of a high order. The poorly or partially prepared staff member lowers the standard of work, retards his own earning power, and fails in a career meant to provide a livelihood and social improvement.
   According to this statement,

    A. an inefficient member of a law enforcement staff will still earn a good livelihood
    B. law enforcement officers move in good social circles
    C. many people fail in law enforcement careers
    D. persons of training and ability are essential to a law enforcement staff

6. In any state, no crime can occur unless there is a written law forbidding the act or the omission in question; and even though an act may not be exactly in harmony with public policy, such act is not a crime unless it is expressly forbidden by legislative statement. According to the above statement,

    A. a crime is committed with reference to a particular law
    B. acts not in harmony with public policy should be forbidden by law
    C. non-criminal activity will promote public welfare
    D. legislative enactments frequently forbid actions in harmony with public policy

7. The unrestricted sale of firearms is one of the main causes of our shameful crime record. According to this statement, one of the causes of our crime record is

    A. development of firepower
    B. ease of securing weapons
    C. increased skill in using guns
    D. scientific perfection of firearms

8. Every person must be informed of the reason for his arrest unless he is arrested in the actual commission of a crime. Sufficient force to effect the arrest may be used, but the courts frown on brutal methods.
   According to this statement, a person does not have to be informed of the reason for his arrest if

    A. brutal force was not used in effecting it
    B. the courts will later turn the defendant loose
    C. the person arrested knows force will be used if necessary
    D. the reason for it is clearly evident from the circumstances

9. An important duty of an officer is to keep order in the court.
   On the basis of this statement, it is PROBABLY true that

    A. it is more important for an officer to be strong than it is for him to be smart
    B. people involved in court trials are noisy if not kept in check
    C. not every duty of an officer is important
    D. the maintenance of order is important for the proper conduct of court business

10. Ideally, a correctional system should include several types of institutions to provide different degrees of custody.
    On the basis of this statement, one could MOST reasonably say that

    A. as the number of institutions in a correctional system increases, the efficiency of the system increases
    B. the difference in degree of custody for the inmate depends on the types of institutions in a correctional system
    C. the greater the variety of institutions, the stricter the degree of custody that can be maintained
    D. the same type of correctional institution is not desirable for the custody of all prisoners

11. The enforced idleness of a large percentage of adult men and women in our prisons is one of the direct causes of the tensions which burst forth in riot and disorder.
    On the basis of this statement, a good reason why inmates should perform daily work of some kind is that

    A. better morale and discipline can be maintained when inmates are kept busy
    B. daily work is an effective way of punishing inmates for the crimes they have committed
    C. law-abiding citizens must work, therefore labor should also be required of inmates
    D. products of inmates' labor will in part pay the cost of their maintenance

11._____

12. With industry invading rural areas, the use of the automobile, and the speed of modern communications and transportation, the problems of neglect and delinquency are no longer peculiar to cities but an established feature of everyday life.
    This statement implies MOST directly that

    A. delinquents are moving from cities to rural areas
    B. delinquency and neglect are found in rural areas
    C. delinquency is not as much of a problem in rural areas as in cities
    D. rural areas now surpass cities in industry

12._____

13. Young men from minority groups, if unable to find employment, become discouraged and hopeless because of their economic position and may finally resort to any means of supplying their wants.
    The MOST reasonable of the following conclusions that may be drawn from this statement only is that

    A. discouragement sometimes leads to crime
    B. in general, young men from minority groups are criminals
    C. unemployment turns young men from crime
    D. young men from minority groups are seldom employed

13._____

14. To prevent crime, we must deal with the possible criminal long before he reaches the prison. Our aim should be not merely to reform the law breakers but to strike at the roots of crime: neglectful parents, bad companions, unsatisfactory homes, selfishness, disregard for the rights of others, and bad social conditions.
    The above statement recommends

    A. abolition of prisons   B. better reformatories
    C. compulsory education   D. general social reform

14._____

15. There is evidence which shows that comic books which glorify the criminal and criminal acts have a distinct influence in producing young criminals.
    According to this statement,

    A. comic books affect the development of criminal careers
    B. comic books specialize in reporting criminal acts
    C. young criminals read comic books exclusively
    D. young criminals should not be permitted to read comic books

15._____

16. Suppose a study shows that juvenile delinquents are equal in intelligence but three school grades behind juvenile non-delinquents.
    On the basis of this information only, it is MOST reasonable to say that

    A. a delinquent usually progresses to the educational limit set by his intelligence
    B. educational achievement depends on intelligence only
    C. educational achievement is closely associated with delinquency
    D. lack of intelligence is closely associated with delinquency

17. There is no proof today that the experience of a prison sentence makes a better citizen of an adult. On the contrary, there seems some evidence that the experience is an unwholesome one that frequently confirms the criminality of the inmate.
    From the above paragraph only, it may be BEST concluded that

    A. prison sentences tend to punish rather than rehabilitate
    B. all criminals should be given prison sentences
    C. we should abandon our penal institutions
    D. penal institutions are effective in rehabilitating criminals

18. Some courts are referred to as *criminal* courts while others are known as *civil* courts. This distinction in name is MOST probably based on the

    A. historical origin of the court
    B. link between the court and the police
    C. manner in which the judges are chosen
    D. type of cases tried there

19. Many children who are exposed to contacts and experiences of a delinquent nature become educated and trained in crime in the course of participating in the daily life of the neighborhood.
    From this statement only, we may reasonably conclude that

    A. delinquency passes from parent to child
    B. neighborhood influences are usually bad
    C. schools are training grounds for delinquents
    D. none of the above conclusions is reasonable

20. Old age insurance, for whose benefits a quarter of a million city employees may elect to become eligible, is one feature of the Social Security Act that is wholly administered by the Federal government.
    On the basis of this paragraph only, it may MOST reasonably be inferred that

    A. a quarter of a million city employees are drawing old age insurance
    B. a quarter of a million city employees have elected to become eligible for old age insurance
    C. the city has no part in administering Social Security old age insurance
    D. only the Federal government administers the Social Security Act

21. An officer's revolver is a defensive, and not offensive, weapon.
    On the basis of this statement only, an officer should BEST draw his revolver to

    A. fire at an unarmed burglar
    B. force a suspect to confess
    C. frighten a juvenile delinquent
    D. protect his own life

22. Prevention of crime is of greater value to the community than the punishment of crime. If this statement is accepted as true, GREATEST emphasis should be placed on

    A. malingering   B. medication
    C. imprisonment   D. rehabilitation

23. The criminal is rarely or never reformed. Acceptance of this statement as true would mean that GREATEST emphasis should be placed on

    A. imprisonment   B. parole
    C. probation   D. malingering

24. The MOST accurate of the following statements about persons convicted of crimes is that

    A. their criminal behavior is almost invariably the result of low intelligence
    B. they are almost invariably legally insane
    C. they are more likely to come from underprivileged groups than from other groups
    D. they have certain facial characteristics which distinguish them from non-criminals

25. Suppose a study shows that the I.Q. (Intelligence Quotient) of prison inmates is 95 as opposed to an I.Q. of 100 for a numerically equivalent civilian group.
A claim, on the basis of this study, that criminals have a lower I.Q. than non-criminals would be

    A. *improper;* prison inmates are criminals who have been caught
    B. *proper;* the study was numerically well done
    C. *improper;* the sample was inadequate
    D. *proper;* even misdemeanors are sometimes penalized by prison sentences

Questions 26-45.

DIRECTIONS: Select the number of the word or expression that MOST NEARLY expresses the meaning of the capitalized word in the group.

26. ABDUCT

    A. lead   B. kidnap   C. sudden   D. worthless

27. BIAS

    A. ability   B. envy   C. prejudice   D. privilege

28. COERCE

    A. cancel   B. force   C. rescind   D. rugged

29. CONDONE

    A. combine   B. pardon   C. revive   D. spice

30. CONSISTENCY

    A. bravery   B. readiness
    C. strain   D. uniformity

31. CREDENCE
    A. belief
    B. devotion
    C. resemblance
    D. tempo

32. CURRENT
    A. backward
    B. brave
    C. prevailing
    D. wary

33. CUSTODY
    A. advisement
    B. belligerence
    C. guardianship
    D. suspicion

34. DEBILITY
    A. deceitfulness
    B. decency
    C. strength
    D. weakness

35. DEPLETE
    A. beg
    B. empty
    C. excuse
    D. fold

36. ENUMERATE
    A. name one by one
    B. disappear
    C. get rid of
    D. pretend

37. FEIGN
    A. allow
    B. incur
    C. pretend
    D. weaken

38. INSTIGATE
    A. analyze
    B. coordinate
    C. oppose
    D. provoke

39. LIABLE
    A. careless
    B. growing
    C. mistaken
    D. responsible

40. PONDER
    A. attack
    B. heavy
    C. meditate
    D. solicit

41. PUGILIST
    A. farmer
    B. politician
    C. prize fighter
    D. stage actor

42. QUELL
    A. explode
    B. inform
    C. shake
    D. suppress

43. RECIPROCAL
    A. mutual
    B. organized
    C. redundant
    D. thoughtful

44. RUSE

    A. burn   B. impolite   C. rot   D. trick

44.____

45. STEALTHY

    A. crazed   B. flowing   C. sly   D. wicked

45.____

Questions 46-50.

DIRECTIONS: Each of the sentences in Questions 46 through 50 may be classified under one of the following four categories:
    A. faulty because of incorrect grammar
    B. faulty because of incorrect punctuation
    C. faulty because of incorrect capitalization or incorrect spelling
    D. correct

Examine each sentence carefully to determine under which of the above four options it is best classified. Then, in the space at the right, print the capital letter preceding the option which is the BEST of the four suggested above. Each faulty sentence contains but one type of error. Consider a sentence to be correct if it contains none of the types of errors mentioned, even though there may be other correct ways of expressing the same thought.

46. They told both he and I that the prisoner had escaped.   46.____

47. Any superior officer, who, disregards the just complaints of his subordinates, is remiss in the performance of his duty.   47.____

48. Only those members of the national organization who resided in the Middle west attended the conference in Chicago.   48.____

49. We told him to give the investigation assignment to whoever was available.   49.____

50. Please do not disappoint and embarass us by not appearing in court.   50.____

KEY (CORRECT ANSWERS)

1. C	11. A	21. D	31. A	41. C
2. A	12. B	22. D	32. C	42. D
3. B	13. A	23. A	33. C	43. A
4. A	14. D	24. C	34. D	44. D
5. D	15. A	25. A	35. B	45. C
6. A	16. C	26. B	36. A	46. A
7. B	17. A	27. C	37. C	47. B
8. D	18. D	28. B	38. D	48. C
9. D	19. D	29. B	39. D	49. D
10. D	20. C	30. D	40. C	50. C

TEST 2

DIRECTIONS: Each question or incomplete statement is followed by several suggested answers or completions. Select the one that BEST answers the question or completes the statement. *PRINT THE LETTER OF THE CORRECT ANSWER IN THE SPACE AT THE RIGHT.*

1. Suppose a man falls from a two-story high scaffold and is unconscious. You should

    A. call for medical assistance and avoid moving the man
    B. get someone to help you move him indoors to a bed
    C. have someone help you walk him around until he revives
    D. hold his head up and pour a stimulant down his throat

1.____

2. For proper first aid treatment, a person who has fainted should be

    A. doused with cold water and then warmly covered
    B. given artificial respiration until he is revived
    C. laid down with his head lower than the rest of his body
    D. slapped on the face until he is revived

2.____

3. If you are called on to give first aid to a person who is suffering from shock, you should

    A. apply cold towels   B. give him a stimulant
    C. keep him awake   D. wrap him warmly

3.____

4. Artificial respiration would NOT be proper first aid for a person suffering from

    A. drowning   B. electric shock
    C. external bleeding   D. suffocation

4.____

5. Suppose you are called on to give first aid to several victims of an accident. First attention should be given to the one who is

    A. bleeding severely   B. groaning loudly
    C. unconscious   D. vomiting

5.____

6. If an officer's weekly salary is increased from $480 to $540, then the percent of increase is _____ percent.

    A. 10   B. 11 1/9   C. 12 1/2   D. 20

6.____

7. Suppose that one-half the officers in a department have served for more than ten years and one-third have served for more than 15 years.
Then, the fraction of officers who have served between ten and fifteen years is

    A. 1/3   B. 1/5   C. 1/6   D. 1/12

7.____

8. In a city prison there are four floors on which prisoners are housed. The top floor houses one-quarter of the inmates, the bottom floor houses one-sixth of the inmates, one-third are housed on the second floor. The rest of the inmates are housed on the third floor. If there are 90 inmates housed on the third floor, the TOTAL number of inmates housed on all four floors together is

    A. 270   B. 360   C. 450   D. 540

8.____

9. Suppose that ten percent of those who commit serious crimes are convicted and that fifteen percent of those convicted are sentenced for more than 3 years.
The percentage of those committing serious crimes who are sentenced for more than 3 years is _____ percent.

   A. 15 B. 1.5 C. .15 D. .015

10. Assume that there are 1,100 employees in a city agency. Of these, 15 percent are officers, 80 percent of whom are attorneys; of the attorneys, two-fifths have been with the agency over five years.
Then, the number of officers who are attorneys and have over five years experience with the agency is MOST NEARLY

    A. 45 B. 53 C. 132 D. 165

11. An employee who has 500 cartons of supplies to pack can pack them at the rate of 50 an hour. After this employee has worked for 1/2 hour, he is joined by another employee who can pack 45 cartons an hour.
Assuming that both employees can maintain their respective rates of speed, then the TOTAL number of hours required to pack all the cartons is

    A. 4 1/2 B. 5 C. 5 1/2 D. 6 1/2

12. Thirty-six officers can complete an assignment in 22 days. Assuming that all officers work at the same rate of speed, the number of officers that would be needed to complete this assignment in 12 days is

    A. 42 B. 54 C. 66 D. 72

Questions 13-15.

DIRECTIONS: Questions 13 through 15 are to be answered on the basis of the table below. Data for certain categories have been omitted from the table. You are to calculate the missing numbers if needed to answer the questions.

	2007	2008	Numerical Increase
Correction Officers	1,226	1,347	
Court Officers		529	34
Deputy Sheriffs	38	40	
Supervisors			
	2,180	2,414	

13. The number in the *Supervisors* group in 2007 was MOST NEARLY

    A. 500 B. 475 C. 450 D. 425

14. The LARGEST percentage increase from 2007 to 2008 was in the group of

    A. Correction Officers   B. Court Officers
    C. Deputy Sheriffs   D. Supervisors

15. In 2008, the ratio of the number of Correction Officers to the total of the other three categories of employees was MOST NEARLY

    A. 1:1 B. 2:1 C. 3:1 D. 4:1

16. A directed verdict is made by a court when

    A. the facts are not disputed
    B. the defendant's motion for a directed verdict has been denied
    C. there is no question of law involved
    D. neither party has moved for a directed verdict

17. Papers on appeal of a criminal case do NOT include one of the following:

    A. Summons
    B. Minutes of trial
    C. Complaint
    D. Intermediate motion papers

18. A pleading titled *Smith vs. Jones, et al* indicates

    A. two plaintiffs
    B. two defendants
    C. more than two defendants
    D. unknown defendants

19. A District Attorney makes a *prima facie* case when

    A. there is proof of guilt beyond a reasonable doubt
    B. the evidence is sufficient to convict in the absence of rebutting evidence
    C. the prosecution presents more evidence than the defense
    D. the defendant fails to take the stand

20. A person is NOT qualified to act as a trial juror in a criminal action if he or she

    A. has been convicted previously of a misdemeanor
    B. is under 18 years of age
    C. has scruples against the death penalty
    D. does not own property of a value at least $500

21. A court clerk who falsifies a court record commits a(n)

    A. misdemeanor
    B. offense
    C. felony
    D. no crime, but automatically forfeits his tenure

22. Insolent and contemptuous behavior to a judge during a court of record proceeding is punishable as

    A. civil contempt
    B. criminal contempt
    C. disorderly conduct
    D. a disorderly person

23. Offering a bribe to a court clerk would not constitute a crime UNLESS the

    A. court clerk accepted the bribe
    B. bribe consisted of money
    C. bribe was given with intent to influence the court clerk in his official functions
    D. court was actually in session

24. A defendant comes to trial in the same court in which he had previously been defendant in a similar case.
    The court officer should

    A. tell him, *Knew we'd be seeing you again*
    B. tell newspaper reporters what he knows of the previous action
    C. treat him the same as he would any other defendant
    D. warn the judge that the man had previously been a defendant

24.____

25. Suppose in conversation with you, an attorney strongly criticizes a ruling of the judge and you believe the attorney to be correct.
    You should

    A. assure him you feel the same way
    B. tell him the judge knows the law
    C. tell him to ask for an exception
    D. refuse to discuss the matter

25.____

26. Assume that you are a court officer. A woman sees you in the hall and attempts to register a complaint that her husband raped her two hours earlier.
    Which one of the following is the MOST appropriate action for you to take FIRST in this case?

    A. Refer her to Family Court.
    B. Advise her that her husband has not committed any crime.
    C. Ask her for additional information about the circumstances surrounding her allegation so that you may refer her to the proper office or agency.
    D. Have her sign a criminal information in the court.

26.____

27. Which one of the following is the BEST example of a privileged communication which is NOT admissible as evidence in a court of law without the consent of the communicator?

    A. Client to his accountant
    B. Informant to a law enforcement officer
    C. Parent to his child
    D. Defendant to his spouse

27.____

28. A court officer has many contacts with the public. In these contacts, it is MOST important that he

    A. be brief and complete in his answers
    B. be courteous and helpful
    C. go along with what they ask
    D. know the law

28.____

29. Suppose a witness becomes engaged in a very heated argument with an attorney who is cross-examining him. The court officer should

    A. ask the attorney to avoid exciting the witness
    B. ask the judge if he wishes any action to be taken
    C. await the judge's order before interceding
    D. caution the witness to be more respectful

29.____

30. Suppose that you are a court officer stationed at the door of the courtroom to prevent anyone from entering while the judge is charging the jury. A man whom you recognize as a City Councilman, accompanied by a woman, attempts to enter the courtroom.
The BEST action for you to take is to

    A. apologize and explain why they cannot be permitted to enter
    B. permit the man to enter since he is a Councilman but exclude the woman
    C. permit them to enter since the judge would surely make an exception for them
    D. send a note in to the judge to find if they may be permitted to enter

31. It is desirable that a court officer acquire a knowledge of the procedures of the court to which he is assigned MAINLY because such knowledge will help him

    A. become familiar with anti-social behavior
    B. discharge his duties properly
    C. gain insight into causes of crime
    D. in any personal legal proceeding

32. Since he is a city employee, a court officer who refuses to waive immunity from prosecution when called on to testify in court automatically terminates his employment. From this statement ONLY, it may be BEST inferred that

    A. a court officer is a city employee
    B. all city employees are court officers
    C. city employees may be fired only for malfeasance
    D. court attendants who waive immunity may not be prosecuted

33. Referees of the Civil Court are former judges of this court who have served at least ten years and whose term of office terminated at the age of 55 or over, or any judge who has served in a court of record and has retired.
According to this statement, a person can be a referee of the Civil Court ONLY if he

    A. has been a judge
    B. has retired
    C. has served at least 10 years in the court
    D. meets certain age requirements

34. Assume that you are assigned to a jury room where you are to guard the jury until 4 P.M. Your relief does not arrive and the jury is still deliberating.
Of the following, the BEST action for you to take is to

    A. ask the foreman of the jury to assume responsibility until your relief arrives
    B. find out what the jurors may need, get it, and then lock them in for the night
    C. inform your supervisor but remain on duty until you are relieved
    D. wait until 5 P.M., your usual closing time, and then leave if the relief has not arrived by then

35. When, at a trial, a piece of evidence is tagged as *Exhibit A,* the CHIEF purpose is to

    A. assure its return to the owner
    B. make it possible to examine it for fingerprints without chance of error
    C. make it possible to identify and refer to it easily
    D. prevent the defendant from denying he had it

36. In one case, a mistrial was declared because the indictment used the pronoun he instead of she.
The MOST useful information a court attendant can derive from this statement is that

    A. accuracy is important
    B. mistrial is a legal term
    C. one must always use good grammar
    D. to misrepresent is criminal

37. Suppose a newspaper reporter asks you for information about what happened at a trial where the judge had ordered the courtroom cleared of reporters and spectators.
You should

    A. give him the information he wants
    B. refer him to the judge for information
    C. refuse to talk to him unless reporters from other papers are present
    D. give him misleading information

38. Assume that you are the court officer on duty outside the judge's chambers in the court house. One day, one of the judges informs you that he will be too busy that day to see any visitors, and he tells you to refer them to his secretary for new appointments. Later in the day, an important visitor comes in and asks to see the judge about urgent business.
Of the following, the BEST course of action for you to take in this situation is to

    A. ask the visitor to come back another day when the judge may be able to see him
    B. call the judge on the phone and tell him that the visitor has urgent business to discuss with him
    C. refer the visitor to one of the other judges who may be present in chambers
    D. tell the visitor that the judge is not available, but his secretary may be able to help him or make a new appointment

39. To gain a verdict against X in a trial, it was necessary to show that he could have been at Y Street at 5 P.M.
It was proven that he was seen at Z Street at 4:45 P.M. The question that MUST be answered to show whether the verdict should be against X is:

    A. How long does it take to get from Z Street to Y Street?
    B. In what sort of neighborhood is Y Street located?
    C. Was X acting suspiciously on the day in question?
    D. Who was with X when he was seen at Z Street at 4:45 P.M.?

40. If, at the instructions of the judge, a court officer calls the name of a defendant in a lawsuit and the person does not answer, the court officer should FIRST

    A. ask the judge if he called the person's name correctly
    B. call the person's name again
    C. look outside the doors of the courtroom for the defendant
    D. tell the judge the person doesn't answer

41. When X is accused of having cheated Y of a sum of money and Y is proven to have been deprived of the money, there is an additional requirement for a verdict against X.
The additional requirement is to prove that

    A. the money was stolen from Y
    B. X had the money after Y had it
    C. X had the money before Y had it
    D. X cheated Y of the money

42. Assume that you are on duty in a courtroom and during the judge's absence one of the witnesses for a pending case becomes very angry about the delay.
Of the following, the BEST action for you to take is to

   A. listen to him until he calms down and then explain the reason for the delay
   B. tell him your court is no different from any other court
   C. walk away from him so that you will not get involved in a dispute
   D. warn him that the judge may be back at any minute and will hold him in contempt

43. Assume that you are assigned to the post outside judge's chambers in the court house. A visitor tells you he has an appointment with Judge Jones who is expected to arrive shortly. He asks for permission to wait in the judge's office which is unoccupied at the present time.
For you to permit him to wait there would be

   A. *wise;* the judge would no doubt wish to speak to the man privately
   B. *wise;* it would keep the anteroom where you are stationed clear, allowing other employees to work without any disturbance
   C. *unwise;* it is rude to allow a visitor to sit alone in an office
   D. *unwise;* there may be confidential material on the judge's desk or bookcases

44. A court officer shall not receive a gift from any defendant or other person on the defendant's behalf.
The BEST explanation for this rule is that

   A. acceptance of a gift has no significance
   B. defendants cannot usually afford gifts
   C. favors may be expected in return
   D. gifts are only an expression of good will

45. When a jury is selected, the attorney for each side has a right to refuse to accept a certain number of prospective jurors without giving any reason therefor.
The reason for this is MAINLY that

   A. attorneys can exclude persons likely to be biased even though no prejudice is admitted
   B. persons who will suffer economically by being summoned for jury duty can be excused forthwith
   C. relatives of the litigants can be excused thus insuring a fair trial for each side
   D. there will be a greater number of people from which the jury can be selected

46. Where the defendant in a criminal case is too poor to afford counsel, the court will assign one and he will be paid by the government.
The principle BEST established by this statement is that

   A. it is improper for the government to provide both prosecuting and defending counsel in a trial
   B. laws are usually violated because of poverty and defendants are too poor to employ counsel
   C. only wealthy law violators may hope to be represented by competent counsel
   D. the government is obligated to shield the innocent as well as punish the guilty

47. If a visitor to the court asks foolish questions, the BEST action for the court officer to take is to   47._____

    A. answer in a brusque manner to discourage further foolish questions
    B. refer the questioner to his supervisor
    C. answer them the same way as he would any other questions
    D. ignore them since the person doesn't really expect an answer

48. A man plus a uniform makes a good court officer. This statement is FALSE because   48._____

    A. a court officer is also required to wear a badge
    B. a good court officer is not made merely by putting on a uniform
    C. it makes no mention of the fact that the uniform must be neat
    D. patrolmen as well as court officers wear uniforms

49. It is a frequent misconception that court officers can be recruited from those registers established for the recruitment of city police or firemen. While it is true that many common qualifications are found in all of these, specific standards for court work are indicated, varying with the size, geographical location, and policies of the court.
    According to this paragraph ONLY, it may BEST be inferred that   49._____

    A. a successful court officer must have some qualifications not required of a policeman or fireman
    B. qualifications which make a successful patrolman will also make a successful fireman
    C. the same qualifications are required of a court officer regardless of the court to which he is assigned
    D. the successful court officer is required to be both more intelligent and stronger than a fireman

50. One of the duties of a court officer is to assist the public with their problems.
    A PROPER exercise of this duty by a court officer would be for the officer to   50._____

    A. advise members of the public to settle their differences out of court
    B. advise a member of the public how to fill out forms required by the court
    C. lend money to a member of the public to pay the required court fees
    D. recommend a lawyer to a member of the public who does not have one

KEY (CORRECT ANSWERS)

1. A	11. C	21. C	31. B	41. D
2. C	12. C	22. B	32. A	42. A
3. D	13. D	23. C	33. A	43. D
4. C	14. D	24. C	34. C	44. C
5. A	15. A	25. D	35. C	45. A
6. C	16. A	26. C	36. A	46. D
7. C	17. D	27. D	37. B	47. C
8. B	18. C	28. B	38. D	48. B
9. B	19. B	29. C	39. A	49. A
10. B	20. B	30. A	40. B	50. B

EXAMINATION SECTION
TEST 1

DIRECTIONS: Each question or incomplete statement is followed by several suggested answers or completions. Select the one that BEST answers the question or completes the statement. *PRINT THE LETTER OF THE CORRECT ANSWER IN THE SPACE AT THE RIGHT.*

1. Which of the following is the LEAST important factor to consider in surveying the physical layout of a building for traffic flow?

    A. Location of windows
    B. Number of entrances
    C. Number of exits
    D. Location of first aid rooms

2. The major purpose of any security program in a large organization is to prevent unlawful acts.
    If adequate patrol coverage is provided at a given location, it is MOST likely that

    A. crimes will not be committed
    B. undesirables will not enter the building
    C. unlawful acts will increase in the long run
    D. there will be less opportunity to commit a crime

3. The MOST frequent cause of fires in public facilities is

    A. incinerators   B. vandalism
    C. electrical sources   D. smoking on the job

4. After bomb threats are received, it is sometimes necessary to evacuate a facility. How long BEFORE the threatened time of explosion should a facility be evacuated?
    At least _____ minutes.

    A. 15   B. 25   C. 50   D. 60

5. Once a facility is evacuated because of a bomb threat, how much time should pass before the public and employees are allowed to enter the building?
    _____ minutes.

    A. 10   B. 20   C. 40   D. 60

6. Of the following locations in public buildings, the one which is the LEAST likely place for bombs to be planted is in

    A. storerooms   B. bathrooms
    C. cafeterias   D. waste receptacles

7. The one of the following that is the surest means of establishing positive identification of someone entering a facility is by

    A. personal recognition   B. I.D. badge
    C. social security card   D. driver's license

8. The one of the following which most probably would NOT be included in a police record report concerning an incident at a facility is the

    A. name of complainant or injured party
    B. name of the investigating officer
    C. statement of each witness
    D. religion of complainant or injured party

9. Preventing trouble is one of the primary concerns of special officers.
   When dealing with unruly groups of people who threaten to become violent, which of the following is a measure which should NOT be taken?

    A. Maintain close surveillance of such groups
    B. Try to contact the leaders of the group regardless of their militancy
    C. Keep the officer force alerted
    D. Have the officer force deal aggressively with provocations

10. Of the following, the MOST important factor to consider in the deployment of officers dealing with a client population is the officers' ability to

    A. remain calm   B. look stern
    C. evaluate personality   D. take a firm stand

11. Assume that an offender is struggling with a group of officers who are trying to arrest him.
    What force, if any, can be used to overcome this resistance?

    A. The amount of force acceptable to the public
    B. The amount of force necessary to restrain the offender and protect the officers
    C. Any amount of force that is acceptable to the officers at the scene
    D. No force may be used until the police arrive

12. Assume that a fire is discovered at your work location. The one of the following actions which would be INAPPROPRIATE for you to take is to

    A. notify the telephone operator
    B. station a reliable person at the entrance
    C. open all windows and doors in the area
    D. start evacuating the area

13. If a person has an object caught in his throat or air passage but is breathing adequately, which one of the following should you do?

    A. Probe for the object
    B. Force him to drink water
    C. Lay him over your arm and slap him between the shoulder blades
    D. Allow him to cough and to assume the position he finds most comfortable

14. The one of the following methods which should NOT be used to report a fire is to

    A. call 911
    B. pull the handle in the red box on the street corner
    C. call the fire department county numbers listed in each county directory
    D. call 411

15. Assume that an officer, alone in a building at night, smells the strong odor of cooking or heating gas. In addition to airing the building and making sure that he is not overcome, it would be BEST for the officer to call

   A. his superior at his home and ask for instructions
   B. for a plumber from the department of public works
   C. 911 for police and fire help
   D. the emergency number at Con Edison

15.____

16. Of the following situations, the one that is MOST dangerous for an officer is when he

   A. investigates suspicious persons and circumstances
   B. finds a burglary in progress or pursues burglary suspects
   C. attempts an arrest or finds a robbery in progress
   D. patrols on the overnight shift

16.____

17. An officer on security patrol generally should spend MOST of his time

   A. checking doors and locks
   B. helping the public and answering questions
   C. chasing criminals and looking for clues
   D. writing reports on unusual incidents

17.____

18. The one of the following that is an ACCEPTABLE way to arrest a person is to

   A. tell him to report to the nearest police precinct
   B. send a summons to his permanent address
   C. tell him in person that he is under arrest
   D. show him handcuffs and ask him to come along

18.____

19. A carbon dioxide fire extinguisher is BEST suited for extinguishing _____ fires.

   A. paper   B. rag   C. rubbish   D. grease

19.____

20. A pressurized water or soda-acid fire extinguisher is BEST suited for extinguishing _____ fires.

   A. wood   B. gasoline
   C. electrical   D. magnesium

20.____

21. The one of the following statements that does NOT apply to the use of handcuffs is that they

   A. are used as temporary restraining devices
   B. eliminate the need for vigilance
   C. cannot be opened without keys
   D. are used to secure a violent person

21.____

22. The one of the following that is GENERALLY a crime against the person is

   A. trespass   B. burglary   C. robbery   D. arson

22.____

23. Of the following, the SAFEST way of escape from an office in a burning building is generally the

    A. stairway
    B. rooftop
    C. passenger elevator
    D. freight elevator

24. In attempting to control a possible riot situation, an officer pushed his way into a crowd gathered outside the building and tried to cause confusion by arguing with members of the group.
    This procedure NORMALLY is considered

    A. *desirable;* any violence that occurs will remain outside the building
    B. *desirable;* the crowd will break into smaller groups and disperse
    C. *undesirable;* to maintain control of the situation, the officer must not become part of the crowd
    D. *undesirable;* the supervisor should stay clear of the scene

25. Which one of the following is MOST effective in making officers more safety-minded?

    A. Maintaining an up-to-date library of the latest safety literature
    B. Reading daily safety bulletins at roll-call
    C. Holding informal group safety meetings periodically
    D. Offering prizes for good safety slogans and displays

KEY (CORRECT ANSWERS)

1.	A	11.	B
2.	D	12.	C
3.	C	13.	D
4.	A	14.	D
5.	D	15.	D
6.	C	16.	C
7.	A	17.	A
8.	D	18.	C
9.	D	19.	D
10.	A	20.	A

21. B
22. C
23. A
24. C
25. C

TEST 2

DIRECTIONS: Each question or incomplete statement is followed by several suggested answers or completions. Select the one that BEST answers the question or completes the statement. *PRINT THE LETTER OF THE CORRECT ANSWER IN THE SPACE AT THE RIGHT.*

1. Assume that an angry crowd of some 75 to 100 people has built up in one of the hallways of a center and that only one superior officer and two subordinate officers are on duty in the building. A glass panel in one of the stairway doors has just been broken under the pressure of the crowd and a bench has been hurled down a flight of stairs. The one of the following actions that the superior officer SHOULD take in this situation is to   1.____

    A. push his way into the crowd and try to reason with them
    B. order the two other officers to try to quiet the crowd
    C. call the police on 911 and meet them outside the building
    D. do nothing at this point in order to avoid a riot

2. One of the duties and responsibilities of a supervisor is to test the knowledge of the officers concerning their post conditions.   2.____
This should be done if the officer's assignment is

    A. fixed only
    B. roving only
    C. roving only in a troublesome spot
    D. either fixed or roving

3. An officer discovers early one morning that an office in the building he guards has been burglarized.   3.____
Of the following, it is important for the officer to FIRST

    A. go through the building and look for suspects
    B. call the police and protect the area and whatever evidence exists until they arrive
    C. allow people into their offices as they come to work
    D. examine, sort, and handle all evidence before the police get there

4. Assume that two officers are interrogating one suspect. How should these officers position themselves during the interrogation?   4.____

    A. One officer should stand on either side of the suspect.
    B. One officer should stand to the right of the suspect, and the other officer should stand behind the suspect.
    C. Both officers should stand to the right of the suspect.
    D. One officer should stand to the right of the suspect, and the other officer should stand in front of the suspect.

5. A witness who takes an oath to testify truly and who states as true any matter which he knows to be false is guilty of   5.____

    A. perjury   B. libel   C. slander   D. fraud

6. An officer checking a substance suspected of containing narcotics should GENERALLY

   A. taste it in small amounts
   B. send it to a laboratory for analysis
   C. smell it for its distinctive odor
   D. examine it for its unusual texture

7. A certain center is situated in an area where frequent outbreaks of hostilities seem to be focused on the center itself.
   Which of the following BEST explains why the center may be a target for hostile acts?
   It

   A. serves community needs
   B. represents governmental authority
   C. represents all ethnic groups
   D. serves as a neutral battlefield

8. An officer often deals with people who might be addicted to drugs.
   The one of the following symptoms which is NOT generally an indication of drug addiction is

   A. dilation of the eye pupils
   B. frequent yawning and sneezing
   C. a deep, rasping cough
   D. continual itching of the arms and legs

9. In emergency situations, panic will MOST probably occur when people are

   A. unexpectedly confronted with a terrorizing condition from which there appears to be no escape
   B. angry and violent
   C. anxious about circumstances which are not obvious, easily visible or within the immediate area
   D. familiar with the effects of the emergency

10. The one of the following actions on the part of a person that would NOT be considered *resisting arrest* is

    A. retreating and running away
    B. saying, *You can't arrest me*
    C. pushing the officer aside
    D. pulling away from an officer's grasp

11. Which of the following items would NOT be considered an APPROPRIATE item of uniform for an officer to wear while on duty?

    A. Reefer type overcoat
    B. Leather laced shoes with flat soles
    C. White socks
    D. Cap cover with cap device displayed

12. What can happen to an officer if the leather thong on his night stick is NOT twisted correctly?
    The

    A. baton may be taken out of the officer's hand
    B. officer's wrist may be broken
    C. leather will tear more easily
    D. officer's arm may be injured

13. The one of the following kinds of information which SHOULD be included in the log book is

    A. any important matter of police information
    B. an item noted in Standard Operating Procedures only
    C. everything of general interest
    D. a crime or offense only

14. While on patrol at your work location, you receive a call that an assault has taken place. Upon your arrival at the scene, the victim, who has severe lacerations, informs you that the assailant ran into a nearby basement.
    After apprehending the suspect, the type of search you should conduct is a _____ search.

    A. wall   B. frisk   C. body   D. strip

15. A tactical force is valuable in MOST emergency situations PRIMARILY because of its

    A. location   B. morale
    C. flexibility   D. size

16. An officer should be encouraged to talk easily and frankly when he is dealing with his superior.
    In order to encourage such free communication, it would be MOST appropriate for a superior to behave in a(n)

    A. *sincere* manner; assure the officer that you will deal with him honestly and openly
    B. *official* manner; you are a superior officer and must always act formally with subordinates
    C. *investigative* manner; you must probe and question to get to a basis of trust
    D. *unemotional* manner; the officer's emotions and background should play no part in your dealings with him

17. Research findings show that an increase in free communication within an agency GENERALLY results in which one of the following?

    A. Improved morale and productivity
    B. Increased promotional opportunities
    C. An increase in authority
    D. A spirit of honesty

18. Assume that you are a superior officer and your superiors have given you a new arrest procedure to be followed. Before passing this information on to your subordinates, the one of the following actions that you should take FIRST is to

    A. ask your superiors to send out a memorandum to the entire staff
    B. clarify the procedure in your own mind
    C. set up a training course to provide instructions on the new procedure
    D. write a memorandum to your subordinates

19. Communication is necessary for an organization to be effective.
    The one of the following which is LEAST important for most communication systems is that

    A. messages are sent quickly and directly to the person who needs them to operate
    B. information should be conveyed understandably and accurately
    C. the method used to transmit information should be kept secret so that security can be maintained
    D. senders of messages must know how their messages were received and acted upon

20. Which one of the following is the CHIEF advantage of listening willingly to subordinate officers and encouraging them to talk freely and honestly?
    It

    A. reveals to superiors the degree to which ideas that are passed down are accepted by subordinates
    B. reduces the participation of subordinates in the operation of the department
    C. encourages officers to try for promotion
    D. enables officers to learn about security leaks on the part of officials

21. A superior may be informed through either oral or written reports.
    Which one of the following is an ADVANTAGE of using oral reports?

    A. There is no need for a formal record of the report.
    B. An exact duplicate of the report is not easily transmitted to others.
    C. A good oral report requires little time for preparation.
    D. An oral report involves two-way communication between a subordinate and his superior.

22. Of the following, the MOST important reason why officers should communicate effectively with the public is to

    A. improve the public's understanding of information that is important for them to know
    B. establish a friendly relationship
    C. obtain information about the kinds of people who come to the center
    D. convince the public that services are adequate

23. Officers should generally NOT use phrases like *too hard, too easy,* and *a lot* principally because such phrases

    A. may be offensive to some minority groups
    B. are too informal

C. mean different things to different people
D. are difficult to remember

24. The ability to communicate clearly and concisely is an important element in effective leadership.
Which of the following statements about oral and written communication is GENERALLY true?

    A. Oral communication is more time-consuming.
    B. Written communication is more likely to be misinterpreted.
    C. Oral communication is useful only in emergencies.
    D. Written communication is useful mainly when giving information to fewer than twenty people.

24.____

25. Rumors can often have harmful and disruptive effects on an organization.
Which one of the following is the BEST way to prevent rumors from becoming a problem?

    A. Refuse to act on rumors, thereby making them less believable
    B. Increase the amount of information passed along by the *grapevine*
    C. Distribute as much factual information as possible
    D. Provide training in report writing

25.____

KEY (CORRECT ANSWERS)

1. C		11. C
2. D		12. A
3. B		13. A
4. B		14. A
5. A		15. C
6. B		16. A
7. B		17. A
8. C		18. B
9. A		19. C
10. B		20. A

21. D
22. A
23. C
24. B
25. C

EXAMINATION SECTION
TEST 1

DIRECTIONS: Each question or incomplete statement is followed by several suggested answers or completions. Select the one that BEST answers the question or completes the statement. *PRINT THE LETTER OF THE CORRECT ANSWER IN THE SPACE AT THE RIGHT.*

1. As a superior officer, you have the responsibility of deciding whether some of your duties should be delegated to subordinate officers.
   The delegation of certain duties to subordinates is GENERALLY considered

   A. *inadvisable;* subordinates should not share your responsibilities
   B. *advisable;* this will help to prevent you from getting bogged down with minor details and problems
   C. *inadvisable;* you can probably do all parts of your job better than anyone else can
   D. *advisable;* more time can therefore be devoted to day-to-day operations and less to long-range planning

   1.___

2. Assume that you are a superior officer and that one of your subordinates is careless in the performance of his job.
   Of the following, it would be MOST important for you, when helping this employee, to realize that

   A. punitive methods produce better long-term results than non-punitive methods
   B. most problem officers require strict supervision rather than counseling and training
   C. the superior can often play a large part in changing employee patterns of work
   D. if orders are given in detail, carelessness will be eliminated

   2.___

3. One of the key qualities of a good superior officer is his ability to balance his work load against the time available to him to complete the job.
   Of the following, the BEST procedure for a superior to follow in establishing his work priorities is to

   A. organize tasks according to urgency without regard to importance
   B. undertake all important, difficult tasks in any order and delegate the routine work to subordinates
   C. assign all work to various subordinates and guide their handling of the problems
   D. delegate those problems that can be solved by others and personally handle the difficult, most pressing issues first

   3.___

4. It is generally CORRECT to state that the planning process within an organization

   A. is a management responsibility and should not involve the participation of operating personnel
   B. should include long-range programs and goals, and should not include activities which can be carried out within a few weeks or months
   C. is to be used in order to develop and improve practices and procedures but is not to be used in applying these procedures in actual operations
   D. should be used at all supervisory levels since each superior officer must determine how to accomplish tasks and what resources are needed

   4.___

5. Assume you are a superior officer and one of your subordinates, who has a low performance rating, has made a good suggestion that will make his job easier.
The BEST course of action for you to take in this situation is to

   A. disregard his suggestion, since he is only trying to do as little work as possible
   B. use his suggestion, since it is a positive suggestion and could motivate him to do better work
   C. use his suggestion, but transfer him to a position where he will not benefit from it
   D. disregard his suggestion, and have a talk with him about his poor performance

6. The use of different criteria to rate employees in different jobs is GENERALLY considered

   A. *desirable,* chiefly because people should be treated as individuals with varying strengths and weaknesses
   B. *undesirable,* chiefly because the use of different criteria results in unfair evaluations
   C. *desirable,* chiefly because people in different jobs cannot always be rated on the basis of the same criteria
   D. *undesirable,* chiefly because ratings that are standardized cannot be compared

7. In preparing an annual division budget for equipment and supplies, the one of the following methods that is MOST appropriate to use is to

   A. combine the previous year's division budget with the estimate of any additional or reduced needs for the coming year
   B. determine what amount the department will approve and use that figure
   C. overestimate division needs by 10% because the department will automatically reduce the figure that is first submitted
   D. underestimate division needs because a reduction in the budget indicates increased efficiency

8. All of the following are objectives of in-service training EXCEPT

   A. discovering and developing skills
   B. providing better service to the public
   C. raising the status of the service
   D. eliminating the need for performance evaluations

9. From a management point of view, the one of the following that is the MOST important advantage of regular personnel performance appraisals is that they

   A. help an officer to prepare for promotion examinations
   B. pinpoint an officer's personality weaknesses
   C. provide an opportunity for regular discussions, including counseling, between an officer and his superior
   D. provide the setting to explain the reasons for disciplinary actions which an officer might not understand

10. Assume that an officer arrests a man for assaulting a woman in the building he is guarding. Later, while the suspect is being searched, the officer finds a switchblade knife, four bags of heroin, and three hypodermic syringes in his clothing.
    In these circumstances, the possession of which of the following items might indicate a violation of some law?

    A. Only the heroin
    B. The heroin, the hypodermic syringes, but not the switchblade knife
    C. The switchblade knife, the heroin, but not the hypodermic syringes
    D. The switchblade knife, the heroin, and the hypodermic syringes

11. Upon arriving at the scene of a serious crime, a superior officer SHOULD instruct his subordinates to

    A. protect the crime scene
    B. collect, mark, and evaluate evidence
    C. brief the news media on the status of the crime
    D. prevent medical personnel from entering the crime scene

12. In standard police terminology, the term *fugitive warrant* refers to

    A. any type of warrant that is not a local warrant
    B. a written request for the detention of a suspect
    C. a warrant for a person who leaves his local jurisdiction and commits an offense in another jurisdiction
    D. a type of booking made when a person wanted by an out-of-state jurisdiction is arrested by local officers

13. The one of the following actions with respect to an offender that an officer should NOT take when an infraction has been committed is to

    A. inform the offender of his rights
    B. punish the offender
    C. warn the offender of possible consequences
    D. apprehend the offender using appropriate force

14. Perimeter barriers, intrusion devices, protective lighting, and a personnel identification system are used for good physical security of a building.
    An objective of personnel identification and control is to

    A. exempt authorized personnel from compliance with annoying entry and departure procedures
    B. detect unauthorized persons who attempt to gain entry
    C. eliminate the need for expensive perimeter barriers and intrusion alarms
    D. allow an increased number of gates and perimeter entrances to be operated at the same time during peak activity hours

15. A true copy of the testimony taken in a criminal action is known as a(n)

    A. verdict B. transcript
    C. judgment D. indictment

16. The process of gathering information during an investigation usually involves interviewing or interrogating witnesses.
Interviews or interrogations are *primarily* used for all of the following purposes EXCEPT to

   A. establish the facts of a possible crime to provide the investigator with leads
   B. verify information already known to the police
   C. secure evidence that may establish the guilt or complicity of a suspect
   D. prevent the person questioned from giving an account of the incident under investigation to newspapers

17. Of the following, the BEST reason to apprehend a narcotics violator out of view of the public is to

   A. prevent the drug user from becoming violent
   B. allow the suspect to *save face* with his friends
   C. prevent the knowledge of his apprehension from reaching any collaborators
   D. keep the suspect from disposing of evidence

18. Assume that you, a superior officer, are planning the physical security operation at a facility. One of the problems you are faced with is that of casual thievery by staff.
Of the following, the BEST means of discouraging such thievery is by establishing

   A. an aggressive security education program
   B. adequate inventory control measures
   C. spot search procedures
   D. an effective key control system

19. Under an officer's scope of authority, all of the following actions would be proper EXCEPT

   A. apprehending persons attempting to gain unauthorized access to any work location
   B. enforcing the traffic control rules applicable to the work location
   C. removing persons suspected of theft with a warning to them not to return
   D. responding to protective alarm signals and other warning devices

20. One of the ways of deploying an officer force at the scene of a demonstration is called *strength in reserve*. This procedure involves having only a few officers police the demonstration while most are being held in reserve. Which one of the following is a DISADVANTAGE of this type of deployment?
It

   A. permits the demonstrators to estimate the number of officers available
   B. might result in a delay between a violent outbreak and the arrival of enough officers to handle the situation
   C. prevents the superior officer from deploying his forces
   D. does not permit rotation of the officers confronting the demonstrators

21. Of the following, the MOST important principle to keep in mind when making arrests is that 21.____

    A. the absence of force will discourage resistance on the part of the offender
    B. the arresting officer should assume, for his own safety, that the person to be arrested is dangerous
    C. once the offender is arrested he should be kept at the scene of the arrest and questioned
    D. in order to prevent violence, it is better to have too few officers making arrests than too many

22. Of the following steps, the one that an officer should take FIRST upon discovering a broken electrical power line while on duty is to 22.____

    A. notify his supervisor
    B. notify the electrical company
    C. determine whether it is a live wire
    D. take measures to protect and barricade the area

23. Assume you are a superior officer interrogating a suspect. 23.____
    The FIRST question you ask him should usually pertain to

    A. his name and address
    B. a package which he may be carrying
    C. where he has been
    D. where he is going

24. Which one of the following statements concerning the interrogation of a juvenile is INCORRECT? 24.____

    A. The juvenile should be advised of his rights.
    B. The juvenile should be told as little as possible about the case.
    C. A bond of mutual interest should be established with the juvenile.
    D. The juvenile should be encouraged to ask the interrogator questions.

25. Assume that an intoxicated man has wandered into a center and is begging for money and harassing clients. Of the following, the MOST effective action to take in this situation would be to 25.____

    A. call immediately for police assistance
    B. take the man aside quietly and try to persuade him to move along
    C. ask two or three male clients to help you take the man outside
    D. arrest the man at once so that drunks will know they should stay away

KEY (CORRECT ANSWERS)

1. B
2. C
3. D
4. D
5. B

6. C
7. A
8. D
9. C
10. D

11. A
12. D
13. B
14. B
15. B

16. D
17. C
18. C
19. C
20. B

21. B
22. D
23. A
24. D
25. B

TEST 2

DIRECTIONS: Each question or incomplete statement is followed by several suggested answers or completions. Select the one that BEST answers the question or completes the statement. *PRINT THE LETTER OF THE CORRECT ANSWER IN THE SPACE AT THE RIGHT.*

1. Assume that you, a superior officer, have received a communication from one of your subordinates that his center has just received a *ticking* package.
   Of the following steps, the one that he should take FIRST is to

   A. notify the Police Department
   B. remove the package and soak it in water
   C. check the contents of the package
   D. evacuate the area

2. Assume that an individual suspected of drug abuse is apprehended. The suspect produces a prescription which he claims is for the drug found on his person.
   Which of the following actions should be taken NEXT?

   A. The prescription should be disregarded and the suspect should be arrested.
   B. Release the individual, but confiscate the drug in order to have a laboratory check its composition.
   C. The opinion of a medical doctor should be obtained.
   D. The suspect should be released since he has a prescription.

3. A mob has been defined as a group of individuals who commit lawless acts under the stimulus of intense excitement or agitation.
   All of the following are generally considered characteristics of a mob EXCEPT

   A. some degree of organization
   B. one or more leaders
   C. a common motive for action
   D. unemotional behavior

4. Which of the following would be IMPROPER for an officer to do while apprehending a suspect?

   A. Maintain a quiet voice and manner
   B. Remove the person from the scene as soon as possible in order to avoid conflict with the suspect and bystanders
   C. Allow the suspect to realize that the officer does not like persons who commit crimes
   D. Direct and accompany the person to an appropriate location

5. Which of the following is MOST appropriate for an officer to do while testifying as a witness in court?

   A. State the facts only of your own knowledge
   B. Argue with the defense attorney in order to show that your actions were proper
   C. Deny that you have discussed the case outside of court even if you have done so only with close friends
   D. Use as much technical language as possible in order to impress the jury with your knowledge

6. It is sometimes inadvisable to arrest the leaders of an unlawful demonstration immediately.
   Of the following, the BEST reason to delay arresting the leaders of a demonstration is to

   A. permit them to restrain their followers who might threaten violence
   B. avoid unfavorable coverage by the press
   C. determine whether there is more than one charge involved
   D. let them get deeper in trouble so they will receive longer sentences when convicted

7. The one of the following approaches which would BEST foster good human relations when dealing with the public is for an officer to

   A. act very self-assured, thus gaining respect
   B. learn how to appeal to the biases and prejudices of others
   C. treat everyone in exactly the same way since everyone has the same needs
   D. appeal to the positive interests of others

8. The causes of many job complaints come not just from wages and working conditions but also from contacts with people on and off the job and from the officer's background and outlook on life.
   Because of this, the BEST of the following ways for a superior officer to handle a complaint from a subordinate is generally to

   A. talk to the officer for the purpose of getting him to withdraw his complaint
   B. get as much information as possible to try to determine the real causes of the complaint
   C. postpone action on the complaint since conditions change so rapidly that it is useless to try to act quickly on a complaint
   D. handle each complaint as quickly as possible without looking into the motives for the complaint

9. In every unit certain officers are more cooperative than others.
   The one of the following that is MOST likely to occur with regard to supervising such cooperative officers is that they

   A. are more easily intimidated
   B. are often assigned to difficult jobs
   C. are unfriendly to the general public
   D. assume a supervisor's position in dealing with others

10. Assume that you are a superior officer and that one of your subordinate officers comes to you with a complaint about an officer under his command. After listening to a few of the details, you suspect that his complaint is not justified.
    Considering this, you should do all of the following during this initial conversation EXCEPT

    A. listen with interest until the subordinate officer finishes making his complaint
    B. tell the subordinate officer that you will investigate the matter further
    C. inform the subordinate that his complaint is invalid
    D. ask the subordinate officer further questions about his complaint

11. As a superior officer, you may receive complaints about the department or individual officers from the public.
Of the following, the PROPER attitude to take with regard to such complaints is that they

   A. are often helpful in determining how to give the public better service
   B. cause poor morale in the service and should not be revealed to subordinates
   C. are useful as a basis for disciplining officers who have been troublesome in the past
   D. take up too much of an officer's time and should not be accepted

12. One of the people present at a local parent-teacher organization meeting complained about the time it took for him to be taken care of at an agency office. A superior officer, present at the meeting, stood up and explained to the person and the group that there was no personal discrimination involved because the normal procedures took a while and that everyone spent about the same amount of time in the office.
In this situation, the action of the superior officer was

   A. *proper,* mainly because it will show the group how much he knows about agency operations
   B. *improper,* mainly because he should tell the man who complained to check first with the agency before complaining
   C. *proper,* mainly because he helped to clear up a misunderstanding
   D. *improper,* mainly because the officer should not discuss his agency in public

13. Assume that you are a superior officer and that you have begun a campaign to encourage your subordinates to be prompt in reporting for work. One of your subordinates requests that he be allowed to arrive a half hour late in the morning while his wife is in the hospital as a maternity patient.
Of the following actions, it would be BEST in this situation for you to

   A. *refuse* the request, claiming it would be unfair to others to make an exception
   B. *grant* the request, telling your other subordinates the reason for this exception
   C. *refuse* the request, blaming the central office for having inflexible rules
   D. *grant* the request, making it clear to all that this will be the last exception

14. Authorities agree that keeping rumors to a minimum is one of the goals of communication.
Which of the following is NOT consistent with this goal?

   A. Distribute information that will tend to make rumors unnecessary
   B. Reduce the social distance between top management and the lower supervisors
   C. Stress the development of downward rather than upward channels of communication
   D. Understand the emotional elements that cause stress

15. Of the following, the MOST important factor in determining the success or failure of communication between officers and the public is the

   A. attitude of the public toward the officers prior to and during the communication
   B. use of proper channels of communication within the organization
   C. use of the mass media to change the public's attitude from negative to positive
   D. increase in opportunities for personal contact between the officers and the public

16. Assume that you are a superior officer concerned with the effective use of praise and criticism to motivate your subordinates.
Of the following statements, the one that is EQUALLY TRUE of praise and criticism is that both should generally be

   A. directed mainly toward the act instead of the person
   B. given often and with no restrictions
   C. given in public for the greatest effect
   D. directed toward group efforts rather than individual efforts

17. Which of the following actions on the part of a superior officer is MOST likely to improve upward communication between his subordinates and himself?

   A. Delay acting on undesirable working conditions until complaints from subordinates have reached top management
   B. Make the time to listen to subordinates' ideas
   C. Resist becoming involved with the personal problems of subordinates
   D. Discourage communications that indicate which policies may have resulted in poor performance

18. Assume that you are a recently appointed superior officer and are told that one of your subordinates is a chronic complainer.
In this situation, which of the following steps should you take FIRST?

   A. Report your subordinate to higher authority
   B. Discipline your subordinate for his poor performance
   C. Change your subordinate's tour of duty
   D. Ask your subordinate for a list of his complaints

19. In addition to formal supervision, every group of officers soon develops informal leaders who influence the other members of the group.
Of the following statements about informal leaders, the one that is GENERALLY correct is that they

   A. provide supervision when the regular supervisor is absent
   B. are entitled to special benefits for their services
   C. can be used to help settle disputes between employees
   D. prevent the rapid transmission of orders

20. The grapevine is a frequently used means of informal communication in any work location.
The one of the following statements that BEST describes the attitude a superior officer should take in relation to the grapevine is that it is

   A. unreliable and should not be trusted
   B. useful and should be recognized
   C. valuable and should be the chief method of transmitting orders
   D. insignificant and should be ignored

21. As a supervising officer, it may be useful for you to conduct periodic interviews with each of your subordinates to discuss his job performance in broad perspective.
All of the following are ground rules to follow during such an interview EXCEPT

    A. showing him how he compares in work performance with other supervisors in your district
    B. giving him a chance to talk
    C. focusing on what can be learned from any mistakes discussed rather than on the mistakes themselves
    D. avoiding a discussion of personalities

22. When you, as a superior officer, are correcting the errors of a supervisor in your district, which of the following is NOT a good point to keep in mind?

    A. Find something on which to compliment the supervisor before you correct him
    B. Watch yourself carefully to avoid the mistake of overcorrecting
    C. Correct the supervisor at the same time as you correct other supervisors who make similar mistakes
    D. Induce the supervisor to correct himself if possible

23. Following are four steps to be used when instructing a subordinate in the performance of his job:
    I. Observe the subordinate doing the job
    II. Compare his performance to established standards
    III. Explain the purpose of the job to the subordinate
    IV. Demonstrate each step of the job

    Which of the following choices lists the CORRECT order in which the above steps should be taken?

    A. III, IV, I, II
    B. IV, III, I, II
    C. III, IV, II, I
    D. IV, III, II, I

24. Of the following leadership characteristics, the one that is generally considered PRIMARY for a supervisor is the ability to

    A. achieve good working relations with fellow supervisors
    B. get subordinates to air their personal problems
    C. take action to get the job done
    D. plan his work efficiently

25. A recently appointed supervising officer is placed in charge of a district which includes several senior employees. He finds that while these subordinates are able to learn new tasks and methods, some of them tend to take longer to learn procedural changes than newer, younger workers.
Of the following, the MAIN reason for this is that senior workers

    A. are embarrassed by younger workers' intelligence
    B. have to *unlearn* what was taught them in the past
    C. form learning blocks when they are supervised by a younger person
    D. are more interested in doing the work than in academic discussion

KEY (CORRECT ANSWERS)

1. D
2. C
3. D
4. C
5. A

6. A
7. D
8. B
9. B
10. C

11. A
12. C
13. B
14. C
15. A

16. A
17. B
18. D
19. C
20. B

21. A
22. C
23. A
24. C
25. B

EXAMINATION SECTION
TEST 1

DIRECTIONS: Each question or incomplete statement is followed by several suggested answers or completions. Select the one that BEST answers the question or completes the statement. *PRINT THE LETTER OF THE CORRECT ANSWER IN THE SPACE AT THE RIGHT.*

1. When training your subordinates in a new method of crowd control, which one of the following techniques SHOULD be used?

    A. Teach them the whole job at one time, whether it contains a great many steps or only a few
    B. Issue orders without giving reasons because this will result in more questions and delays
    C. Explain and demonstrate, one step at a time
    D. Use technical language in order to make instructions precise

1.____

2. It is sometimes necessary to provide additional training for staff members who are poor in their performance of specific tasks.
Of the following, the MOST effective way of improving staff performance is to

    A. use visual aids along with reading material to train staff on the general subject involved
    B. train subordinates to perform only those tasks which they normally perform
    C. plan and carry out programs to meet the subordinates' real work needs
    D. provide training only for staff members performing critical tasks

2.____

3. Assume that as a superior officer you confront one of your subordinate officers with the fact that he is not performing his job effectively. The officer tries to avoid the blame and shifts the criticism to other officers including yourself.
Which one of the following is NOT a good way of handling this situation?

    A. Speaking and acting in an impartial and fair-minded manner
    B. Trying to determine why the officer finds it difficult to accept justifiable criticism
    C. Calling in the other officers whom this subordinate has criticized and having them discuss the matter with him
    D. Listening to the officer, at least at the outset, rather than interrupting his statement

3.____

4. For a superior officer to discuss a subordinate's performance evaluation with him is GENERALLY

    A. *inadvisable;* such a discussion will discourage a good worker
    B. *advisable;* the subordinate must know about the quality of his performance for improvement to occur
    C. *inadvisable;* a good performance evaluation will result in the subordinate's asking for more responsibility
    D. *advisable;* such discussions generally lead to a change in the subordinate's evaluation

4.____

5. The one of the following which is the MAJOR cause of employee lateness is

   A. low morale
   B. excessive fatigue
   C. accidents
   D. sickness

6. For officers to work together smoothly, teamwork is necessary.
   Which one of the following statements BEST describes the relationship between leadership and teamwork?

   A. Leadership cannot exist without teamwork.
   B. Teamwork cannot exist without leadership.
   C. Leadership and teamwork are one and the same.
   D. There is no relationship between leadership and teamwork.

7. For superiors who wish to achieve proper discipline among subordinates, it is generally MOST difficult to

   A. obtain rapid compliance with orders and directives
   B. prevent subordinates from questioning orders that are issued to them
   C. achieve compliance with orders while encouraging individual initiative
   D. use punishment to prevent infractions of the rules

8. Of the following, it is MOST likely that laxity in administering discipline will result in

   A. a loss of respect for their superior on the part of subordinates
   B. the satisfactory completion of the organization's job
   C. an increase in the number of disturbances at centers
   D. the establishment of proper conditions for successful administration

9. In dealing with a subordinate who shows a lack of interest in performing his duties, a superior officer should GENERALLY

   A. assign to him all the difficult work
   B. give him more responsibility
   C. inspect his performance more often than usual
   D. give him direct, detailed orders

10. A superior officer who has a highly motivated group of officers under his command GENERALLY

    A. shows an interest in how they are doing and is willing to back them up
    B. spends most of his time in closely supervising his subordinates
    C. supervises mainly through one of his subordinate officers
    D. is management-oriented rather than subordinate-oriented

11. As a superior, you might have to supervise subordinate officers who are very enthusiastic and ambitious.
    Which one of the following is the BEST reason for carefully watching the work of such officers?
    They

    A. may produce so much work that other officers resent them
    B. may appear to be overly concerned about being promoted
    C. might make decisions before obtaining the necessary information
    D. may be seeking the superior's job

12. In dealing with the public, officers should behave with courtesy.
    Which one of the following practices would be LEAST effective in promoting courtesy?

    A. Giving advice on subjects about which you are not well informed
    B. Learning to take constructive criticism intelligently
    C. Avoiding discussions of a personal nature
    D. Treating members of the public as you would like to be treated

    12.____

13. When directing the officers under your command, which one of the following is generally the MOST effective method of supervision?

    A. Provide your directions through written orders to prevent misunderstanding
    B. Supervise every detail of the work closely so that it is carried out exactly as you want it
    C. Limit your concern to getting the job done and not to the people doing the work
    D. Set up general standards and goals so that officers have leeway as to how to achieve them

    13.____

14. Leadership is particularly important in the security field.
    Of the following, people GENERALLY expect their leader to

    A. state, *Do as I say, not as I do*
    B. refuse to allow changes in orders
    C. get many of his ideas from his subordinates
    D. take his feelings out on those who make mistakes

    14.____

15. The MOST important single factor in the selection of a person for assignment to a position of greater responsibility should be his

    A. demonstrated ability to do the job
    B. schooling, both civilian and military
    C. training and experience on the job
    D. length of service

    15.____

16. Security training received by security officers and noted in their personnel charts or records should NOT be used as a basis for

    A. indicating individual degrees of skill
    B. assigning officers to particular shifts
    C. establishing priorities of instruction
    D. presenting a consolidated picture of the training status

    16.____

17. As a superior officer, you note that one of your subordinates has not been performing his job properly. You discover that the cause of this problem seems to be that he drinks excessively when off duty.
    Of the following, the BEST way to handle this situation is to

    A. discipline the officer to the fullest extent possible
    B. discuss the problem and possible solutions with the officer's fellow workers
    C. wait until the officer has straightened himself out and then counsel him
    D. have a blunt and firm talk with the officer and direct him to seek treatment

    17.____

18. Officers who are overly sensitive to criticism are one of the problems that superiors must deal with.
    Of the following, which is the BEST way to handle such officers?
    They should

    A. not be talked to differently from other officers
    B. be criticized only on serious mistakes
    C. not be criticized at all
    D. be reassured of their worth to their unit

19. A superior officer who suspects an employee of petty office theft calls the employee to his office and questions him directly.
    In this situation, the superior's action is

    A. *desirable,* primarily because the subordinate should be allowed to answer these accusations privately
    B. *desirable,* primarily because confrontation will persuade the employee to tell the truth
    C. *undesirable,* primarily because line department personnel should handle such matters
    D. *undesirable,* primarily because direct confrontation might unnecessarily embarrass the employee

20. Assume that a certain superior officer assigns a task, without explanation, to a new subordinate who is not yet accepted by the work group.
    Of the following, the MOST likely result of this action would be to

    A. encourage the subordinate to perform at his best
    B. make the subordinate feel insecure about proving himself
    C. stimulate other officers to do their best to impress the new staff member
    D. cause the experienced officers to feel inferior

21. A newly appointed superior officer often faces the problem of supervising officers who were formerly close personal friends of his.
    In this situation, the one of the following which is the BEST approach to take toward these officers is to

    A. break all ties with former friends
    B. stay personally close with friends as this is always an advantage on the job
    C. maintain a relationship of easy, occasional familiarity
    D. become businesslike on the job but remain close socially

22. Assume that you, as a superior officer, are talking over a proposed change in procedure with your subordinates which would require their full cooperation.
    Which one of the following actions would be MOST appropriate for you to take if your subordinates suggest modifications in the procedure?

    A. Prepare arguments against your subordinates' suggestions while you are listening to them
    B. Refuse to accept suggestions for changes since procedures can't be modified
    C. Listen carefully since your subordinates' suggestions may have merit
    D. Accept the recommendations of your more experienced subordinates

23. The successful supervisor should be aware that two of his most important assets are patience and understanding.
Of the following actions by a supervisor, the one that is LEAST likely to demonstrate these qualities would be to

    A. make deadlines realistic and reachable
    B. reprimand an employee the minute he makes a mistake
    C. assist employees in work-related problems
    D. discuss changes in procedures with subordinates

24. One of a supervisor's goals should be to create and maintain a force of loyal subordinates with high morale. This objective is likely to be achieved by all of the following EXCEPT

    A. making subordinate officers feel that their job is an important one
    B. encouraging supervisors to be concerned with the individual needs of subordinates
    C. giving subordinate officers an opportunity to express their thoughts, likes, and interests to their supervisors
    D. having supervisors rely only on the advice of trusted employees when resolving disputes between subordinates

25. One of a supervisor's major responsibilities is to evaluate the performance of his subordinates.
Which one of the following practices would be LEAST productive in developing meaningful evaluations from performance interviews?

    A. Make positive statements only
    B. Outline the points to discuss
    C. Adjust to the individual and situation
    D. Allow the employee to participate

KEY (CORRECT ANSWERS)

1.	C	11.	C
2.	C	12.	A
3.	C	13.	D
4.	B	14.	C
5.	A	15.	A
6.	B	16.	B
7.	C	17.	D
8.	A	18.	D
9.	B	19.	A
10.	A	20.	B

21. C
22. C
23. B
24. D
25. A

TEST 2

DIRECTIONS: Each question or incomplete statement is followed by several suggested answers or completions. Select the one that BEST answers the question or completes the statement. *PRINT THE LETTER OF THE COREECT ANSWER IN THE SPACE AT THE RIGHT.*

1. Assume that you are a superior officer concerned with improving the attitude of your subordinates toward their work.
   Of the following, the action that is MOST likely to improve this attitude would be for you to

   A. allow your subordinates to take extra time off
   B. interpret rules and regulations leniently
   C. request a merit increase in salary for your subordinates
   D. train your subordinates to perform at the highest possible level

   1.____

2. Assume that two of the officers under your command are hotly disputing the accuracy of a log book entry. One of the officers asks for your opinion.
   Which of the following would be LEAST advisable for you to do in this situation?

   A. Ask the officers to present their views calmly
   B. Keep your temper and remain impartial
   C. Stop the argument and then give your decision
   D. Judge the argument in proportion to its importance

   2.____

3. A superior officer notices that one of his subordinates is not doing his job.
   In this situation, it would be MOST appropriate for the superior officer to

   A. caution the subordinate officer promptly
   B. ignore the incident this time
   C. check on the subordinate officer's behavior in an hour
   D. warn the subordinate officer at the end of his work day that a report may be filed

   3.____

4. A recently appointed superior officer finds it difficult to make the decisions required in his new position.
   Which one of the following suggestions would be MOST helpful to him in overcoming this problem?

   A. Don't be concerned because everyone makes mistakes, and any mistake caused by your decisions will be ignored.
   B. Remember that you will be judged by the long-range soundness of all of your decisions.
   C. Since you are now in charge of a number of officers, let them bear the decision-making responsibility.
   D. Remember that you have a superior and that he can make the decision for you.

   4.____

5. Of the following, the BEST reason for a superior officer to nake inspections and rounds is to

   A. observe the physical appearance of personnel
   B. determine whether communication equipment is working properly

   5.____

C. decide whether adequate records are being kept
D. see that the performance of subordinates conforms with departmental standards

6. Assume that you, as a superior officer, have made an inspection and have submitted recommendations for improvements.
Which one of the following actions should be taken to assure that the desired results are obtained from the inspection?
You should

   A. distribute copies of the recommendations to all members of the force
   B. follow-up to determine whether the recommended improvements have been made
   C. give credit to other officers when it is due in order to help increase morale
   D. set up a schedule so that you inspect once a week

7. Assume that you have noticed that one of your subordinates has been quiet and rather depressed for two to three days with no change in his usual satisfactory job performance.
Of the following, the BEST action for you to take in this situation is to

   A. ask him to describe his feelings in detail
   B. act as if you noticed no change in the subordinate's behavior
   C. tell him to forget what's bothering him
   D. recommend that he seek professional guidance

8. Assume that you wish to introduce a change in your subordinates' work procedures in order to improve their performance.
Of the following, the BEST way to gain acceptance of this change is for you to

   A. stress its positive aspects
   B. downgrade past practices
   C. delay discussing it for a while
   D. order your subordinates to follow the new procedure at once

9. Suppose you come across two of your subordinate officers having an argument about the boundaries of their patrol posts.
Which of the following is the LEAST advisable course of action for you to take after stopping the argument?

   A. Tell the officers to speak with you individually
   B. Have the officers submit their views in writing for you to evaluate properly when you have time
   C. Meet with both officers in your office after they finish their tours
   D. Tell the officers to consult you on such matters in the future

10. Assume that a superior officer is explaining a new rule to his men at roll call. One officer states that he does not like the rule. The superior tells the officer that he agrees with him, but that the rule must be followed anyway. In this situation, the superior officer's statement was

    A. *proper*, chiefly because the men should know where superiors stand on rules and regulations
    B. *improper*, chiefly because superiors should not indicate disagreement with a change in rules since they must enforce them

C. *proper,* chiefly because efficiency improves when supervisors and subordinates agree on new rules
D. *improper,* chiefly because questions regarding rule changes should be answered at staff meetings rather than at roll call

11. Assume that you find that several of your subordinate officers have not performed satisfactorily during the last few emergency situations at your work location. The one of the following actions which is LEAST likely to improve their performance is for you to 11.____

   A. keep the subordinates informed about how they performed after each emergency
   B. stay alert for officers who are having difficulty with their work
   C. circulate among the officers at emergencies
   D. avoid the use of criticism

12. Of the following qualifications for an officer, the one that is MOST important is the ability to 12.____

   A. understand and get along with people
   B. write a good report
   C. overcome resistance to arrest
   D. solve crimes

13. Assume that you have noticed that one of your subordinate officers makes errors when questioning clients. You discuss with him the proper method to use when questioning clients. 13.____
   Of the following, your NEXT step should be to

   A. ask another officer to check on your subordinate's procedure when questioning clients
   B. tell the officer to discuss with others how they question clients
   C. have the officer report regularly to you about the clients he questions
   D. watch the officer to see how he questions clients

14. One of the MOST important rules to follow when communicating with your superior is: 14.____

   A. Report everything that happens at your work location to him
   B. Pass on to him rumors and gossip heard within your center
   C. Let him hear from you first about any unusual success, problem or error
   D. Assign to one of your subordinates the responsibility of communicating with your supervisor

15. A superior officer may be required to instruct subordinates in the performance of their tasks. 15.____
   Which of the following would NOT be proper when instructing a small group of employees?

   A. Use simple language
   B. Explain the procedure and the reason for the procedure
   C. Demonstrate one step at a time
   D. Use the lecture method instead of the discussion method whenever possible

16. Assume that a new officer has joined your unit. Which of the following approaches should you, as his superior officer, use in introducing him to the job?

    A. Put him right to work; he will learn best through his mistakes
    B. Act sternly, thereby gaining his respect and indicating the proper supervisor-subordinate relationship
    C. Give him the overall picture of the department and unit he is in
    D. Praise him, even when he makes errors, in order to gain his confidence

17. When a new officer begins work, he will often perform tasks ineffectively, thus requiring corrective action by his supervisor.
    In this situation, which one of the following represents the MOST desirable course of action for the supervisor?

    A. Point out specific errors in performance and how to correct them
    B. Tell the new officer that he is not doing the job properly and assign him to a new task
    C. Avoid criticism in the beginning since it may result in bitterness
    D. Do not criticize because criticism is not currently considered an acceptable tool of management

18. Of the following types of work, the one that is MOST likely to lead to dissatisfaction is work that is

    A. difficult to perform   B. tiring to complete
    C. uncomplicated   D. unimportant

19. When instructing subordinates to perform new tasks, the one of the following that is LEAST important in helping then to learn is to

    A. explain the procedure to them in a step-by-step manner
    B. show them what they must do
    C. let them do the task under guidance
    D. have them perform the task without supervision so they may learn from their mistakes

20. Which one of the following is the MOST important single thing to bear in mind about giving orders?

    A. An order should be given to a capable employee, not an uncooperative one.
    B. If an order is given correctly, you will not have to check the work.
    C. An order should be given in as forceful a manner as possible to assure that it is understood.
    D. An order is given because it is necessary to bring about certain results.

21. Suppose that a subordinate asks you about a rumor he has heard. The rumor deals with a subject which your superiors consider *confidential*.
    Which of the following BEST describes how you should answer the officer?
    Tell

    A. the officer that you don't make the rules and that he should speak to higher ranking officers
    B. the officer that you will ask your superior for information

C. him only that you cannot comment on the matter
D. him the rumor is not true

22. Superior officers often find it difficult to *get their message across* when instructing newly appointed officers in their various duties.
The MAIN reason for this is generally that the

   A. duties of the officers have increased
   B. superior officer is often so expert in his area that he fails to see it from the learner's point of view
   C. superior officer adapts his instruction to the slowest learner in the group
   D. new officers are younger, less concerned with job security, and more interested in fringe benefits

23. Assume that you are discussing a security problem with an officer under your command. During the discussion, you see that the officer's eyes are turning away from you and that he is not paying attention.
In order to get the officer's attention, you should FIRST

   A. ask him to look you in the eye
   B. talk to him about sports
   C. tell him he is being very rude
   D. change your tone of voice

24. As a superior officer, you may find it necessary to conduct meetings with your subordinates.
Of the following, which would be MOST helpful in assuring that a meeting accomplishes the purpose for which it was called?

   A. Give notice of the conclusions you would like to reach at the start of the meeting
   B. Delay the start of the meeting until everyone is present
   C. Write down points to be discussed in proper sequence
   D. Make sure everyone is clear on whatever conclusions have been reached and on what must be done after the meeting

25. Every superior officer will occasionally be called upon to deliver a reprimand to a subordinate. If done properly, this can greatly help an officer improve his performance.
Which one of the following is NOT a good practice to follow when giving a reprimand?

   A. Maintain your composure and temper
   B. Reprimand a subordinate in the presence of other officers so they can learn the same lesson
   C. Try to understand why the officer was not able to perform satisfactorily
   D. Let your knowledge of the officer involved determine the exact nature of the reprimand

KEY (CORRECT ANSWERS)

1. D
2. C
3. A
4. B
5. D

6. B
7. B
8. A
9. B
10. B

11. D
12. A
13. D
14. C
15. D

16. C
17. A
18. D
19. D
20. D

21. B
22. B
23. D
24. D
25. B

———

TEST 3

DIRECTIONS: Each question or incomplete statement is followed by several suggested answers or completions. Select the one that BEST answers the question or completes the statement. *PRINT THE LETTER OF THE CORRECT ANSWER IN THE SPACE AT THE RIGHT.*

1. Of the following, the PRIMARY purpose of communications between subordinates and superiors is to

    A. develop language skills
    B. enable subordinates to air their grievances
    C. help establish friendly ties
    D. solve job problems

    1.____

2. Of the following, the MOST necessary elements of good communication are

    A. openness and form
    B. details and subjectivity
    C. speed and dependability
    D. length and appearance

    2.____

3. Of the following, the MOST important role of a supervisor is that of

    A. being able to understand how his men feel about their assignments
    B. establishing good contacts with the administration
    C. fulfilling his responsibility to the assigned position
    D. presenting a good public image on the behalf of his organization

    3.____

4. Of the following, the LEAST desirable behavior of a senior officer would be for him to

    A. attempt to gain the respect of superiors
    B. attempt to find causes of high employee turnover
    C. ignore infrequent latenesses
    D. ignore suggestions which may prove unworthy

    4.____

5. A senior officer who consults with his subordinates about operational planning is GENERALLY

    A. attempting to prove his supervisory ability
    B. developing their job participation and cooperation
    C. passing down his responsibilities to others
    D. searching for an employee with supervisory ability

    5.____

6. If a senior officer conducted supervision and inspection programs in order to become aware of his men's conduct, he would GENERALLY be considered to be

    A. excessively strict and authoritarian
    B. looking for potential troublemakers
    C. overconscientious in his work
    D. performing a vital duty

    6.____

7. Of the following, the BEST reason for a supervisor's evaluation of his own on-the-job performance is to enable him to

    A. find the best methods of supervising his men and in getting the job done
    B. give the impression that he is sincere in trying to become a better supervisor

    7.____

C. make a favorable impression on his superiors
D. make his work seem more important than it actually is

8. Assume that you are a senior officer making a performance evaluation of an officer. The reason for NOT drawing conclusions too quickly is CHIEFLY that

   A. without due consideration of all the facts, you are likely to evaluate the officer on biased personal judgment
   B. evaluation reports take a great deal of time and thought
   C. senior officers must consult with superiors before drawing conclusions about a subordinate's performance
   D. the officer might try to disprove any wrong information which you may have obtained about him

9. A senior officer notices two officers, known to be good workers, playing practical jokes and pranks on the other employees.
   In this case, disciplinary action is

   A. *desirable,* chiefly because horseplay on the job is not, strictly speaking, against the rules
   B. *undesirable,* chiefly because good workers tend to correct their own improper actions
   C. *desirable,* chiefly because horseplay could provoke other employees and that would disrupt normal work routine
   D. *undesirable,* chiefly because a supervisor should not get involved with employees' affairs

10. Resistance to or resentment of training is likely to be an attitude shown by many officers. Therefore, it is important for a senior officer to understand the causes of his men's attitudes and learn how to deal with them. Of the following, which is the BEST method of lessening an officer's resentment of training?

    A. Give the officers extra time off for taking part in the training program
    B. Openly criticize the officer who often makes mistakes during training
    C. Recommend promotions for those who complete the training program quickest
    D. Explain that the purpose of the training is to help them perform their jobs more efficiently

11. A senior officer required all officers under his supervision to submit a weekly report based on information from their daily log (memo) entries. The senior officer did not examine these reports, but he did file them as proof that the officers were not *sleeping* on the job.
    In general, this practice of the senior officer is considered

    A. *correct,* chiefly because the senior officer has little need of the reports since he is usually on the scene to observe the performance of his men
    B. *incorrect,* chiefly because, if the senior officer asked for reports, he should read or use the information they contain
    C. *correct,* chiefly because any information an officer had could only be based on daily occurrences
    D. *incorrect,* chiefly because the senior officer is placing too much emphasis on accuracy of paper work

12. Selecting an employee to be trained for performing the supervisor's duties is generally considered

    A. *desirable*, chiefly because it allows the supervisor to avoid many of his duties
    B. *undesirable*, chiefly because it creates the impression that the supervisor is showing favoritism
    C. *desirable*, chiefly because supervisory coverage is assured in the absence of the supervisor
    D. *undesirable*, chiefly because the trainee will cause the supervisor to worry about possible competition and thus neglect the performance of his duties

13. When discussing lateness with an employee, a supervisor should take the employee to an area where the problem can be discussed privately
    Generally, this practice is considered

    A. *desirable*, chiefly because it gives the employee an opportunity to converse with the supervisor in a very casual way
    B. *desirable*, chiefly because it keeps the problem from being discussed in front of an audience
    C. *undesirable*, chiefly because isolating an employee from his co-workers causes the *rumor-mongers* to spread false gossip about the matter
    D. *undesirable*, chiefly because trivial matters can be mentioned in the open without any repercussions

14. When an officer shows a pattern of abuse in his use of sick leave, a senior officer should

    A. ask the officer for medical proof of all future illnesses
    B. discourage other officers from abusing sick leave by giving the offending officer a public warning
    C. interview the officer and inquire about the reasons for his behavior
    D. acknowledge the officer's right to sick leave as set forth in departmental rules and regulations

15. Of the following, the MAJOR reason why grapevines generally develop in an agency is that

    A. employees have too much idle time
    B. employees want to socialize and gossip with other employees while working
    C. superior officers avoid reporting bad news downward from management to subordinates
    D. there is a communication gap between management and employees

16. If a newly-assigned senior officer is doubtful about the exact details of the assignment he is about to give to an officer, he should GENERALLY

    A. ask to speak to the officer in private and give him another assignment
    B. delay giving the assignment until he clears up his own doubt
    C. attempt to explain to the officer what he knows about the assignment in the best possible way
    D. put the assignment in writing

17. Of the following situations, which one would justify a supervisor's giving direct orders to another supervisor's subordinate?

    A. A supervisor away from his normal assignment observes a serious disturbance and gives orders to the officers in that area.
    B. A supervisor foresees a problem that will arise the next day in another district and immediately proceeds to inform the other supervisor's officers of the action they should take.
    C. A supervisor tells an officer under another supervisor to perform a duty a week from today because he feels it is an urgent matter.
    D. None of the above situations would justify direct supervision by any senior officer.

18. In the planning process, which of the following is NOT a recommended practice in preparing your final plan of action?

    A. Obtain all important available facts related to the problem
    B. Clarify the problem before any plan is created
    C. Make the plan easy to understand so that it can be carried out efficiently
    D. Never make assumptions or forecasts about what could occur

19. Of the following, the BEST way for a senior officer to get his subordinates to carry out his orders is to

    A. explain whenever possible why the orders are being given
    B. let subordinates know in advance the penalties for disobeying his orders
    C. describe the steps that must be followed in performing each order
    D. issue all orders in the form of direct and positive commands

20. It is MOST correct to state that race prejudice is to the GREATEST extent

    A. an inborn human characteristic
    B. the result of training and group association
    C. the product of ghetto areas
    D. a condition limited to adults only

21. *Scapegoating* is a form of prejudice which results MAINLY from

    A. degrading minority groups in an effort to secure status for one's own group
    B. shifting the blame for social inadequacies and ills from oneself to others
    C. thinking of people not as individual persons but rather placing them in carelessly formed, all-embracing classifications
    D. maintaining the existing order to prevent other groups from rising in social and economic status

22. The MOST important step in democratic supervision is

    A. allowing the employee a chance to apologize whenever he makes an error
    B. keeping tight control over employees
    C. making the employee realize that he needs your approval in order to keep his position
    D. showing an interest in the welfare of the employee

23. Evaluating a subordinate's likes and dislikes concerning his work is GENERALLY considered to be 23._____

   A. valuable in assigning work details to the subordinate
   B. necessary only when the subordinate complains of dissatisfaction with his daily duties
   C. unnecessary and a waste of time
   D. useful only in establishing a good relationship with the subordinate

24. Employee motivation is very critical in keeping up the morale of employees. 24._____
    Of the following, which is generally the BEST method of supervision which both motivates and maintains high morale?

   A. Aid employees in finding satisfaction in their assignments even if it requires extra time and responsibility
   B. Allow employees to work with a free hand and without daily interruptions
   C. Don't get involved or become concerned with interests or problems of employees outside the job
   D. Prove your friendship to a select number of employees so that the remainder of the staff will feel you are a *good guy* to work for

25. When attempting to motivate an experienced individual, it is BEST for a senior officer to appeal to the person's 25._____

   A. emotions   B. positive interests
   C. negative feelings   D. inhibitions

KEY (CORRECT ANSWERS)

1.	D	11.	B
2.	C	12.	C
3.	C	13.	B
4.	D	14.	C
5.	B	15.	D
6.	D	16.	B
7.	A	17.	A
8.	A	18.	D
9.	C	19.	A
10.	D	20.	B

21. B
22. D
23. A
24. A
25. B

EXAMINATION SECTION
TEST 1

DIRECTIONS: Each question or incomplete statement is followed by several suggested answers or completions. Select the one that BEST answers the question or completes the statement. *PRINT THE LETTER OF THE CORRECT ANSWER IN THE SPACE AT THE RIGHT.*

1. Suppose that one of the forms you fill out daily requires some information which you know is unnecessary.
   Which is the BEST action to take?
   A. Refuse to supply the information you think is unnecessary.
   B. Continue to fill out the form as required, even though the information is unnecessary.
   C. Suggest to your supervisor that the form be revised to reflect useful information.
   D. Suggest that fewer copies of the form be required.

   1.____

2. Of the following, the MOST likely reason for recommending that your department establish a standard form for recording certain information would be that this information
   A. will be produced at some disciplinary hearing
   B. concerns a secret or confidential record about an unusual incident at the garage
   C. contains a detailed explanation of a complex procedure
   D. must be taken from a large number of people on a regular basis

   2.____

3. If the four steps listed below for processing records were given in logical sequence, the one that would be the THIRD step is
   A. coding the records, using a chart or classification system
   B. inspecting the records to make sure they have been released for filing
   C. preparing cross-reference sheets or cards
   D. skimming the records to determine filing captions

   3.____

4. Which of the following BEST describes "office work simplification"?
   A. An attempt to increase the rate of production by speeding up the movements of employees
   B. Eliminating wasteful steps in order to increase efficiency
   C. Making jobs as easy as possible for employees so they will not be overworked
   D. Eliminating all difficult tasks from an office and leaving only simple ones

   4.____

2 (#1)

5. The use of the same method of recordkeeping and reporting by all sections is
   A. *desirable*, mainly because it saves time in section operations
   B. *undesirable*, mainly because it kills the initiative of the individual section foreman
   C. *desirable*, mainly because it will be easier for the superior to evaluate and compare section operations
   D. *undesirable*, mainly because operations vary from section to section and uniform recordkeeping and reporting is not appropriate

5.____

6. The GREATEST benefit the section officer will have from keeping complete and accurate records of section operations is that
   A. he will find it easier to run his section efficiently
   B. he will need less equipment
   C. he will need less manpower
   D. the section will run smoothly when he is out

6.____

7. You have prepared a report to your superior and are ready to send it forward. But on reading it, you think some parts are not clearly expressed and the superior may have difficulty getting your point.
   Of the following, it would be BEST for you to
   A. give the report to one of your men to read, and, if he has no trouble understanding it, send it through
   B. forward the report and call the superior the next day to ask if it was all right
   C. forward the report as is; higher echelons should be able to understand any report prepared by a section officer
   D. do the report over, re-writing the sections you are doubtful of

7.____

8. Of the following, a flow chart is BEST described as a chart which shows
   A. the places through which work moves in the course of the job process
   B. which employees perform specific functions leading to the completion of a job
   C. the schedules for production and how they eliminate waiting time between jobs
   D. how work units are affected by the actions of related work units

8.____

9. A superior decided to hold a problem-solving conference with his entire staff and distributed an announcement and agenda one week before the meeting.
   Of the following, the BEST reason for providing each participate with an agenda is that
   A. participants will feel that something will be accomplished
   B. participants may prepare for the conference
   C. controversy will be reduced
   D. the top man should state the expected conclusions

9.____

10. The one of the following activities which is generally the LEAST proper function of a centralized procedures section is
    A. issuing new and revised procedural instructions
    B. coordinating forms revision and procedural changes
    C. accepting or rejecting authorized procedural changes
    D. controlling standard numbering systems for procedural releases

10.____

11. Assume that it is the policy of an operating unit to act on all requests received within five working days. Several operations are involved in acting on these requests. Each operation is performed by a separate sub-unit. The staff of the unit is reasonable adequate to handle this workload.
    If only one of the following can be done, the MOST effective procedure for maintaining adherence to the unit's five-day processing policy is to
    A. maintain a central "tickler" file in each sub-unit for the requests received daily in that sub-unit
    B. prepare a "tickler" card for each request and follow it up five days later to determine whether action has been taken
    C. rely on standards of production for each operation as an incentive to the employees of each sub-unit to meet the schedule
    D. schedule the operations on a timetable basis so that the request will be forwarded from one sub-unit to another within specified time limits

11.____

12. When one or two simple changes are needed in a memo to another unit or in a letter to a citizen, a unit head follows the practice of making such simple changes neatly in ink.
    This practice is GENERALLY
    A. *poor*, chiefly because it reflects unfavorably on the originating unit's ability to make a decision
    B. *good*, chiefly because the department's public image is likely to be improved when people see it as trying to save money and speed up its processes
    C. *poor*, chiefly because a letter or document prepared in final form represents an investment of department time and effort and should go out only as a perfect finished product
    D. *good*, chiefly because the document may be important, and sending it back for retyping may delay it too long to achieve its purpose

12.____

13. Suppose that one of the office machines in your unit is badly in need of replacement.
    Of the following, the MOST important reason for postponing immediate purchase of a new machine would be that
    A. a later model of the machine is expected on the market in a few months
    B. the new machine is more expensive than the old machine
    C. the operator of the present machine will have to be instructed by the manufacturer in the operation of the new machine
    D. the employee operating the old machine is not complaining

13.____

14. To avoid cutting off parts of letters when using an automatic letter opener, it is BEST to
    A. arrange all of the letters so that the addresses are right side up
    B. hold the envelopes up to the light to make sure their contents have not settled to the side that is to be opened
    C. strike the envelopes against a table or desktop several times so that the contents of all the envelopes settle to one side
    D. check the enclosures periodically to make sure that the machine has not been cutting into them

15. Of the following, the BEST reason for setting up a partitioned work area for the typists in our office is that
    A. an uninterrupted flow of work among the typists will be possible
    B. complaints about ventilation and lighting will be reduced
    C. the first-line supervisor will have more direct control over the typists
    D. the noise of the typewriters will be less disturbing to other workers

16. From the viewpoint of use of a typewriter to fill in a form, the MOST important design factor to consider is
    A. standard spacing
    B. box headings
    C. serial numbering
    D. vertical guide lines

17. Requests to repair office equipment which appears to be unsafe should be given priority MAINLY because, if repairs are delayed,
    A. there may be injuries to staff
    B. there may be further deterioration of the equipment
    C. work flow may be interrupted
    D. the cost of repair may increase

18. A clerk is asked to complete two assignments – transcribe a handwritten business letter and create a spreadsheet. Which two computer programs would the clerk use?
    A. Microsoft Word and Microsoft Excel
    B. Microsoft Word and Microsoft PowerPoint
    C. Google Docs and Google Chrome
    D. Adobe Reader and Microsoft PowerPoint

19. Generally, the actual floor space occupied by a standard letter-size office file cabinet, when closed, is MOST NEARLY
    A. ½ square foot
    B. 3 square feet
    C. 7 square feet
    D. 11 square feet

20. Suppose a clerk under your supervision accidentally opens a personal letter while handling office mail.
    Under such circumstances, you should tell the clerk to put the letter back into the envelope and
    A. take the letter to the person to whom it belongs and make sure he understands that the clerk did not read it
    B. try to seal the envelope so it won't appear to have been opened

5 (#1)

    C. write on the envelope "Sorry – opened by mistake," and put his initials on it
    D. write on the envelope "Sorry – opened by mistake," but not put his initials on it

21. Standard forms frequently call for entries on them to be printed.   21._____
The MAIN reason for this practice is that printing, as compared to writing, is GENERALLY
    A. more compact   B. more legal
    C. more legible   D. easier to do

22. After a stenographer types a letter which has been dictated, the finished   22._____
letter should be carefully read for errors.
If he dictator follows the procedure of carefully reading each transcribed letter, a stenographer, under your supervision, should, unless you instruct her otherwise
    A. not take time to proofread transcribed letters
    B. continue to carefully proofread transcribed letters
    C. review transcribed letters for meaning rather than for errors in typing or transcription
    D. review transcribed letters for errors in typing rather than for errors in transcription

23. In transcribing a letter, the secretary notes that the dictator said, "The series   23._____
of conferences are planned to be relevant to today's problems." In such a case, the secretary should
    A. type the sentence as it appears in the notes
    B. check with the dictator to see whether he would prefer a different grammatical construction
    C. change the noun so that it is correct
    D. revise the sentence as much as necessary to make it read better

24. Of the following, the BEST procedure for your staff to follow in transcribing   24._____
several letters that were dictated is to
    A. transcribe first the letters that are most difficult so that they can return immediately to the dictator with any questions
    B. read through the notes for each letter to be sure they have all the information needed before preparing the transcript
    C. transcribe first those letters that are shortest and simplest in order to get them out of the way
    D. read all the notes aloud to a co-worker to see whether they sound right

25. In typing long letters, which of the following is generally considered the   25._____
LEAST desirable practice?
    A. Numbering the second and succeeding pages of the letter
    B. Typing a single line of a new paragraph as the last line of a page
    C. Dividing a word at the end of a line of typing
    D. Typing the name of the recipient of the letter on the second and succeeding pages

KEY (CORRECT ANSWERS)

1.	C	11.	D
2.	D	12.	B
3.	D	13.	A
4.	B	14.	C
5.	C	15.	D
6.	A	16.	A
7.	D	17.	A
8.	A	18.	A
9.	B	19.	B
10.	C	20.	C

21. C
22. B
23. B
24. B
25. B

TEST 2

DIRECTIONS: Each question or incomplete statement is followed by several suggested answers or completions. Select the one that BEST answers the question or completes the statement. *PRINT THE LETTER OF THE CORRECT ANSWER IN THE SPACE AT THE RIGHT.*

1. The use of a microfilm system for information storage and retrieval would make the MOST sense in an office where
   A. a great number of documents must be kept available for permanent reference
   B. documents are ordinarily kept on file for less than six months
   C. filing is a minor and unimportant part of the office work
   D. most of the records on file are working forms on which additional entries are frequently made

   1.____

2. Of the following concepts, the one which CANNOT be represented suitably by a pie chart is
   A. percent shares
   B. shares in absolute units
   C. time trends
   D. successive totals over time, with their shares

   2.____

3. A pictogram is ESSENTIALLY another version of a(n) _____ chart.
   A. plain bar   B. component bar
   C. pie   D. area

   3.____

4. A time series for a certain cost is presented in a graph. It is drawn so that the vertical (cost) axis starts at a point well above zero. This is a legitimate method of presentation for some purposes, but it may have the effect of
   A. hiding fixed components of the cost
   B. exaggerating changes which, in actual amounts, may be insignificant
   C. minimizing variable components of the cost
   D. impairing correlation analysis

   4.____

5. Certain budgetary data may be represented by bar, area, or volume charts. Which one of the following BEST expressed the most appropriate order of usefulness?
   A. Descends from bar to volume and area charts, the last two being about the same
   B. Descends from volume to area, to bar charts
   C. Depends on the nature of the data presented
   D. Descends from bar to area to volume charts

   5.____

6. One weekend, you develop a painful infection in one hand. You know that your typing speed will be much slower than normal and the likelihood of your making mistakes will be increased.
   Of the following, the BEST course of action for you to take in this situation is to
   A. report to work as scheduled and do your typing assignments as best you can without complaining
   B. report to work as scheduled and ask your co-workers to divide your typing assignments until your hand heals
   C. report to work as scheduled and ask your supervisor for non-typing assignments until your hand heals
   D. call in sick and remain on medical leave until your hand is completely healed so that you can perform your normal duties

7. When filling out a departmental form during an interview concerning a citizen complaint, an interviewer should know the purpose of each question that he asks the citizen. For such information to be supplied by your department is
   A. *advisable*, because the interviewer may lose interest in the job if he is not fully informed about the questions he has to ask
   B. *inadvisable*, because the interviewer may reveal the true purpose of the questions to the citizens
   C. *advisable*, because the interviewer might otherwise record superficial or inadequate answers if he does not fully understand the questions
   D. *inadvisable*, because the information obtained through the form may be of little importance to the interviewer

8. The one of the following which is the BEST reason for placing the date and time of receipt on incoming mail is that this procedure
   A. aids the filing of correspondence in alphabetical order
   B. fixes responsibility for promptness in answering correspondence
   C. indicates that the mail has been checked for the presence of a return address
   D. makes it easier to distribute the main in sequence

9. Which one of the following is the FIRST step that you should take when filing a document by subject?
   A. Arrange related documents by date with the latest date in front
   B. Check whether the document has been released for filing
   C. Cross-reference the document if necessary
   D. Determine the category under which the document will be filed

10. The one of the following which is NOT generally employed to keep track of frequently used material requiring future attention is a
    A. card tickler file   B. dated follow-up folder
    C. periodic transferal of records   D. signal folder

11. Which one of the following is NOT a useful filing practice? 11.____
    A. Filing active records in the most accessible parts of the file cabinet
    B. Filing a file drawer to capacity in order to save space
    C. Gluing small documents to standard-size paper before filing
    D. Using different colored labels for various filing categories

12. The one of the following cases in which you would NOT place a special notation in the left margin of a letter that you have typed is when 12.____
    A. one of the copies is intended for someone other than the addressee of the letter
    B. you enclose a flyer with the letter
    C. you sign your superior's name to the letter, at his or her request
    D. the letter refers to something being sent under separate cover

13. Suppose that you accidentally cut a letter or enclosure as you are opening an envelope with a paper knife. The one of the following that you should do FIRST is to 13.____
    A. determine whether the document is important
    B. clip or staple the pieces together and process as usual
    C. mend the cut document with transparent tape
    D. notify the sender that the communication was damaged and request another copy

14. It is generally advisable to leave at least six inches of working space in a file drawer. This procedure is MOST useful in 14.____
    A. decreasing the number of filing errors
    B. facilitating the sorting of documents and folders
    C. maintaining a regular program of removing inactive records
    D. preventing folders and papers from being torn

15. Of the following, the MOST important reason to sort large volumes of documents before filing is that sorting 15.____
    A. decreases the need for cross-referencing
    B. eliminates the need to keep the filing up-to-date
    C. prevents overcrowding of the file drawers
    D. saves time and energy in filing

16. When typing a preliminary draft of a report, the one of the following which you should generally NOT do is to 16.____
    A. erase typing errors and deletions rather than "X"ing them out
    B. leave plenty of room at the top, bottom, and sides of each page
    C. make only the number of copies that you are asked to make
    D. type double or triple space

17. When printing a 500-page office manual, the most efficient method is to use 17._____
    which of the following office machines?
    A. Inkjet printer
    B. Copy machine
    C. Word processor
    D. All-in-one scanner/fax/copier

18. When typing name or titles on a roll of folder labels, the one of the following 18._____
    which it is MOST important to do is to type the caption
    A. as it appears son the papers to be placed in the folder
    B. in capital letters
    C. in exact indexing or filing order
    D. so that it appears near the bottom of the folder tab when the label is
       attached

19. The MOST important reason for having color cartridges on hand for an office copier 19._____
    even though most prints are black and white is because
    A. color ink is used for all copies
    B. some copiers or printers will not print black and white if any of the color
       cartridges are empty
    C. black ink is cheaper when purchasing along with color cartridges
    D. lack of color ink can cause copier malfunctions

20. All of the following pertain to the formatting of word-processing documents EXCEPT 20._____
    A. headers and footers
    B. rows and columns
    C. indents and page breaks
    D. alignment and justified type

KEY (CORRECT ANSWERS)

1.	A	11.	B
2.	C	12.	C
3.	A	13.	C
4.	B	14.	D
5.	D	15.	D
6.	C	16.	A
7.	C	17.	B
8.	B	18.	C
9.	B	19.	B
10.	C	20.	B

READING COMPREHENSION
UNDERSTANDING AND INTERPRETING WRITTEN MATERIAL
EXAMINATION SECTION
TEST 1

DIRECTIONS: Each question or incomplete statement is followed by several suggested answers or completions. Select the one that *BEST* answers the question or completes the statement. *PRINT THE LETTER OF THE CORRECT ANSWER IN THE SPACE AT THE RIGHT.*

Questions 1-5.

DIRECTIONS: The following passage is to be used as the *SOLE* basis for answering Questions 1 to 5. Read the selection carefully and base your answers *ONLY* on the information contained therein.

PASSAGE

Politicians, preachers, and moralists frequently inveigh against the breakdown of family and community morality. According to one variant of this position, it is because of a "moral breakdown" that we find so much "crime in the streets." This line of reasoning has a persuasive message for many white Americans – it carries surface plausibility and underlying racial prejudice. Family "breakdown," "immoral" delinquent gangs and African-Americans are all disproportionately found in the urban slums. There is, however, an important flaw in the implied argument of this modern morality tale. It is apparent that lower-class families have difficulty in maintaining control over their children. According to the modern morality tale, if parents were more responsible and less perverse, and exercised control over their children, there would be less delinquency. The parents, and later their children, are the villains. But the lack of control stems not from parental perversity but from parental poverty, that is, from the deprivations of lower-class status. Of course, personalities do vary, even in their degree of "perversity"; and there are undoubtedly elements of "perversity" among some parents who do not maintain control over their children. But the magnitude of the problem stems from major social forces that have a pervasive influence over the lives of so many people.

By increasing the amount and awareness of legitimate opportunities, and reducing the attractiveness of delinquent gangs and illegitimate behavior, it may be possible to reduce delinquency. But overcoming these deprivations may also have an indirect effect upon delinquency by influencing family structure. The key problem in the lower class family is the weak occupational economic position of the man. Since, in the United States, the man is expected to be the breadwinner above all else, he performs inadequately at his major role within the family. As a result the lower class man is not esteemed, even within his own family. Under these circumstances, he may also leave his family. It can therefore be expected that improvements made in occupational and economic opportunities for lower class men will strengthen their position within the family and thereby strengthen the stability of the family as a whole. It will also heighten the attractiveness of the father and the family in the eyes of the children and make additional resources available within the family. Such changes will make it possible for the family to maintain stronger controls over its children.

Some argue that the provision of opportunities is not enough–that lower class people differ in their subculture, or values, or goals, or motivations so that they would not take advantage of these opportunities. Although value modifications generally take place within the lower class to make life's values more in accord with life's circumstances, it appears that middle class values and goals are still retained. Lower class people frequently find it necessary to stretch their values and aspirations downward to accord with realistic opportunities, but they do not abandon middle class values. They may lessen their commitment to values so that some of the sting will be taken out of life's deprivations, but they do not abandon all values. In short, providing additional opportunities seems to be the key area for change.

QUESTIONS

1. According to the passage, which of the following statements concerning street crime and moral breakdown is CORRECT?

    A. The irresponsibility of parents in slum-areas is the root cause of moral breakdown and street crime.
    B. Moral breakdown is basically a result of street crime.
    C. Moral breakdown and street crime are aspects of larger and widespread social problems.
    D. Street crime is basically a result of moral breakdown.
    E. Moral breakdown and street crime are a response to the prejudice of many white Americans.

2. According to the passage, the problem of juvenile delinquency is basically a result of

    A. the overrepresentation of minority groups in lower class neighborhoods
    B. the poor social and economic conditions that are an inherent part of lower class life
    C. the unwillingness of parents to accept their responsibilities and exercise discipline
    D. the breakdown in family morality that is most pervasive among the lower class
    E. personality variations among lower class parents which prevent them from maintaining control over their children

3. According to the passage, the *central* problem of the lower class family is the

    A. absence of goal motivated behavior
    B. failure to develop a distinct subculture within poor communities
    C. dissatisfaction with middle class values
    D. inability of the father to adequately support his family
    E. attractiveness of delinquency and illegitimate behavior

4. According to the passage, providing greater occupational opportunities for lower class men will result in all of the following EXCEPT

    A. allowing families to maintain greater control over their children
    B. improving the standing of lower class fathers within their families
    C. reducing the amount of juvenile delinquency so that lower class neighborhoods are as safe as others in the city
    D. increasing the stability of lower class families
    E. enhancing the image of the family itself for lower class children

5. According to the passage, lower class people often make adjustments in their values. As a result, their values *generally* 5.____

    A. reflect the opportunities that are actually available to the lower class
    B. coincide exactly with middle class values
    C. depend upon a family structure that lacks a strong father figure
    D. include goals and aspirations that exceed their economic situation
    E. deny responsibility for the delinquent behavior of their children

Questions 6-10.

DIRECTIONS: Questions 6 to 10 are to be answered *SOLELY* on the basis of the following passage.

PASSAGE

Of all the groups claiming interference by restrictions on the dissemination of news, the one with the most pressing claim is the law enforcement agency. Due to the combination of a morbid interest in crimes of violence and fear that a vicious criminal may be at large, there is a demand by the public for a showing by the police of capability in solving a crime. Perhaps unwilling to acknowledge the existence of, and accept responsibility for, a degenerate element in its midst, the public tends to cast the blame for a successful crime on police failure to prevent it. Thus there is constant pressure on the police to demonstrate that the case is nearing solution and that the perpetrator will soon be in custody. To avoid the accusation of suppressing information to cover up malfeasance, there is a legitimate tendency on the part of the police to cooperate with the press and thus escape being cast in an unfavorable light. The ideal solution – from the point of view of the police – would be to allow them free rein in releasing information to reassure the public. However, this would not be consonant with the right of the accused to a fair trial with the presumption of innocence.

A distinguished committee of lawyers and jurists has developed a comprehensive code for police and law enforcement agencies. The committee's recommendations include the following:

A. Concerning the Defendant

   1. The release of information concerning the defendant shall be limited to his name, age, occupation, marital status, and personal data not related to the crime or the character of the defendant. His criminal record, prior medical and psychiatric history, or military disciplinary record, if any, shall not be released. No other information that is clearly prejudicial to the defendant shall be released.
   2. No statement of any nature made by the defendant, or the substance thereof, shall be released. No reference shall be made to any test taken by the defendant or that he has refused to take.
   3. The announcement of the arrest of the defendant may include, in addition to the information authorized above, the time, place, and manner of apprehension as well as the text or summary of the charge, information, or indictment. No comments shall be made relating to his guilt or innocence.
   4. News media shall not be permitted to interview the defendant with or without his attorney's consent, while he is in police custody.
   5. News media shall not be permitted to photograph or televise the defendant while he is in police custody except in a public place. This prohibition extends to such instances as where he is being interrogated, where he is being processed ("booked") following arrest, where he is in a lockup or detention facility, or where he is at a hospital bedside for identification purposes.
   6. Where the defendant is still at large, and it appears that he is a fugitive from justice, additional information that may reasonably and directly aid in effecting his apprehension, including his photograph, may be released.

B. Concerning the Crime, the Investigation, and the Arrest
   1. A general description of the crime shall be made available to the news media. Gruesome or sordid aspects which tend unduly to inflame public emotions shall not be released. Witnesses shall not be identified by name or otherwise, nor shall any comment be made concerning their credibility, their testimony, or their identification of the defendant.
   2. No comment on the apparent motivation or character of the perpetrator shall be made.
   3. No information concerning scientific evidence such as laboratory or ballistics tests or fingerprints shall be released.
C. General
   1. A member of the police agency shall be designated as the Information Officer responsible for the dissemination of all information to the news media. It will be the responsibility of the Information Officer to supervise the enforcement of these regulations and to solicit and encourage full cooperation of news media. No member of a police agency may furnish any information to news media without prior approval by the Information Officer. No interviews shall be permitted with investigating or arresting officers.
   2. Wherever feasible, the Information Officer will encourage news media to enter into pool arrangements so as to reduce confusion and interference with the orderly processes of law enforcement. It shall be a prime responsibility of the Information Officer to insure a calm and orderly atmosphere during the dissemination of information to the news media.

QUESTIONS

6. According to the passage, the tendency of the police to cooperate with the press by releasing information is based on the

   A. public's desire for evidence that the police are able to bring criminals to justice
   B. deterrent effect on other criminals which results from reports of police efficiency
   C. requirement of the courts for full disclosure of pertinent information
   D. assistance which unrestricted publicity provides in apprehending perpetrators who are still at large
   E. belief that charges of corruption cannot be avoided in any other way

7. Of the following, the *BASIC* purpose of the recommendations contained in the passage is to

   A. satisfy the public's curiosity concerning crime
   B. expedite the dissemination of information to the news media
   C. protect the defendant's right to a fair trial
   D. enhance the reputation of the police
   E. reduce interference by the news media in essential police functions

8. According to the recommendations contained in the passage, it would *NOT* be proper for a law enforcement agency to

   A. release information pertaining to how the defendant was caught
   B. discuss the testimony given by eyewitnesses
   C. distribute a written copy or synopsis of the indictment
   D. provide a general description of the crime in question
   E. disclose the occupation and marital status of the defendant

9. According to the recommendations contained in the passage, law enforcement agencies, under certain circumstances, would be able to

   A. permit a defendant to make a statement to the news media
   B. release information concerning the defendant's medical history which is not pertinent to the case
   C. describe to the news media evidence against the defendant in terms of probable guilt or innocence
   D. allow a defendant to be televised while in their custody in a non-public place
   E. provide a photograph of the defendant to the news media

10. According to the passage, the Information Officer in a police department is responsible for all of the following EXCEPT

    A. coordinating interviews of arresting officers by members of the news media
    B. enforcing regulations concerning dissemination of information to the news media
    C. fostering the use of pool arrangements by the news media
    D. approving in advance all requests by the news media for information
    E. preventing hectic and unruly situations when information is provided to the news media.

KEY (CORRECT ANSWERS)

1.	C	6.	A
2.	B	7.	C
3.	D	8.	B
4.	C	9.	E
5.	A	10.	A

TEST 2

DIRECTIONS: Each question or incomplete statement is followed by several suggested answers or completions. Select the one that *BEST* answers the question or completes the statement. *PRINT THE LETTER OF THE CORRECT ANSWER IN THE SPACE AT THE RIGHT.*

Questions 1-5.

DIRECTIONS: Questions 1 to 5 are to be answered *SOLELY* on the basis of the following passage.

PASSAGE

There is a hazy boundary between grateful citizens paying their respects to a proud profession, and "good" citizens involved in corruption, wishing to buy future favors. Once begun, however, the acceptance of small bribes and favors or similar practices can become "norms" or informal standards of cliques of policemen. A recruit can be socialized into accepting these illegal practices by mild, informal negative sanctions such as the withholding of group acceptance. If these unlawful practices are embraced, the recruit's membership group – the police force – and his reference group – the clique involved in illegal behavior – are no longer one and the same. In such circumstances the norms of the reference group (the illegal-oriented clique) would clearly take precedence over either the formal requisites of the membership group (police department regulations) or the formalized norms (legal statutes) of the larger society. When such conflicts are apparent a person can

1. conform to one, take the consequences of non-conformity to the other;
2. seek a compromise position by which he attempts to conform in part, though not wholly, to one or more sets of role expectations, in the hope that sanctions applied will be minimal.

If these reference group norms involving illegal activity become routinized with use they become an identifiable informal "code." Such codes are not unique to the police profession. A fully documented case study of training at a military academy, in which an informal pattern of behavior was assimilated along with the formal standards, clearly outlined the function of the informal norms, their dominance when in conflict with formal regulations, and the secretive nature of their existence to facilitate their effectiveness and subsequent preservation. This same secrecy could be demanded of a police "code" to insure its preservation. Although within the clique the code must be well defined, the ignorance of the lay public to even its existence would be a requisite to its continuous and effective use. Through participation in activity regimented by the "code," an increased group identity and cohesion among "code" practitioners would emerge.

Group identity requires winning of acceptance as a member of the inner group and, thereby, gaining access to the secrets of the occupation which are acquired through informal contacts with colleagues. Lack of this acceptance not only bars the neophyte from the inner secrets of the profession, but may isolate him socially and professionally from his colleagues and even his superiors. There is the added fear that, in some circumstances in which he would need their support, they would avoid becoming involved, forcing him to face personal danger or public ridicule alone.

QUESTIONS

1. According to the passage, the reference group of a recruit who accepts corrupt practices is

   A. the police force of which the recruit is a member
   B. a loosely-structured group from which the recruit learns both formal and informal norms
   C. the coterie of officers who are involved in illegal activities
   D. society as a whole, of which the police are a component
   E. a professional organization which instructs the recruit in his responsibilities

2. According to the passage, allegiance by policemen to informally codified standards of behavior is *most likely* to result in

   A. increased attempts by most citizens to bribe police officers
   B. a decrease of mutual support among policemen
   C. greater awareness on the part of the public of such behavior
   D. decreased secrecy about police department practices
   E. stronger group identification among such policemen

3. According to the passage, the police recruit who is NOT accepted by the group which is involved in illegal behavior will

   A. be prevented from learning many confidential aspects of police work
   B. face less risk of public ridicule or personal danger
   C. be held in high esteem by his superiors
   D. gain social and professional stature among his colleagues
   E. be more likely to expose the activities of the group to the public

4. According to the passage, informal codes of illegal behavior function effectively only when they

   A. are tacitly accepted by the entire society
   B. permit formal standards to predominate whenever there is a conflict
   C. exist without being known to outsiders
   D. minimize the use of informal negative sanctions
   E. complement pre-existing norms within the police profession

5. According to the passage, a recruit who must deal with conflicting norms of different groups may

   A. not be able to distinguish between ordinary citizens and those involved in graft
   B. try to accommodate himself to the different roles he is expected to play
   C. be unaware of the informal codes of behavior within the police department
   D. accept one set of standards and thereby avoid any unpleasant consequences
   E. find that he is able to solve the problem by bringing the competing norms into conformity

Questions 6-10.

DIRECTIONS: Questions 6 to 10 are to be answered *SOLELY* on the basis of the following passage.

PASSAGE
THE CONCEPT OF AN OFFENSIVELY DEPLOYED PATROL FORCE

Police forces, in general, are defensively deployed, both in their organization and operation. That is, they are principally designed to act efficiently during or after the commission of a crime. This concept becomes quite clear when the distribution of available manpower of a police force is examined.

The defensive enforcement attitude is prevalent in the philosophy of the individual policeman. Most law enforcement officers seem to view the making of an arrest as one of their major goals. The reason for this attitude is obvious. Police administrators do not have available a measuring technique for evaluating an officer's crime prevention efforts, while an arrest is a measure of his defensive effectiveness.

One of the most serious drawbacks for any police force that is committed to a defensive action during a period of rising crime, is that it becomes, of necessity, a retrograde operation; that is, as more crime is committed, more manpower is utilized for investigation, with a corresponding decrease in crime prevention activities, thus encouraging more crime, more manpower for investigation, etc., etc. The logical extension of this situation is a police force that is completely overloaded with investigations, while crime runs rampant.

It is now appropriate to inquire into the effectiveness of defensive police strategy in the present crime situation. Determining the effectiveness of a police system and its strategy requires the use of absolute measurements. In particular, the effectiveness should be measured in terms of how well it attains its goals. By these measures, the defensive strategy used by the police does not appear to be effective.

If the goal of police action is to eliminate or substantially reduce crime, it is not succeeding. The number of crimes as well as the crime rate is increasing.

It seems completely self-evident that if it were possible to station a policeman at or about every house and building in the city, the amount of crime would be significantly reduced. It would be reduced not because a criminal would be caught after he committed a crime, but because he would not commit the crime, because of the fear of being caught. Thus the crime rate would be reduced by preventing the crime from happening, not by punishing the criminal (if caught) after the crime has been committed.

The solution is, of course, not a practical one but, nevertheless, it should serve as an ideal for an offensively deployed police force. In practice, the force should create the appearance of being everywhere at once.

In contrast to the defensive force, whose operation is retrograde, such an offensive force would be progressive in nature; that is, by preventing a crime from occurring, the manpower required for investigation would be reduced. Hence, it could be diverted toward the prevention of more crime, which would further reduce the investigations and manpower needed, etc. The logical extension of this situation is a force that is completely deployed to prevent crime.

The offensive force depicted above is, of course, a patrol force, but not in the sense of the conventional police patrol, which is very inflexible with regard to the time and place it can be deployed, which is heavily committed to answering complaints, and which is managed by "seat of the pants" techniques.

The specifications for an offensively deployed patrol force are as follows:
1. A patrol unit must pass by every point in the city, on the average of once every ten minutes.

2. The patrol unit must not be sent on a complaint, unless the complaint can be disposed of in less than ten minutes, or there is a crime or equivalent emergency situation in progress. If a unit does become involved, its territory must be covered by adjacent patrol units.
3. The patrol force must be deployed with due regard to the expected type and location of crime, based on an analysis of previous criminal activity for the particular season of the year, day of the week, hour of the day, etc.

QUESTIONS

6. Assume that a certain city has changed the nature of its motor patrol force from a defensive force to offensive deployment.
Which one of the following results will *MOST* logically follow if the patrol force is functioning in line with the principles discussed in the passage? The

   A. arrest rate for burglary will decrease
   B. number of complaints received will increase
   C. number of aggravated assaults will increase
   D. number of miles that the patrol vehicles travel will increase
   E. number of complaints answered by the patrol force will increase

7. According to the passage, which one of the following *MOST* accurately states the underlying purpose of offensively deployed patrol? To

   A. leave the patrol unit free to perform offensive patrol
   B. increase the number of criminals that are caught and punished
   C. catch so many criminals that the criminals are afraid to commit offenses
   D. make offenders so fearful of being caught that they refrain from committing offenses
   E. have a patrol unit pass every point in the city on the average of once every ten minutes

8. A certain police department has accepted the concept of offensive deployment. In implementing this concept, it has adopted a policy defining the basic responsibility for making initial investigations or crimes.
Which one of the following is *MOST* likely the policy this department has adopted, if it followed the terms of the passage?

   A. Basic responsibility for initial investigation of crimes is assigned to the patrol force.
   B. Basic responsibility for initial criminal investigation is assigned somewhere other than to the patrol units.
   C. As crime increases above normal levels, the basic responsibility for initial investigation of crime retrogrades to the patrol force.
   D. As crime increases above normal levels, the basic responsibility for initial investigation of crime retrogrades to the Detective Division.
   E. When crime is normal, basic responsibility for initial investigation of crime is divided between the Detective Division and the patrol force, depending on the availability of manpower in each.

9. Assume the following facts: The police department of a certain city has implemented the concept of an offensively deployed police force based on the recommendations contained in the passage.
Which one of the following results would MOST logically indicate that the patrol force is functioning ineffectively? The

   A. crime rate has decreased
   B. number of crime investigations by the patrol units has increased
   C. percentage of crimes cleared by arrest has increased
   D. number of prosecutions for crimes cleared by arrest has increased
   E. average amount of time spent by the average officer answering complaints has decreased

10. According to the passage, which one of the following is the MOST probable reason why many individual policemen have accepted the philosophy of defensive enforcement? Because

   A. of the retrograde philosophy
   B. no technique exists for evaluating an officer's offensive efforts
   C. most policemen believe in the effectiveness of the crime-investigation cycle
   D. the goal of police action is to eliminate or substantially reduce crime
   E. the effectiveness of defensive police strategy has never been evaluated

KEY (CORRECT ANSWERS)

1. C
2. E
3. A
4. C
5. B

6. D
7. D
8. B
9. B
10. B

EVALUATING CONCLUSIONS IN LIGHT OF KNOWN FACTS
EXAMINATION SECTION
TEST 1

DIRECTIONS: Each question or incomplete statement is followed by several suggested answers or completions. Select the one that BEST answers the question or completes the statement. *PRINT THE LETTER OF THE CORRECT ANSWER IN THE SPACE AT THE RIGHT.*

Questions 1-9.

DIRECTIONS: In Questions 1 through 9, you will read a set of facts and a conclusion drawn from them. The conclusion may be valid or invalid, based on the facts—it's your task to determine the validity of the conclusion.

For each question, select the letter before the statement that BEST expresses the relationship between the given facts and the conclusion that has been drawn from them. Your choices are:
  A. The facts prove the conclusion;
  B. The facts disprove the conclusion; or
  C. The facts neither prove nor disprove the conclusion.

1. FACTS: If the supervisor retires, James, the assistant supervisor, will not be transferred to another department. James will be promoted to supervisor if he is not transferred. The supervisor retired.

   CONCLUSION: James will be promoted to supervisor.
   A. The facts prove the conclusion.
   B. The facts disprove the conclusion.
   C. The facts neither prove nor disprove the conclusion.

1.____

2. FACTS: In the town of Luray, every player on the softball team works at Luray National Bank. In addition, every player on the Luray softball team wear glasses.

   CONCLUSIONS: At least some of the people who work at Luray National Bank wear glasses.
   A. The facts prove the conclusion.
   B. The facts disprove the conclusion.
   C. The facts neither prove nor disprove the conclusion.

2.____

3. FACTS: The only time Henry and June go out to dinner is on an evening when they have childbirth classes. Their childbirth classes meet on Tuesdays and Thursdays.

3.____

113

2 (#1)

CONCLUSION: Henry and June never go out to dinner on Friday or Saturday.
   A. The facts prove the conclusion.
   B. The facts disprove the conclusion.
   C. The facts neither prove nor disprove the conclusion.

4. FACTS: Every player on the field hockey team has at least one bruise. Everyone on the field hockey team also has scarred knees.

   CONCLUSION: Most people with both bruises and scarred knees are field hockey players.
   A. The facts prove the conclusion.
   B. The facts disprove the conclusion.
   C. The facts neither prove nor disprove the conclusion.

4.____

5. FACTS: In the chess tournament, Lance will win his match against Jane if Jane wins her match against Mathias. If Lance wins his match against Jane, Christine will not win her match against Jane.

   CONCLUSION: Christine will not win her match against Jane if Jane wins her match against Mathias.
   A. The facts prove the conclusion.
   B. The facts disprove the conclusion.
   C. The facts neither prove nor disprove the conclusion.

5.____

6. FACTS: No green lights on the machine are indicators for the belt drive status. Not all of the lights on the machine's upper panel are green. Some lights on the machine's lower panel are green.

   CONCLUSION: The green lights on the machine's lower panel may be indicators for the belt drive status.
   A. The facts prove the conclusion.
   B. The facts disprove the conclusion.
   C. The facts neither prove nor disprove the conclusion.

6.____

7. FACTS: At a small, one-room country school, there are eight students: Amy, Ben, Carla, Dan, Elliot, Francine, Greg, and Hannah. Each student is in either the 6th, 7th, or 8th grade. Either two or three students are in each grade. Amy, Dan, and Francine are all in different grades. Ben and Elliot are both in the 7th grade. Hannah and Carl are in the same grade.

   CONCLUSION: Exactly three students are in the 7th grade.
   A. The facts prove the conclusion.
   B. The facts disprove the conclusion.
   C. The facts neither prove nor disprove the conclusion.

7.____

8. FACTS: Two married couples are having lunch together. Two of the four people are German and two are Russian, but in each couple the nationality of the spouse is not necessarily the same as the other's. One person in the group is a teacher, the other a lawyer, one an engineer, and the other a writer. The teacher is a Russian man. The writer is Russian, and her husband is an engineer. One of the people, Mr. Stern, is German.

   CONCLUSION: Mr. Stern's wife is a writer.
   A. The facts prove the conclusion.
   B. The facts disprove the conclusion.
   C. The facts neither prove nor disprove the conclusion.

   8.____

9. FACTS: The flume ride at the county fair is open only to children who are at least 36 inches tall. Lisa is 30 inches tall. John is shorter than Henry, but more than 10 inches taller than Lisa.

   CONCLUSION: Lisa is the only one who can't ride the flume ride.
   A. The facts prove the conclusion.
   B. The facts disprove the conclusion.
   C. The facts neither prove nor disprove the conclusion.

   9.____

Questions 10-17.

DIRECTIONS: Questions 10 through 17 are based on the following reading passage. It is not your knowledge of the particular topic that is being tested, but your ability to reason based on what you have read. The passage is likely to detail several proposed courses of action and factors affecting these proposals. The reading passage is followed by a conclusion or outcome based on the facts in the passage, or a description of a decision taken regarding the situation. The conclusion is followed by a number of statements that have a possible connection to the conclusion. For each statement, you are to determine whether:
   A. The statement proves the conclusion.
   B. The statement supports the conclusion but does not prove it.
   C. The statement disproves the conclusion.
   D. The statement weakens the conclusion but does not disprove it.
   E. The statement has no relevance to the conclusion.

Remember that the conclusion after the passage is to be accepted as the outcome of what actually happened, and that you are being asked to evaluate the impact each statement would have had on the conclusion.

PASSAGE:

The Grand Army of Foreign Wars, a national veteran's organization, is struggling to maintain its National Home, where the widowed spouses and orphans of deceased members are housed together in a small village-like community. The Home is open to spouses and children who are bereaved for any reason, regardless of whether the member's death was related to military service, but a new global conflict has led to a dramatic surge in the number of members' deaths: many veterans who re-enlisted for the conflict have been killed in action.

The Grand Army of Foreign Wars is considering several options for handling the increased number of applications for housing at the National Home, which has been traditionally supported by membership due. At its national convention, it will choose only one of the following:

The first idea is a one-time $50 tax on all members, above and beyond the dues they pay already. Since the organization has more than a million member, this tax should be sufficient for the construction and maintenance of new housing for applicants on the existing grounds of the National Home. The idea is opposed, however, by some older members who live on fixed incomes. These members object in principle to the taxation of Grand Army members. The Grand Army has never imposed a tax on its members.

The second idea is to launch a national fundraising drive the public relations campaign that will attract donations for the National Home. Several national celebrities are members of the organization, and other celebrities could be attracted to the cause. Many Grand Army members are wary of this approach, however: in the past, the net receipts of some fundraising efforts have been relatively insignificant, given the costs of staging them.

A third approach, suggested by many of the younger members, is to have new applicants share some of the costs of construction and maintenance. The spouses and children would pay an up-front "enrollment" fee, based on a sliding scale proportionate to their income and assets, and then a monthly fee adjusted similarly to contribute to maintenance costs. Many older members are strongly opposed to this idea, as it is in direct contradiction to the principles on which the organization was founded more than a century ago.

The fourth option is simply to maintain the status quo, focus the organization's efforts on supporting the families who already live at the National Home, and wait to accept new applicants based on attrition.

CONCLUSION: At its annual national convention, the Grand Army of Foreign Wars votes to impose a one-time tax of $10 on each member for the purpose of expanding and supporting the National Home to welcome a larger number of applicants. The tax is considered to be the solution most likely to produce the funds needed to accommodate the growing number of applicants.

10. Actuarial studies have shown that because the Grand Army's membership consists mostly of older veterans from earlier wars, the organization's membership will suffer a precipitous decline in numbers in about five years.
    A. The statement proves the conclusion.
    B. The statement supports the conclusion but does not prove it.
    C. The statement disproves the conclusion.
    D. The statement weakens the conclusion but does not disprove it.
    E. The statement has no relevance to the conclusion.

11. After passage of the funding measure, a splinter group of older members appeals for the "sliding scale" provision to be applied to the tax, so that some members may be allowed to contribute less based on their income.
    A. The statement proves the conclusion.
    B. The statement supports the conclusion but does not prove it.
    C. The statement disproves the conclusion.
    D. The statement weakens the conclusion but does not disprove it.
    E. The statement has no relevance to the conclusion.

5 (#1)

12. The original charter of the Grand Army of Foreign Wars specifically states that the organization will not levy taxes or duties on its members beyond its modest annual dues. It takes a super-majority of attending delegates at the national convention to make alterations to the charter.
    A. The statement proves the conclusion.
    B. The statement supports the conclusion but does not prove it.
    C. The statement disproves the conclusion.
    D. The statement weakens the conclusion but does not disprove it.
    E. The statement has no relevance to the conclusion.

12.____

13. Six months before Grand Army of Foreign Wars' national convention, the Internal Revenue Service rules that because it is an organization that engages in political lobbying, the Grand Army must no longer enjoy its own federal tax-exempt status.
    A. The statement proves the conclusion.
    B. The statement supports the conclusion but does not prove it.
    C. The statement disproves the conclusion.
    D. The statement weakens the conclusion but does not disprove it.
    E. The statement has no relevance to the conclusion.

13.____

14. Two months before the national convention, Dirk Rockwell, arguably the country's most famous film actor, announces in a nationally televised interview that he has been saddened to learn of the plight of the National Home, and that he is going to make it his own personal crusade to see that it is able to house and support a greater number of widowed spouses and orphans in the future.
    A. The statement proves the conclusion.
    B. The statement supports the conclusion but does not prove it.
    C. The statement disproves the conclusion.
    D. The statement weakens the conclusion but does not disprove it.
    E. The statement has no relevance to the conclusion.

14.____

15. The Grand Army's final estimate is that the cost of expanding the National Home to accommodate the increased number of applicants will be about $61 million.
    A. The statement proves the conclusion.
    B. The statement supports the conclusion but does not prove it.
    C. The statement disproves the conclusion.
    D. The statement weakens the conclusion but does not disprove it.
    E. The statement has no relevance to the conclusion.

15.____

16. Just before the national convention, the Federal Department of Veterans Affairs announces steep cuts in the benefits package that is currently offered to the widowed spouses and orphans of veterans.
    A. The statement proves the conclusion.
    B. The statement supports the conclusion but does not prove it.
    C. The statement disproves the conclusion.
    D. The statement weakens the conclusion but does not disprove it.
    E. The statement has no relevance to the conclusion.

16.____

17. After the national convention, the Grand Army of Foreign Wars begins charging a modest "start-up" fee to all families who apply for residence at the national home.
    A. The statement proves the conclusion.
    B. The statement supports the conclusion but does not prove it.
    C. The statement disproves the conclusion.
    D. The statement weakens the conclusion but does not disprove it.
    E. The statement has no relevance to the conclusion.

Questions 18-25.

DIRECTIONS: Questions 18 through 25 each provide four factual statements and a conclusion based on these statements. After reading the entire question, you will decide whether:
    A. The conclusion is proved by statements I-IV;
    B. The conclusion is disproved by statements I-IV.
    C. The facts are not sufficient to prove or disprove the conclusion.

18. FACTUAL STATEMENTS:
    I. In the Field Day high jump competition, Martha jumped higher than Frank.
    II. Carl jumped higher than Ignacio.
    III. Ignacio jumped higher than Frank.
    IV. Dan jumped higher than Carl.

    CONCLUSION: Frank finished last in the high jump competition.
    A. The conclusion is proved by statements I-IV;
    B. The conclusion is disproved by statements I-IV.
    C. The facts are not sufficient to prove or disprove the conclusion.

19. FACTUAL STATEMENTS:
    I. The door to the hammer mill chamber is locked if light 6 is red.
    II. The door to the hammer mill chamber is locked only when the mill is operating.
    III. If the mill is not operating, light 6 is blue.
    IV. Light 6 is blue.

    CONCLUSION: The door to the hammer mill chamber is locked.
    A. The conclusion is proved by statements I-IV;
    B. The conclusion is disproved by statements I-IV.
    C. The facts are not sufficient to prove or disprove the conclusion.

20. FACTUAL STATEMENTS:
    I. Ziegfried, the lion tamer at the circus, has demanded ten additional minutes of performance time during each show.
    II. If Ziegfried is allowed his ten additional minutes per show, he will attempt to teach Kimba the tiger to shoot a basketball.
    III. If Kimba learns how to shoot a basketball, then Ziegfried was not given his ten additional minutes.
    IV. Ziegfried was given his ten additional minutes.

7 (#1)

CONCLUSION: Despite Ziegfried's efforts, Kimba did not learn how to shoot a basketball.
   A. The conclusion is proved by statements I-IV;
   B. The conclusion is disproved by statements I-IV.
   C. The facts are not sufficient to prove or disprove the conclusion.

21. FACTUAL STATEMENTS:
    I. If Stan goes to counseling, Sara won't divorce him.
    II. If Sara divorces Stan, she'll move back to Texas.
    III. If Sara doesn't divorce Stan, Irene will be disappointed.
    IV. Stan goes to counseling.

    CONCLUSION: Irene will be disappointed.
    A. The conclusion is proved by statements I-IV;
    B. The conclusion is disproved by statements I-IV.
    C. The facts are not sufficient to prove or disprove the conclusion.

22. FACTUAL STATEMENTS:
    I. If Delia is promoted to district manager, Claudia will have to be promoted to team leader.
    II. Delia will be promoted to district manager unless she misses her fourth-quarter sales quota.
    III. If Claudia is promoted to team leader, Thomas will be promoted to assistant team leader.
    IV. Delia meets her fourth-quarter sales quota.

    CONCLUSION: Thomas is promoted to assistant team leader.
    A. The conclusion is proved by statements I-IV;
    B. The conclusion is disproved by statements I-IV.
    C. The facts are not sufficient to prove or disprove the conclusion.

23. FACTUAL STATEMENTS:
    I. Clone D is identical to Clone B.
    II. Clone B is not identical to Clone A.
    III. Clone D is not identical to Clone C.
    IV. Clone E is not identical to the clones that are identical to Clone B.

    CONCLUSION: Clone E is identical to Clone D.
    A. The conclusion is proved by statements I-IV;
    B. The conclusion is disproved by statements I-IV.
    C. The facts are not sufficient to prove or disprove the conclusion.

24. FACTUAL STATEMENTS:
    I. In the Stafford Tower, each floor is occupied by a single business.
    II. Big G Staffing is on a floor between CyberGraphics and MainEvent.
    III. Gasco is on the floor directly below CyberGraphics and three floors above Treehorn Audio.
    IV. MainEvent is five floors below EZ Tax and four floors below Treehorn Audio.

8 (#1)

CONCLUSION: EZ Tax is on a floor between Gasco and MainEvent.
  A. The conclusion is proved by statements I-IV;
  B. The conclusion is disproved by statements I-IV.
  C. The facts are not sufficient to prove or disprove the conclusion.

25. FACTUAL STATEMENTS: 25._____
  I. Only county roads lead to Nicodemus.
  II. All the roads from Hill City to Graham County are federal highways.
  III. Some of the roads from Plainville lead to Nicodemus.
  IV. Some of the roads running from Hill City lead to Strong City.

CONCLUSION: Some of the roads from Plainville are county roads.
  A. The conclusion is proved by statements I-IV;
  B. The conclusion is disproved by statements I-IV.
  C. The facts are not sufficient to prove or disprove the conclusion.

KEY (CORRECT ANSWERS)

1.	A		11.	A
2.	A		12.	D
3.	A		13.	E
4.	C		14.	D
5.	A		15.	B
6.	B		16.	B
7.	A		17.	C
8.	A		18.	A
9.	A		19.	B
10.	E		20.	A

21.	A
22.	A
23.	B
24.	A
25.	A

SOLUTIONS TO PROBLEMS

1. **CORRECT ANSWER: A**
   Given Statement 3, we deduce that James will not be transferred to another department. By Statement 2, we can conclude that James will be promoted.

2. **CORRECT ANSWER: A**
   Since every player on the softball team wears glasses, these individuals compose some of the people who work at the bank. Although not every person who works at the bank plays softball, those bank employees who do play softball wear glasses.

3. **CORRECT ANSWER: A**
   If Henry and June go out to dinner, we conclude that it must be on Tuesday or Thursday, which are the only two days when they have childbirth classes. This implies that if it is not Tuesday or Thursday, then this couple does not go out to dinner.

4. **CORRECT ANSWER: C**
   We can only conclude that if a person plays on the field hockey team, then he or she has both bruises and scarred knees. But there are probably a great number of people who have both bruises and scarred knees but do not play on the field hockey team. The given conclusion can neither be proven or disproven.

5. **CORRECT ANSWER: A**
   From statement 1, if Jane beats Mathias, then Lance will beat Jane. Using statement 2, we can then conclude that Christine will not win her match against Jane.

6. **CORRECT ANSWER: B**
   Statement 1 tells us that no green light can be an indicator of the belt drive status. Thus, the given conclusion must be false.

7. **CORRECT ANSWER: A**
   We already know that Ben and Elliot are in the 7th grade. Even though Hannah and Carl are in the same grade, it cannot be the 7th grade because we would then have at least four students in this 7th grade. This would contradict the third statement, which states that either two or three students are in each grade. Since Amy, Dan, and Francine are in different grade, exactly one of them must be in the 7th grade. Thus, Ben, Elliot, and exactly one of Amy, Dan, and Francine are the three students in the 7th grade.

8. **CORRECT ANSWER: A**
   One man is a teacher, who is Russian. We know that the writer is female and is Russian. Since her husband is an engineer, he cannot be the Russian teacher. Thus, her husband is of German descent, namely Mr. Stern. This means that Mr. Stern's wife is the writer. Note that one couple consists of a male Russian teacher and a female German lawyer. The other couple consists of a male German engineer and a female Russian writer.

9. CORRECT ANSWER: A
Since John is more than 10 inches taller than Lisa, his height is at least 46 inches. Also, John is shorter than Henry, so Henry's height must be greater than 46 inches. Thus, Lisa is the only one whose height is less than 36 inches. Therefore, she is the only one who is not allowed on the flume ride.

18. CORRECT ANSWER: A
Dan jumped higher than Carl, who jumped higher than Ignacio, who jumped higher than Frank. Since Martha jumped higher than Frank, every person jumped higher than Frank. Thus, Frank finished last.

19. CORRECT ANSWER: B
If the light is red, then the door is locked. If the door is locked, then the mill is operating. Reversing the logical sequence of these statements, if the mill is not operating, then the door is not locked, which means that the light is blue. Thus, the given conclusion is disproved.

20. CORRECT ANSWER: A
Using the contrapositive of statement III, Ziegfried was given his ten additional minutes, then Kimba did not learn how to shoot a basketball. Since statement IV is factual, the conclusion is proved.

21. CORRECT ANSWER: A
From Statements IV and I, we conclude that Sara doesn't divorce Stan. Then statement III reveals that Irene will be disappointed. Thus, the conclusion is proved.

22. CORRECT ANSWER: A
Statement II can be rewritten as "Delia is promoted to district manager or she misses her sales quota." Furthermore, this statement is equivalent to "If Delia makes her sales quota, then she is promoted to district manager." From statement I, we conclude that Claudia is promoted to team leader. Finally, by statement III, Thomas is promoted to assistant team leader.

23. CORRECT ANSWER: B
By statement IV, Clone E is not identical to any clones identical to Clone B. Statement I tells us that Clones B and D are identical. Therefore, Clone E cannot be identical to Clone D. The conclusion is disproved.

24. CORRECT ANSWER: A
Based on all four statements, CyberGraphics is somewhere below MainEvent. Gasco is one floor below CyberGraphics. EZ Tax is two floors below Gasco. Treehorn Audio is one floor below EZ Tax. MainEvent is four floors below Treehorn Audio. Thus, EZ Tax is two floors below Gasco and five floors above MainEvent. The conclusion is proved.

25. CORRECT ANSWER: A
From statement III, we know that some of the roads from Plainville lead to Nicodemus. But statement I tells us that only county roads lead to Nicodemus. Therefore, some of the roads from Plainville must be county roads. The conclusion is proved.

TEST 2

DIRECTIONS: Each question or incomplete statement is followed by several suggested answers or completions. Select the one that BEST answers the question or completes the statement. *PRINT THE LETTER OF THE CORRECT ANSWER IN THE SPACE AT THE RIGHT.*

Questions 1-9.

DIRECTIONS: In Questions 1 through 9, you will read a set of facts and a conclusion drawn from them. The conclusion may be valid or invalid, based on the facts—it's your task to determine the validity of the conclusion.

For each question, select the letter before the statement that BEST expresses the relationship between the given facts and the conclusion that has been drawn from them. Your choices are:
  A. The facts prove the conclusion;
  B. The facts disprove the conclusion; or
  C. The facts neither prove nor disprove the conclusion.

1. FACTS: Some employees in the testing department are statisticians. Most of the statisticians who work in the testing department are projection specialists. Tom Wilks works in the testing department.

   CONCLUSION: Tom Wilks is a statistician.
     A. The facts prove the conclusion.
     B. The facts disprove the conclusion.
     C. The facts neither prove nor disprove the conclusion.

2. FACTS: Ten coins are split among Hank, Lawrence, and Gail. If Lawrence gives his coins to Hank, then Hank will have more coins than Gail. If Gail gives her coins to Lawrence, then Lawrence will have more coins than Hank.

   CONCLUSION: Hank has six coins.
     A. The facts prove the conclusion.
     B. The facts disprove the conclusion.
     C. The facts neither prove nor disprove the conclusion.

3. FACTS: Nobody loves everybody. Janet loves Ken. Ken loves everybody who loves Janet.

   CONCLUSION: Everybody loves Janet.
     A. The facts prove the conclusion.
     B. The facts disprove the conclusion.
     C. The facts neither prove nor disprove the conclusion.

123

4. FACTS: Most of the Torres family lives in East Los Angeles. Many people in East Los Angeles celebrate Cinco de Mayo. Joe is a member of the Torres family.

   CONCLUSION: Joe lives in East Los Angeles.
   A. The facts prove the conclusion.
   B. The facts disprove the conclusion.
   C. The facts neither prove nor disprove the conclusion.

5. FACTS: Five professionals each occupy one story of a five-story office building. Dr. Kane's office is above Dr. Assad's. Dr. Johnson's office is between Dr. Kane's and Dr. Conlon's. Dr. Steen's office is between Dr. Conlon's and Dr. Assad's. Dr. Johnson is on the fourth story.

   CONCLUSION: Dr. Kane occupies the top story.
   A. The facts prove the conclusion.
   B. The facts disprove the conclusion.
   C. The facts neither prove nor disprove the conclusion.

6. FACTS: To be eligible for membership in the Yukon Society, a person must be able to either tunnel through a snowbank while wearing only a T-shirt and short, or hold his breath for two minutes under water that is 50°F. Ray can only hold his breath for a minute and a half.

   CONCLUSION: Ray can still become a member of the Yukon Society by tunneling through a snowbank while wearing a T-shirt and shorts.
   A. The facts prove the conclusion.
   B. The facts disprove the conclusion.
   C. The facts neither prove nor disprove the conclusion.

7. FACTS: A mark is worth five plunks. You can exchange four sharps for a tinplot. It takes eight marks to buy a sharp.

   CONCLUSION: A sharp is the most valuable.
   A. The facts prove the conclusion.
   B. The facts disprove the conclusion.
   C. The facts neither prove nor disprove the conclusion.

8. FACTS: There are gibbons, as well as lemurs, who like to play in the trees at the monkey house. All those who like to play in the trees at the monkey house are fed lettuce and bananas.

   CONCLUSION: Lemurs and gibbons are types of monkeys.
   A. The facts prove the conclusion.
   B. The facts disprove the conclusion.
   C. The facts neither prove nor disprove the conclusion.

9. FACTS: None of the Blackfoot tribes is a Salishan Indian tribe. Salishan Indians came from the northern Pacific Coast. All Salishan Indians live each of the Continental Divide.

9.____

CONCLUSION: No Blackfoot tribes live east of the Continental Divide.
   A. The facts prove the conclusion.
   B. The facts disprove the conclusion.
   C. The facts neither prove nor disprove the conclusion.

Questions 10-17.

DIRECTIONS: Questions 10 through 17 are based on the following reading passage. It is not your knowledge of the particular topic that is being tested, but your ability to reason based on what you have read. The passage is likely to detail several proposed courses of action and factors affecting these proposals. The reading passage is followed by a conclusion or outcome based on the facts in the passage, or a description of a decision taken regarding the situation. The conclusion is followed by a number of statements that have a possible connection to the conclusion. For each statement, you are to determine whether:
   A. The statement proves the conclusion.
   B. The statement supports the conclusion but does not prove it.
   C. The statement disproves the conclusion.
   D. The statement weakens the conclusion but does not disprove it.
   E. The statement has no relevance to the conclusion.

Remember that the conclusion after the passage is to be accepted as the outcome of what actually happened, and that you are being asked to evaluate the impact each statement would have had on the conclusion.

PASSAGE:

On August 12, Beverly Willey reported that she was in the elevator late on the previous evening after leaving her office on the 16th floor of a large office building. In her report, she states that a man got on the elevator at the 11th floor, pulled her off the elevator, assaulted her, and stole her purse. Ms. Willey reported that she had seen the man in the elevators and hallways of the building before. She believes that the man works in the building. Her description of him is as follows: he is tall, unshaven, with wavy brown hair and a scar on his left cheek. He walks with a pronounced limp, often dragging his left foot behind his right.

CONCLUSION: After Beverly Willey makes her report, the police arrest a 43-year-old man, Barton Black, and charge him with her assault.

10. Barton Black is a former Marine who served in Vietnam, where he sustained shrapnel wounds to the left side of his face and suffered nerve damage in his left leg.
    A. The statement proves the conclusion.
    B. The statement supports the conclusion but does not prove it.
    C. The statement disproves the conclusion.
    D. The statement weakens the conclusion but does not disprove it.
    E. The statement has no relevance to the conclusion.

11. When they arrived at his residence to question him, detectives were greeted at the door by Barton Black, who was tall and clean-shaven.
    A. The statement proves the conclusion.
    B. The statement supports the conclusion but does not prove it.
    C. The statement disproves the conclusion.
    D. The statement weakens the conclusion but does not disprove it.
    E. The statement has no relevance to the conclusion.

12. Barton Black was booked into the county jail several days after Beverly Willey's assault.
    A. The statement proves the conclusion.
    B. The statement supports the conclusion but does not prove it.
    C. The statement disproves the conclusion.
    D. The statement weakens the conclusion but does not disprove it.
    E. The statement has no relevance to the conclusion.

13. Upon further investigation, detectives discover that Beverly Willey does not work at the office building.
    A. The statement proves the conclusion.
    B. The statement supports the conclusion but does not prove it.
    C. The statement disproves the conclusion.
    D. The statement weakens the conclusion but does not disprove it.
    E. The statement has no relevance to the conclusion.

14. Upon further investigation, detectives discover that Barton Black does not work at the office building.
    A. The statement proves the conclusion.
    B. The statement supports the conclusion but does not prove it.
    C. The statement disproves the conclusion.
    D. The statement weakens the conclusion but does not disprove it.
    E. The statement has no relevance to the conclusion.

15. In the spring of the following year, Barton Black is convicted of assaulting Beverly Willey on August 11.
    A. The statement proves the conclusion.
    B. The statement supports the conclusion but does not prove it.
    C. The statement disproves the conclusion.
    D. The statement weakens the conclusion but does not disprove it.
    E. The statement has no relevance to the conclusion.

16. During their investigation of the assault, detectives determine that Beverly Willey 16.____
was assaulted on the 12th floor of the office building.
    A. The statement proves the conclusion.
    B. The statement supports the conclusion but does not prove it.
    C. The statement disproves the conclusion.
    D. The statement weakens the conclusion but does not disprove it.
    E. The statement has no relevance to the conclusion.

17. The day after Beverly Willey's assault, Barton Black fled the area and was never 17.____
seen again.
    A. The statement proves the conclusion.
    B. The statement supports the conclusion but does not prove it.
    C. The statement disproves the conclusion.
    D. The statement weakens the conclusion but does not disprove it.
    E. The statement has no relevance to the conclusion.

Questions 18-25.

DIRECTIONS: Questions 18 through 25 each provide four factual statements and a conclusion based on these statements. After reading the entire question, you will decide whether:
    A. The conclusion is proved by statements I-IV;
    B. The conclusion is disproved by statements I-IV.
    C. The facts are not sufficient to prove or disprove the conclusion.

18. FACTUAL STATEMENTS: 18.____
    I. Among five spice jars on the shelf, the sage is to the right of the parsley.
    II. The pepper is to the left of the basil.
    III. The nutmeg is between the sage and the pepper.
    IV. The pepper is the second spice from the left.

    CONCLUSION: The safe is the farthest to the right.
        A. The conclusion is proved by statements I-IV;
        B. The conclusion is disproved by statements I-IV.
        C. The facts are not sufficient to prove or disprove the conclusion.

19. FACTUAL STATEMENTS: 19.____
    I. Gear X rotates in a clockwise direction if Switch C is in the OFF position.
    II. Gear X will rotate in a counter-clockwise direction is Switch C is ON.
    III. If Gear X is rotating in a clockwise direction, then Gear Y will not be rotating at all.
    IV. Switch C is ON.

    CONCLUSION: Gear X is rotating in a counter-clockwise direction.
        A. The conclusion is proved by statements I-IV;
        B. The conclusion is disproved by statements I-IV.
        C. The facts are not sufficient to prove or disprove the conclusion.

20. FACTUAL STATEMENTS: 20.____
    I. Lane will leave for the Toronto meeting today only if Terence, Rourke, and Jackson all file their marketing reports by the end of the work day.
    II. Rourke will file her report on time only if Ganz submits last quarter's data.
    III. If Terence attends the security meeting, he will attend it with Jackson, and they will not file their marketing reports by the end of the work day.

    CONCLUSION: Lane will leave for the Toronto meeting today.
    A. The conclusion is proved by statements I-IV;
    B. The conclusion is disproved by statements I-IV.
    C. The facts are not sufficient to prove or disprove the conclusion.

21. FACTUAL STATEMENTS: 21.____
    I. Bob is in second place in the Boston Marathon.
    II. Gregory is winning the Boston Marathon.
    III. There are four miles to go in the race, and Bob is gaining on Gregory at the rate of 100 yards every minute.
    IV. There are 1760 yards in a mile and Gregory's usual pace during the Boston Marathon is one mile every six minutes.

    CONCLUSION: Bob wins the Boston Marathon.
    A. The conclusion is proved by statements I-IV;
    B. The conclusion is disproved by statements I-IV.
    C. The facts are not sufficient to prove or disprove the conclusion.

22. FACTUAL STATEMENTS: 22.____
    I. Four brothers are named Earl, John, Gary, and Pete.
    II. Earl and Pete are unmarried.
    III. John is shorter than the youngest of the four.
    IV. The oldest brother is married, and is also the tallest.

    CONCLUSION: Gary is the oldest brother.
    A. The conclusion is proved by statements I-IV;
    B. The conclusion is disproved by statements I-IV.
    C. The facts are not sufficient to prove or disprove the conclusion.

23. FACTUAL STATEMENTS: 23.____
    I. Brigade X is ten miles from the demilitarized zone.
    II. If General Woundwort gives the order, Brigade X will advance to the demilitarized zone, but not quickly enough to reach the zone before the conflict begins.
    III. Brigade Y, five miles behind Brigade X, will not advance unless General Woundwort gives the order.
    IV. Brigade Y advances.

7 (#2)

CONCLUSION: Brigade X reaches the demilitarized zone before the conflict begins.
    A. The conclusion is proved by statements I-IV;
    B. The conclusion is disproved by statements I-IV.
    C. The facts are not sufficient to prove or disprove the conclusion.

24. FACTUAL STATEMENTS: 24.____
    I. Jerry has decided to take a cab from Fullerton to Elverton.
    II. Chubby Cab charges $5 plus $3 a mile.
    III. Orange Cab charges $7.50 but gives free mileage for the first 5 miles.
    IV. After the first 5 miles, Orange Cab charges $2.50 a mile.

    CONCLUSION: Orange Cab is the cheaper fare from Fullerton to Elverton.
    A. The conclusion is proved by statements I-IV;
    B. The conclusion is disproved by statements I-IV.
    C. The facts are not sufficient to prove or disprove the conclusion.

25. FACTUAL STATEMENTS: 25.____
    I. Dan is never in class when his friend Lucy is absent.
    II. Lucy is never absent unless her mother is sick.
    III. If Lucy is in class, Sergio is in class also.
    IV. Sergio is never in class when Dalton is absent.

    CONCLUSION: If Lucy is absent, Dalton may be in class.
    A. The conclusion is proved by statements I-IV;
    B. The conclusion is disproved by statements I-IV.
    C. The facts are not sufficient to prove or disprove the conclusion.

KEY (CORRECT ANSWERS)

1. C
2. B
3. B
4. C
5. A

6. A
7. B
8. C
9. C
10. B

11. E
12. B
13. D
14. E
15. A

16. E
17. C
18. B
19. A
20. C

21. C
22. A
23. B
24. A
25. B

SOLUTIONS TO PROBLEMS

1. CORRECT ANSWER: C
    Statement 1 only tells us that some employees who work in the Testing Department are statisticians. This means that we need to allow the possibility that at least one person in this department is not a statistician. Thus, if a person works in the Testing Department, we cannot conclude whether or not this individual is a statistician.

2. CORRECT ANSWER: B
    If Hank had six coins, then the total of Gail's collection and Lawrence's collection would be four. Thus, if Gail gave all her coins to Lawrence, Lawrence would only have four coins. Thus, it would be impossible for Lawrence to have more coins than Hank.

3. CORRECT ANSWER: B
    Statement 1 tells us that nobody loves everybody. If everybody loved Janet, then Statement 3 would imply that Ken loves everybody. This would contradict statement 1. The conclusion is disproved.

4. CORRECT ANSWER: C
    Although most of the Torres family lives in East Los Angeles, we can assume that some members of this family do not live in East Los Angeles. Thus, we cannot prove or disprove that Joe, who is a member of the Torres family, lives in East Los Angeles.

5. CORRECT ANSWER: A
    Since Dr. Johnson is on the 4th floor, either (a) Dr. Kane is on the 5th floor and Dr. Conlon is on the 3rd floor, or (b) Dr. Kane is on the 3rd floor and Dr. Conlon is on the 5th floor. If option (b) were correct, then since Dr. Assad would be on the 1st floor, it would be impossible for Dr. Steen's office to be between Dr. Conlon and Dr. Assad's office. Therefore, Dr. Kane's office must be on the 5th floor. The order of the doctors' offices, from 5th floor down to the 1st floor is: Dr. Kane, Dr. Johnson, Dr. Conlon, Dr. Steen, Dr. Assad.

6. CORRECT ANSWER: A
    Ray does not satisfy the requirement of holding his breath for two minutes under water, since he can only hold is breath for one minute in that setting. But if he tunnels through a snowbank with just a T-shirt and shorts, he will satisfy the eligibility requirement. Note that the eligibility requirement contains the key word "or." So only one of the two clauses separated by "or" need to be fulfilled.

7. CORRECT ANSWER: B
    Statement 2 says that four sharps is equivalent to one tinplot. This means that a tinplot is worth more than a sharp. The conclusion is disproved. We note that the order of these items, from most valuable to least valuable are: tinplot, sharp, mark, plunk.

8. CORRECT ANSWER: C
    We can only conclude that gibbons and lemurs are fed lettuce and bananas. We can neither prove nor disprove that these animals are types of monkeys.

9. CORRECT ANSWER: C
We know that all Salishan Indians live east of the Continental Divide. But some non-members of this tribe of Indians may also live east of the Continental Divide. Since none of the members of the Blackfoot tribe belong to the Salishan Indian tribe, we cannot draw any conclusion about the location of the Blackfoot tribe with respect to the Continental Divide.

18. CORRECT ANSWER: B
Since the pepper is second from the left and the nutmeg is between the sage and the pepper, the positions 2, 3, and 4 (from the left) are pepper, nutmeg, sage. By statement II, the basil must be in position 5, which implies that the parsley is in position 1. Therefore, the basil, not the sage, is farthest to the right. The conclusion disproved.

19. CORRECT ANSWER: A
Statement II assures us that if switch C is ON, then Gear X is rotating in a counterclockwise direction. The conclusion is proved.

20. CORRECT ANSWER: C
Based on Statement IV, followed by Statement II, we conclude that Ganz and Rourke will file their reports on time. Statement III reveals that if Terence and Jackson attend the security meeting, they will fail to file their reports on time. We have no further information if Terence and Jackson attended the security meeting, so we are not able to either confirm or deny that their reports were filed on time. This implies that we cannot know for certain that Lane will leave for his meeting in Toronto.

21. CORRECT ANSWER: C
Although Bob is in second place behind Gregory, we cannot deduce how far behind Gregory he is running. At Gregory's current pace, he will cover four miles in 24 minutes. If Bob were only 100 yards behind Gregory, he would catch up to Gregory in one minute. But if Bob were very far behind Gregory, for example 5 miles, this is the equivalent of (5)(1760) = 8800 yards. Then Bob would need 8800/100 = 88 minutes to catch up to Gregory. Thus, the given facts are not sufficient to draw a conclusion.

22. CORRECT ANSWER: A
Statement II tells us that neither Earl nor Pete could be the oldest; also, either John or Gary is married. Statement IV reveals that the oldest brother is both married and the tallest. By Statement III, John cannot be the tallest. Since John is not the tallest, he is not the oldest. Thus, the oldest brother must be Gary. The conclusion is proved.

23. CORRECT ANSWER: B
By Statements III and IV, General Woundwort must have given the order to advance. Statement II then tells us that Brigade X will advance to the demilitarized zone, but not soon enough before the conflict begins. Thus, the conclusion is disproved.

11 (#2)

24. CORRECT ANSWER: A
If the distance is 5 miles or less, then the cost for the Orange Cab is only $7.50, whereas the cost for the Chubby Cab is $5 + 3x, where x represents the number of miles traveled. For 1 to 5 miles, the cost of the Chubby Cab is between $8 and $20. This means that for a distance of 5 miles, the Orange Cab costs $7.50, whereas the Chubby Cab costs $20. After 5 miles, the cost per mile of the Chubby Cab exceeds the cost per mile of the Orange Cab. Thus, regardless of the actual distance between Fullerton and Elverton, the cost for the Orange Cab will be cheaper than that of the Chubby Cab.

25. CORRECT ANSWER: B
It looks like "Dalton" should be replaced by "Dan" in the conclusion. Then by statement I, if Lucy is absent, Dan is never in class. Thus, the conclusion is disproved.

EXAMINATION SECTION
TEST 1

DIRECTIONS: Each question or incomplete statement is followed by several suggested answers or completions. Select the one that BEST answers the question or completes the statement. *PRINT THE LETTER OF THE CORRECT ANSWER IN THE SPACE AT THE RIGHT.*

Questions 1-9.

DIRECTIONS: Questions 1 through 9 measure your ability to (1) determine whether statements from witnesses say essentially the same thing, and (2) determine the evidence need to make it reasonably certain that a particular conclusion is true.

1. Which of the following pairs of statements say essentially the same thing in two different ways?   1.____
   I. The only time the machine's red light is on is when the door is locked.
      If the machine's door is locked, the red light is on.
   II. Some gray-jacketed cables are connected to the blower.
      If a cable is connected to the blower, it must be gray-jacketed.
   The CORRECT answer is:
      A. I only   B. I and II   C. II only   D. Neither I nor II

2. Which of the following pairs of statements say essentially the same thing in two different ways?   2.____
   I. If you live on Maple Street, your child is in the Valley District.
      If your child is in the Valley District, you must live on Maple Street.
   II. All the Smith children are brown-eyed.
      If a child is brown-eyed, it is not one of the Smith children.
   The CORRECT answer is:
      A. I only   B. I and II   C. II only   D. Neither I nor II

3. Which of the following pairs of statements say essentially the same thing in two different ways?   3.____
   I. If it's Monday, Mrs. James will be here.
      Mrs. James is here every Monday.
   II. Most people in the Drama Club do not have stage fright, but everyone in the Drama Club wants to be noticed.
      Some people in the Drama Club have stage fright and want to be noticed.
   The CORRECT answer is:
      A. I only   B. I and II   C. II only   D. Neither I nor II

135

4. Which of the following pairs of statements say essentially the same thing in two different ways?
   I. If you are older than 65, you will get a senior's discount.
      Either you will get a senior's discount, or you are not older than 65.
   II. Every cadet in Officer Johnson's class has passed the firearms safety course.
      No cadet that has failed the firearms safety course is in Officer Johnson's class.

   The CORRECT answer is:
   A. I only   B. I and II   C. II only   D. Neither I nor II

5. Summary of Evidence Collected to Date:
   Most people in the Greenlawn housing project do not have criminal records.
   Prematurely Drawn Conclusion:
   Some people in Greenlawn who have been crime victims have criminal records themselves.
   Which of the following pieces of evidence, if any, would make it *reasonably certain* that the conclusion drawn is TRUE?
   A. Some of those who live in the Greenlawn project have been arrested or convicted of "victimless" crimes.
   B. Most people in Greenlawn have been the victims of crime.
   C. Everyone in Greenlawn has been the victim of crime.
   D. None of the above

6. Summary of Evidence Collected to Date:
   Every drug dealer in the Oak Lawn neighborhood wears blue and carries a Glock.
   Prematurely Drawn Conclusion:
   A person in the Oak Lawn neighborhood who carries a Glock is a drug dealer.
   Which of the following pieces of evidence, if any, would make it *reasonably certain* that the conclusion drawn is TRUE?
   A. In the Oak Lawn neighborhood, only drug dealers wear blue.
   B. Drug dealers in Oak Lawn only carry Glocks when they're dealing drugs.
   C. In the Oak Lawn neighborhood, only drug dealers carry Glocks.
   D. None of the above

7. Summary of Evidence Collected to Date:
   I. Dr. Jones is older than Dr. Gupta.
   II. Dr. Gupta and Dr. Unruh were born on the same day.
   Prematurely Drawn Conclusion:
   Dr. Gupta does not work in the emergency room.
   Which of the following pieces of evidence, if any, would make it *reasonably certain* that the conclusion drawn is TRUE?
   A. Dr. Jones is older than Dr. Unruh.
   B. Dr. Jones works in the emergency room.
   C. Every doctor in the emergency room is older than Dr. Unruh.
   D. None of the above

8. Summary of Evidence Collected to Date:
   I. On the street, a "dose" of a certain drug contains four "drams."
   II. A person can trade three "rolls" of a drug for a "plunk."
   Prematurely Drawn Conclusion:
   A plunk is the most valuable amount of the drug on the street.
   Which of the following pieces of evidence, if any, would make it *reasonably certain* that the conclusion drawn is TRUE?
   A. A person can trade five doses for two rolls.
   B. A dram contains two rolls.
   C. A roll is larger than a dram.
   D. None of the above

   8.____

9. Summary of Evidence Collected to Date:
   Sam is a good writer and editor.
   Prematurely Drawn Conclusion:
   Sam is qualified for the job.
   Which of the following pieces of evidence, if any, would make it *reasonably certain* that the conclusion drawn is TRUE?
   A. The job calls for good writing and editing skills.
   B. A person who is not a good editor could still apply for the job on the strength of his/her writing skills.
   C. If Sam applies for the job, he must be both a good writer and editor.
   D. None of the above

   9.____

Questions 10-14.

DIRECTIONS: Questions 10 through 14 refer to Map #7 and measure your ability to orient yourself within a given section of town, neighborhood or particular area. Each of the questions describes a starting point and a destination. Assume that you are driving a car in the area shown on the map accompanying the questions. Use the map as a basis for the shortest way to get from one point to another without breaking the law.
On the map, a street marked by arrows, or by arrows and the words "One Way," indicates one-way travel, and should be assumed to be one-way for the entire length, even when there are breaks or jogs in the street. EXCEPTION: A street that does not have the same name over the full length.

Map #7.

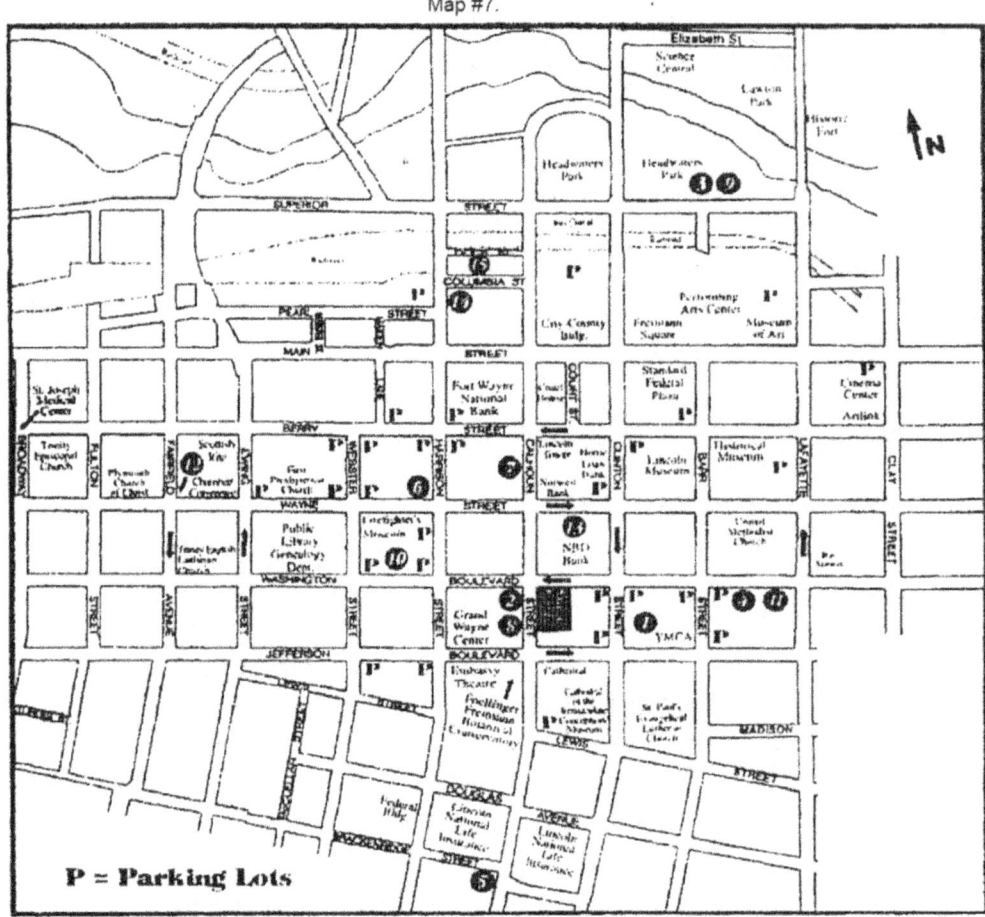

10. The SHORTEST legal way from Trinity Episcopal Church to Science Central is 10.____
    A. east on Berry, north on Clinton, east on Elizabeth
    B. east on Berry, north on Lafayette, west on Elizabeth
    C. north on Fulton, east on Main, north on Lafayette, west on Elizabeth
    D. north on Fulton, east on Main, north on Calhoun

11. The SHORTEST legal way from the Grand Wayne Center to the Museum of 11.____
    Art is
    A. north on Harrison, east on Superior, south on Lafayette
    B. east on Washington Blvd., north on Lafayette
    C. east on Jefferson Blvd., north on Clinton, east on Main
    D. east on Jefferson Blvd., north on Lafayette

12. The SHORTEST legal way from the Embassy Theatre too the City/County 12.____
    Building is
    A. west on Jefferson Blvd., north on Ewing, east on Main
    B. east on Jefferson Blvd., north on Lafayette, west on Main
    C. east on Jefferson Blvd., north on Clinton
    D. north on Harrison, east on Main

5 (#1)

13. The SHORTEST legal way from the YMCA to the Firefighter's Museum is   13.____
    A. west on Jefferson Blvd., north on Webster
    B. north on Barr, west on Washington Blvd., north on Webster
    C. north on Barr, west on Wayne
    D. north on Barr, west on Berry, south on Webster

14. The SHORTEST legal way from the Historic Fort to Freimann Square is   14.____
    A. north on Lafayette, west on Elizabeth, south on Clinton
    B. north on Lafayette, west on Elizabeth, west/south on Calhoun, east on Main
    C. south on Lafayette, west on Main
    D. south on Lafayette, west on Superior, south on Clinton

Questions 15-19.

DIRECTIONS: Questions 15 through 19 refer to Figure #7, on the following page, and measure your ability to understand written descriptions of events. Each question presents a description of an accident or event and asks you which of the five drawings in Figure #7 BEST represents it.

In the drawings, the following symbols are used:

Moving Vehicle: ◯   Non-moving Vehicle: ▮

Pedestrian or Bicyclist: ●

The path and direction of travel of a vehicle or pedestrian is indicated by a solid line.

The path and direction of travel of each vehicle or pedestrian directly involved in a collision from the point of impact is indicated by a dotted line.

In the space at the right, print the letter of the drawing that BEST fits the descriptions written below:

15. A driver headed northeast on Cary strikes a car in the intersection and is   15.____
    diverted north, where he collides with the rear of a car that is traveling north on Park. The northbound car is knocked into the rear of another car that is traveling north ahead of it.

16. A driver headed northeast on Cary strikes a car in the intersection and is   16.____
    diverted north, where he collides head-on with a car stopped at a traffic light in the southbound lane on Park.

17. A driver headed northeast on Cary strikes a car in the intersection and is   17.____
    diverted east, where he collides head-on with a car stopped at a traffic light in the westbound lane on Roble.

139

18. A driver headed east on Roble collides with the left front of a car that is turning right from Knox onto Roble. The driver swerves right after the collision and collides head-on with another car headed north on Park.   18.____

19. A driver headed northeast on Cary strikes a car in the intersection and is diverted north, where he collides with the rear of a car parked on the northbound lane on Park.   19.____

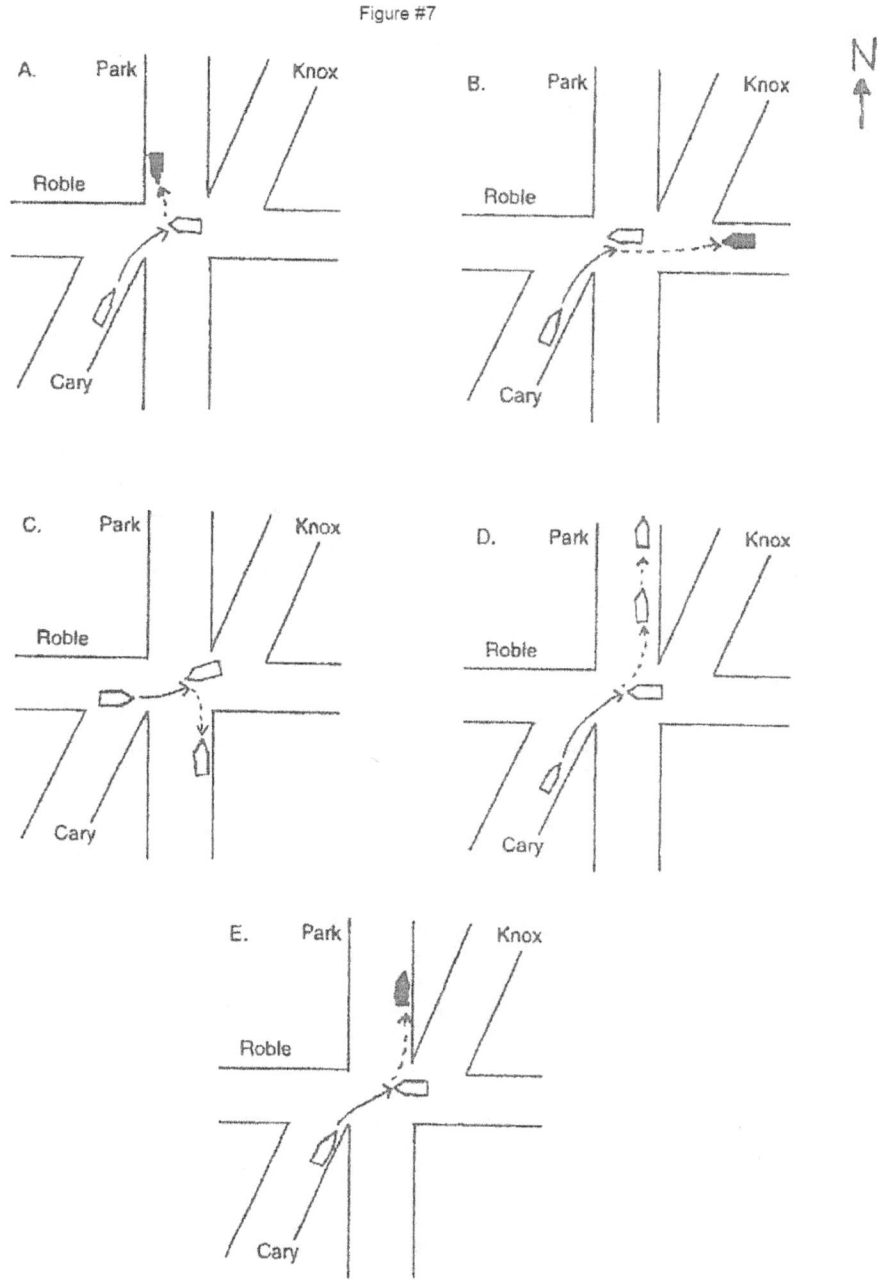

Figure #7

Questions 20-22.

DIRECTIONS: In Questions 20 through 22, choose the word or phrase CLOSEST in meaning to the word or phrase printed in capital letters.

20. JURISDICTION　　　　　　　　　　　　　　　　　　　　　　　　　　　　　　20.____
    A. authority　　　B. decision　　　C. judgment　　　D. argument

21. PROXY　　　　　　　　　　　　　　　　　　　　　　　　　　　　　　　　　21.____
    A. neighbor　　　B. agent　　　C. enforcer　　　D. impostor

22. LARCENY　　　　　　　　　　　　　　　　　　　　　　　　　　　　　　　　22.____
    A. theft　　　B. assault　　　C. deceit　　　D. gentleness

Questions 23-25.

DIRECTIONS: Questions 22 through 25 measure your ability to do fieldwork-related arithmetic. Each question presents a separate arithmetic problem for you to solve.

23. Mr. Long has 14 employees. He has four more male employees than female employees.　　23.____
    How many female employees does he have?
    A. 4　　　B. 5　　　C. 9　　　D. 10

24. A box of latex gloves costs $18. A crate has 12 boxes, each of which contains 48 gloves.　　24.____
    How much does a crate of latex gloves cost?
    A. $216　　　B. $328　　　C. $576　　　D. $864

25. In a single week, the Department of Parking collected 540 quarter, 623 dimes, and 146 nickels from its parking meters.　　25.____
    What was the TOTAL revenue collected from the meters during the week?
    A. $135.00　　　B. $154.00　　　C. $204.60　　　D. $270.30

KEY (CORRECT ANSWERS)

1.	A		11.	D
2.	D		12.	D
3.	B		13.	B
4.	B		14.	A
5.	C		15.	D
6.	C		16.	A
7.	C		17.	B
8.	A		18.	C
9.	A		19.	E
10.	C		20.	A

21. B
22. A
23. B
24. A
25. C

9 (#1)

SOLUTIONS (QUESTIONS 1-9)

P implies Q = original statement

Not Q implies not P = contrapositive of the original statement. A statement and its contrapositive are logically equivalent.

Q implies P = converse of the original statement.

Not P implies not Q = inverse of the original statement. The converse and inverse of an original statement are logically equivalent.

P implies Q = Not P or Q

1. CORRECT ANSWER: A
   For Item I, the equivalent of the first statement would be "If the red light is on, the door is locked." This is the converse of the second statement, so it is not equivalent to the first statement. For Item II, the first statement does not guarantee that all cables that are connected to the blower must be gray-jacketed. There may very well be other cables that are connected to the blower that are not gray-jacketed. Equally possible, some gray-jacketed cables are not necessarily connected to the blower.

2. CORRECT ANSWER: D
   For Item I, the second statement is the converse of the first statement, so it is not logically equivalent. For Item II, the equivalent of the first statement is "If a child is not brown-eyed, then it is not one of the Smith children." Thus, statement II as it stands is not equivalent to statement I.

3. CORRECT ANSWER: B
   For Item I, Mrs. James is here every Monday, so we conclude that if it is Monday, she is here. (She may be here on other days as well.) For Item II, we can conclude that there are some people in the Drama Club who do have stage fright. Since everyone in the Drama Club wants to be noticed, this would include those who have stage fright.

4. CORRECT ANSWER: B
   For Item I, these two statements represent "P implies Q" and "Not P or Q," where P = Older than 65 and Q = Get a senior discount. These are equivalent statements. For Item II, these statements are contrapositive of each other and so must be equivalent. (P = Cadet in Johnson's class and Q = Passes the safety course.)

5. CORRECT ANSWER: C
   If everyone in the housing project has been a victim of crime and most of these people do not have a criminal record, we can conclude that some of them do have a criminal record. Thus, we have the situation that some of the people who live in this housing project are both a victim of crime as well as a perpetrator of crime.

6. CORRECT ANSWER: C
This choice can be written as "In this neighborhood, if a person carries a Glock, he is a drug dealer." This would lead directly to the drawn conclusion.

7. CORRECT ANSWER: C
We know that every doctor in the emergency room is older than Dr. Unruh; it is not possible for Dr. Gupta to be working in the emergency room since he is the same age as Dr. Unruh.

8. CORRECT ANSWER: A
From statement I, a dose is worth more than a dram. If 5 doses is equal to 2 rolls, then a roll is worth more than a dose. So of these three, a roll is worth the most. Finally, statement II tells us that a plunk is worth more than a roll. This means that a plunk is worth the most among all four of these categories.

9. CORRECT ANSWER: A
Sam has the qualifications of being a good writer and editor, which is exactly what is needed for the job. Therefore, Sam is qualified for this job.

TEST 2

DIRECTIONS: Each question or incomplete statement is followed by several suggested answers or completions. Select the one that BEST answers the question or completes the statement. *PRINT THE LETTER OF THE CORRECT ANSWER IN THE SPACE AT THE RIGHT.*

Questions 1-9.

DIRECTIONS: Questions 1 through 9 measure your ability to (1) determine whether statements from witnesses say essentially the same thing, and (2) determine the evidence need to make it reasonably certain that a particular conclusion is true.

To do well on this part of the test, you do NOT have to have a working knowledge of police procedures and techniques. Nor do you have to have any more familiarity with criminals and criminal behavior than that acquired from reading newspapers, listening to radio or watching TV. To do well in this part, you must read and reason carefully.

1. Which of the following pairs of statements say essentially the same thing in two different ways?   1.____
   I. If the garbage is collected today, it is definitely Wednesday.
      The garbage is collected every Wednesday.
   II. Nobody has no answer to the question.
       Everybody has at least one answer to the question.
   The CORRECT answer is:
   A. I only   B. I and II   C. II only   D. Neither I nor II

2. Which of the following pairs of statements say essentially the same thing in two different ways?   2.____
   I. If it rains, the streets will be wet.
      If the streets are wet, it has rained.
   II. All of the Duluth Five are immune from prosecution.
       No member of the Duluth Five can be prosecuted.
   The CORRECT answer is:
   A. I only   B. I and II   C. II only   D. Neither I nor II

3. Which of the following pairs of statements say essentially the same thing in two different ways?   3.____
   I. Ms. Friar will accept her promotion if and only if she is offered a 10% raise.
      For Ms. Friar to accept her promotion, it is necessary that she be offered a 10% raise.
   II. If the hydraulic lines are flushed, it is definitely inspection day.
       The hydraulic lines are flushed only on inspection days.
   The CORRECT answer is:
   A. I only   B. I and II   C. II only   D. Neither I nor II

4. Which of the following pairs of statements say essentially the same thing in two different ways?
   I. If you are tall you will get onto the basketball team.
      Unless you are tall, you will not get onto the basketball team.
   II. That raven is black.
       If that bird is black, it's a raven.
   The CORRECT answer is:
   A. I only   B. I and II   C. II only   D. Neither I nor II

5. Summary of Evidence Collected to Date:
   Every member of the Rotary Club is retired.
   Prematurely Drawn Conclusion:
   At least some people in the planning commission are retired.
   Which of the following pieces of evidence, if any, would make it *reasonably certain* that the conclusion drawn is TRUE?
   A. Retirement is a condition for membership in the Rotary Club.
   B. Every member of the planning commission has been in the Rotary Club at one time.
   C. Every member of the Rotary Club is also on the planning commission.
   D. None of the above

6. Summary of Evidence Collected to Date:
   Some of the SWAT team snipers have poor aim.
   Prematurely Drawn Conclusion:
   The snipers on the SWAT team with the worst aim also have 20/20 vision.
   Which of the following pieces of evidence, if any, would make it *reasonably certain* that the conclusion drawn is TRUE?
   A. Some of the SWAT team snipers have 20/20 vision.
   B. Every sniper on the SWAT team has 20/20 vision.
   C. Some snipers on the SWAT team wear corrective lenses.
   D. None of the above

7. Summary of Evidence Collected to Date:
   The only time Garson hears voices is on a day when he doesn't take his medication.
   Prematurely Drawn Conclusion:
   On Fridays, Garson never hears voices.
   Which of the following pieces of evidence, if any, would make it *reasonably certain* that the conclusion drawn is TRUE?
   A. Garson is supposed to take his medication every day.
   B. Garson usually undergoes shock therapy on Fridays.
   C. Garson usually takes his medication and undergoes shock therapy on Fridays.
   D. None of the above

8. **Summary of Evidence Collected to Date:**
   Among the three maintenance workers, Frank, Lily and Jean, Frank is not the tallest.
   Prematurely Drawn Conclusion:
   Lily is the tallest.
   Which of the following pieces of evidence, if any, would make it *reasonably certain* that the conclusion drawn is TRUE?
   - A. Jean is not the tallest.
   - B. Frank is the shortest.
   - C. Jean is the shortest.
   - D. None of the above

   8.____

9. **Summary of Evidence Collected to Date:**
   Doctor Lyons went to the cafeteria for lunch today and did not eat dessert.
   Prematurely Drawn Conclusion:
   The cafeteria did not serve dessert.
   Which of the following pieces of evidence, if any, would make it *reasonably certain* that the conclusion drawn is TRUE?
   - A. Dr. Lyons never eats dessert.
   - B. When the cafeteria serves dessert, Dr. Lyons always eats it.
   - C. The cafeteria rarely serves dessert when Dr. Lyons eats there.

   9.____

Questions 10-14.

DIRECTIONS: Questions 10 through 14 refer to Map #8 and measure your ability to orient yourself within a given section of town, neighborhood or particular area. Each of the questions describes a starting point and a destination. Assume that you are driving a car in the area shown on the map accompanying the questions. Use the map as a basis for the shortest way to get from one point to another without breaking the law.
On the map, a street marked by arrows, or by arrows and the words "One Way," indicates one-way travel, and should be assumed to be one-way for the entire length, even when there are breaks or jogs in the street. EXCEPTION: A street that does not have the same name over the full length.

Map #8

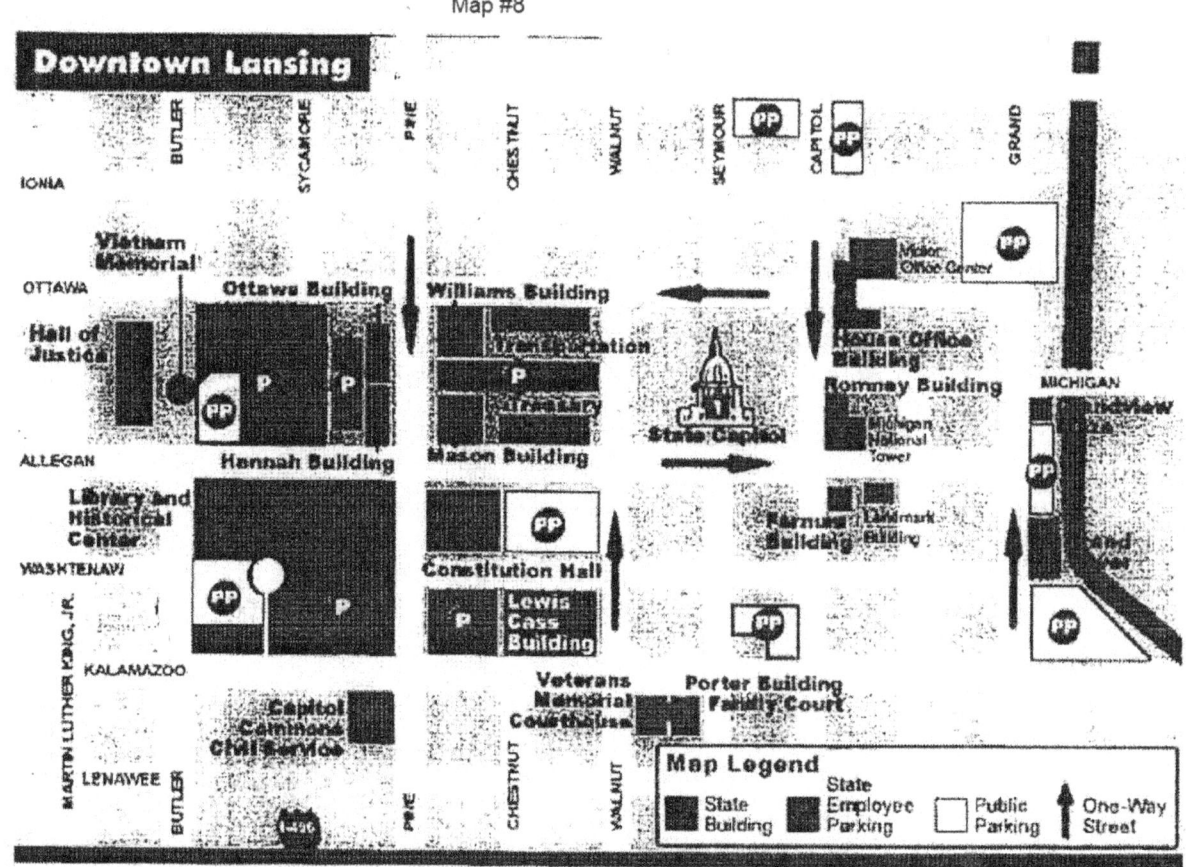

10. The SHORTEST legal way from the Library and Historical Center to Grandview Plaza is
    A. south on Butler, east on Kalamazoo, north on Grand
    B. east on Allegan, north on Grand
    C. north on Butler, east on Ionia, south on Grand
    D. north on Martin Luther King, Jr., east on Ottawa, south on Pine, east on Allegan, north on Grand

11. The SHORTEST legal way from the Victor Office Center to the Mason Building is
    A. west on Ottawa, south on Pine
    B. south on Capitol, west on Allegan, north on Pine
    C. south on Capitol, west on Washtenaw, north on Walnut, west on Allegan
    D. west on Ottawa, north on Seymour, west on Ionia, south on Pine

12. The SHORTESST legal way from the Treasury to the Hall of Justice is
    A. north on Walnut, west on Ottawa, south on Martin Luther King, Jr.
    B. west on Allegan
    C. east on Allegan, north on Grand, west on Ottawa, south on Martin Luther King. Jr.
    D. south on Walnut, west on Kalamazoo, north on Martin Luther King, Jr.

5 (#2)

13. The SHORTEST legal way from the Veterans Memorial Courthouse to the   13.____
    House Office Building is
    A. north on Walnut, east on Ottawa
    B. east on Kalamazoo, north on Capitol
    C. east on Kalamazoo, north on Grand, west on Ottawa
    D. north on Walnut, east on Allegan, north on Capitol

14. The SHORTEST legal way from Grand Tower to Constitution Hall is   14.____
    A. west on Washtenaw
    B. north on Grand, west on Allegan, south on Pine
    C. north on Grand, west on Ottaway, south on Pine
    D. south on Grand, west on Kalamazoo, north on Pine

Questions 15-19.

DIRECTIONS: Questions 15 through 19 refer to Figure #8, on the following page, and measure your ability to understand written descriptions of events. Each question presents a description of an accident or event and asks you which of the five drawings in Figure #8 BEST represents it.

In the drawings, the following symbols are used:

Moving Vehicle: ◯   Non-moving Vehicle: ▮

Pedestrian or Bicyclist: ●

The path and direction of travel of a vehicle or pedestrian is indicated by a solid line.

The path and direction of travel of each vehicle or pedestrian directly involved in a collision from the point of impact is indicated by a dotted line.

In the space at the right, print the letter of the drawing that BEST fits the descriptions written below:

15. A driver headed west on Holly runs a red light and turns left. He sideswipes   15.____
    a car headed south in the intersection, and then flees south on Bay. The
    southbound car is diverted into the rear end of a car parked in the southbound
    lane on Bay.

16. A driver headed east on Holly runs a red light. Another driver headed south   16.____
    through the intersection slams on her brakes just in time to avoid a serious
    collision. The eastbound driver glances off the front of the southbound car and
    continues east, where he collides with a car parked in the eastbound lane on
    Holly.

17. A driver headed east on Holly runs a red light. She strikes the left front of a   17.____
    westbound car that is turning left from Holly onto Bay, and then veers left and
    strikes the rear end of a car parked in the northbound lane on Bay.

18. A driver headed north on Bay strikes the right front of a car heading south in the intersection of Bay and Holly. After the collision, the driver veers left and collides with the rear end of a car parked in the westbound lane of Holly. The southbound car veers left and collides with the rear end of a car in the eastbound lane on Holly.

18.____

19. A driver headed north on Bay strikes the left front of a car heading south in the intersection of Bay and Holly. After the collision, the driver continues north and collides with the rear end of a car parked in the northbound lane. The southbound car continues south and collides with the rear end of a car in the southbound lane.

19.____

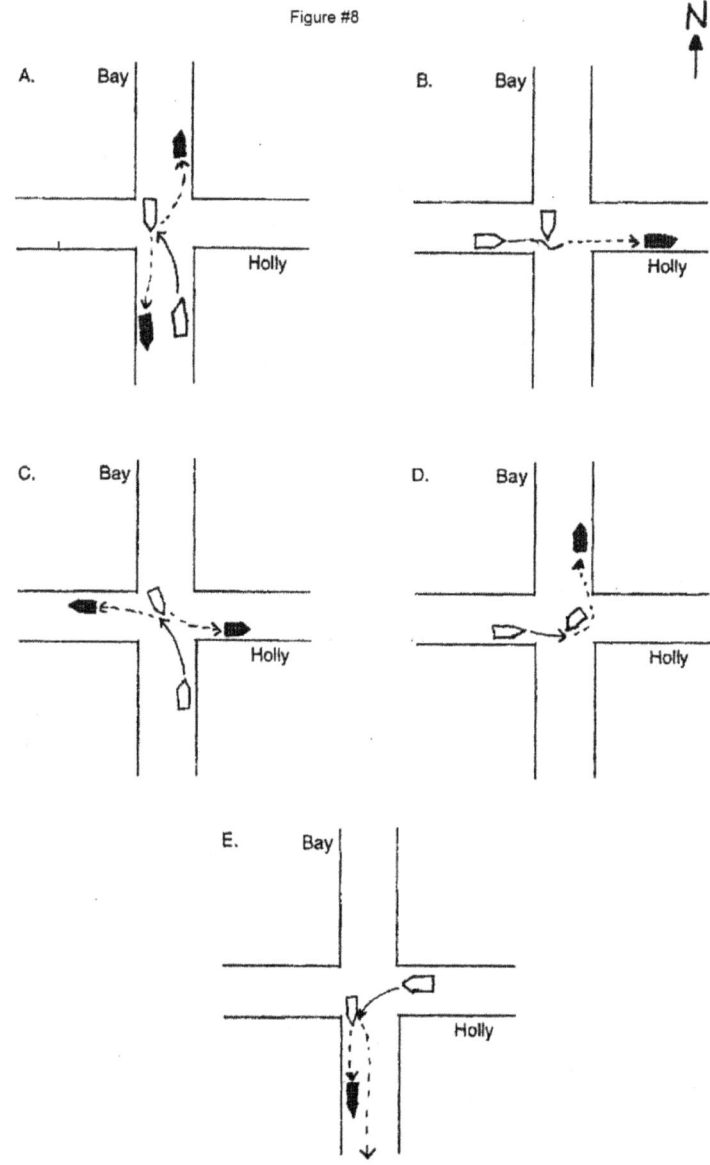

Figure #8

Questions 20-22.

DIRECTIONS: In Questions 20 through 22, choose the word or phrase CLOSEST in meaning to the word or phrase printed in capital letters.

20. LIABLE
    A. sensitive   B. dishonest   C. responsible   D. valid
20.____

21. CLAIM
    A. debt   B. period   C. denial   D. banishment
21.____

22. ADMISSIBLE
    A. false   B. conclusive   C. acceptable   D. indsputable
22.____

Questions 23-25.

DIRECTIONS: Questions 22 through 25 measure your ability to do fieldwork-related arithmetic. Each question presents a separate arithmetic problem for you to solve.

23. Three departments divide an $800 payment. Department 1 takes $270, and Department 2 takes $150 more than Department 3.
How much does Department 2 take?
    A. $150   B. $190   C. $340   D. $490
23.____

24. Detective Smalley cleared 100 murder cases in five years. Each year he cleared six more than he cleared in the previous year.
How many cases did he clear during the first year?
    A. 6   B. 8   C. 12   D. 18
24.____

25. The purchasing agent bought three binders for $2 each, four reams of copier paper for $3 each and five packs of black pens for $7 each.
How much did the agent spend?
    A. $12.00   B. $25.20   C. $53.00   D. $72.00
25.____

KEY (CORRECT ANSWERS)

1. B
2. C
3. B
4. D
5. C

6. B
7. D
8. A
9. B
10. B

11. A
12. A
13. C
14. A
15. E

16. B
17. D
18. C
19. A
20. C

21. A
22. C
23. C
24. B
25. C

SOLUTIONS (QUESTIONS 1-9)

P implies Q = original statement

Not Q implies not P = contrapositive of the original statement. A statement and its contrapositive are logically equivalent.

Q implies P = converse of the original statement.

Not P implies not Q = inverse of the original statement. The converse and inverse of an original statement are logically equivalent.

P implies Q = Not P or Q

1. CORRECT ANSWER: B
   For Item I, we can conclude that it is Wednesday if and only if the garbage is collected. For Item II, the phrase "nobody has no" is equivalent to everybody has at least one."

2. CORRECT ANSWER: C
   For Item I, each statement is the converse of the other. Thus, they are not equivalent. For Item II, each statement says that each member of the Duluth Five is immune from prosecution.

3. CORRECT ANSWER: B
   For Item I, accepting a promotion is a necessary and sufficient condition for receiving a 10% raise. For Item II, we have the P implies Q condition, where P = hydraulic lines are flushed and Q = it is an inspection day.

4. CORRECT ANSWER: D
   For Item I, each statement is the converse of the other (so they are not equivalent). For Item II, the first statement simply states that a particular raven is black. The second statement says that all black birds are ravens. They are not equivalent.

5. CORRECT ANSWER: C
   The two scenarios are (a) a Rotary Club member is a subset of the set of all retirees, which is a subset of all planning commission member or (b) a Rotary Club member is a subset of all planning commission members, which is a subset of all retirees.

6. CORRECT ANSWER: B
   We know that some SWAT sniper members have poor aim. If we also know that all snipers on the SWAT team also have 20/20 vision, then we conclude that any sniper (including those with the worst aim) must have 20/20 vision.

7. CORRECT ANSWER: D
   The only way that Garson will not hear voices is if he takes his medication. The premature conclusion can only be correct if he takes his medication every Friday. None of choices A, B, or C mentions this specifically.

8. CORRECT ANSWER: A
If Frank is not the tallest and Jean is not the tallest, then the conclusion that Lily is the tallest is correct. This is a reasonable conclusion, unless all three are the same height (very unlikely).

9. CORRECT ANSWER: B
We are given that Dr. Lyons went to the cafeteria for lunch and that he did not have dessert. If Dr. Lyons always eats dessert when it is served in the cafeteria, we can conclude that the cafeteria did not serve dessert.

MEMORY FOR FACTS AND INFORMATION

EXAMINATION SECTION
TEST 1

DIRECTIONS: Questions 1 through 15 test your ability to remember key facts and details. You are given a rather long reading passage, which you will have approximately ten minutes to read. The reading selection should then be turned over. Then immediately answer the fifteen questions that refer to this passage. Please do NOT refer back to the reading passage at any time while you are answering the questions. Select the letter that represents the BEST of the four possible choices.

THE CASE OF THE MISSING OVERTIME WAGES

Melba Tolliber is a new Labor Standards Investigator assigned to investigate a complaint of nonpayment of some overtime wages. The complaint came in the form of a telephone call from Albert Brater, employed by the Whizzer Audio and Video Store in Dorchester. Whizzer Audio and Video, Inc. is a fast-growing and very successful chain in the Northeast. Their headquarters is in Dorchester.

Melba Tolliber drives the eight miles to Dorchester on a breezy Monday morning. She meets with Albert Brater, the employee who called. He is employed in the warehouse unit.

Hello, Mr. Brater, my name is Melba Tolliber, and I'm here to investigate whether you've been paid the proper amount of overtime wages.

Nice to meet you, Ms. Tolliber. I'm not the only one with this problem. Two salesclerks in the Dorchester store, Mary and Martin, have also gotten less for overtime than they should have.

Can I talk with them, too? Melba asks.

Well, the problem is, we're worried about getting into a lot of trouble with, the company. We were hoping you could talk just to me. I'm a little worried about talking with you myself.

This is a confidential interview; don't worry. It would be very helpful, however, if I could at least get copies of their pay stubs.

Albert hesitates and then says, *Gee, I hope I can find my last paystub. Anyway, we've been working forty-six hours a week the last four weeks, but only getting paid our usual rate of $5.25 an hour.*

Melba says, *But that's below the minimum wage.*

Maybe it's $5.35; I get confused; I'll have to check. I think it's $5.35. Yeah, I'm pretty sure it's $5.35. But you know what else? I was promised a raise of $.50 per hour after eight months of working here, and that's up next week. We'll see if I get it or not.

155

Have the other employees here gotten the raises they were promised?

Yeah, I think they have. But I know of at least one person, a truckdriver, who hasn't gotten his raise yet.

Do you know his name?

Just his first name. But the next time I see him, I'll ask him if he's gotten the raise yet. I'll let you know if he hasn't.

What day would be good for you to drop off the paystubs and have a second interview?

Well, you have to give me some time to get them from Mary and Martin, too. How about this Thursday afternoon at one?

Fine, heres my card. I'll see you this Thursday at one.

At the beginning of their next meeting, Albert gives Melba the paystubs for the last month's work for all three employees.

Let's do you first, Albert. What have your hours been each week for the last four weeks?

I've worked the same schedule for the past month, my usual forty hours - 8 to 5 with an hour for lunch, which I don't like, on Mondays, Tuesdays, and Thursdays. Wednesdays and Fridays I've worked from 8 A.M. to 9 P.M. because those are the days we do our most shipping. They give us from 5 to 6 P.M. as a dinner break on those days.

So that adds up to forty-six hours. Give me a few minutes to go over these figures with my calculator.

That's a great calculator; it's so small. Looks like a credit card.

Thanks, but I have to be careful how I hit the numbers; there's not much room.... Well, according to my calculations, you're owed $48.15 in overtime pay for the last four weeks. But there's something else wrong, too. It looks like they've been taking out a little too much money for Social Security. Let me recheck this.

1. In the passage, Melba Tolliber visited

    A. Midwood
    C. Midale
    B. Dorchester
    D. Midville

2. In the passage, Melba talked with

    A. Albert who works in the warehouse unit
    B. Albert who works in the warehouse unit and in the store
    C. Robert who works in the warehouse
    D. Robert, Martin, and Mary who work in the warehouse and the store

3. The organization whose payment of overtime wages is in question　　　　　3.____

    A. is struggling to succeed
    B. is the most successful of the new audio-visual store chains in the Northeast
    C. has its headquarters in the town that Melba travels to
    D. has successfully switched from selling just records to selling records, tapes, and video equipment

4. During their initial discussion, how sure of his rate of pay was the employee to whom Melba spoke?　　　　　4.____

    A. Not sure at all　　　　　　　B. Very sure
    C. Pretty sure　　　　　　　　D. Totally unsure

5. What day of the week did Melba conduct the initial interview?　　　　　5.____

    A. Monday　　　　　　　　　B. Wednesday
    C. Tuesday　　　　　　　　　D. Thursday

6. When did Melba conduct the second interview?　　　　　6.____

    A. Monday at 1 P.M.　　　　　B. Thursday at 1 P.M.
    C. Wednesday at 1 P.M.　　　D. Friday at 1 P.M.

7. In order to calculate how much money the employee should have received, Melba used a　　　　　7.____

    A. credit card
    B. calculator
    C. credit card/calculator/watch combination
    D. desk top personal computer

8. According to the passage, what did Melba do to try to make the employee feel more at ease?　　　　　8.____
    She

    A. gave him time to collect his thoughts
    B. assured him that she believed what he said
    C. assured him that the interview was confidential
    D. asked if she could speak with the other two employees affected

9. The initial complaint from the employee　　　　　9.____

    A. resulted in his receiving back pay
    B. came in the form of a phone call
    C. was anonymous
    D. resulted in a large-scale investigation

10. The name of the establishment the employee works for is the　　　　　10.____

    A. Whizzer
    B. Genuine Article
    C. Electronic Era
    D. Gizmos etcetera

11. The other two employees who have questions about their overtime pay 11.____

    A. are truckdrivers B. work in the warehouse
    C. are salesclerks   D. work in maintenance

12. The organization told the employee he would receive a 12.____

    A. $.60 per hour raise after eight months
    B. $.60 per hour raise after five months
    C. $.50 per hour raise after six months
    D. $.50 per hour raise after eight months

13. How many hours a week have the employees who are questioning their pay been working for the last month? 13.____

    A. Forty-four   B. Forty-five
    C. Forty-six   D. Forty-eight

14. In the last month, what hours did the employee Melba interviewed work on Wednesdays? 14.____

    A. 8 A.M. to 5 P.M.   B. 9 A.M. to 10 P.M.
    C. 9 A.M. to 5 P.M.   D. 8 A.M. to 9 P.M.

15. At the start of the second interview, 15.____

    A. the employee gives Melba the paystubs for the last month for all three workers involved
    B. the employee gives Melba the paystubs for the last month for all three workers involved, with the exception of his last paystub
    C. the employee gives Melba only his paystubs from the last month
    D. it cannot be determined if the employee gives Melba any paystubs

---

KEY (CORRECT ANSWERS)

1. B
2. A
3. C
4. C
5. A

6. B
7. B
8. C
9. B
10. A

11. C
12. D
13. C
14. D
15. A

TEST 2

DIRECTIONS: Questions 1 through 15 test your ability to remember key facts and details. You are given a rather long reading passage, which you will have approximately ten minutes to read. The reading selection should then be turned over. Then immediately answer the fifteen questions that refer to this passage. Please do NOT refer back to the reading passage at any time while you are answering these questions. Select the letter that represents the BEST of the four possible choices.

THE CASE OF THE DELINQUENT TAXPAYER

David Owens has been a Tax Investigator for five years. His unit has received another anonymous tip about possible sales tax abuse, and David's supervisor, William, has assigned David to conduct the investigation. The organization in question is Bob's News, a 24-hour newsstand and variety store. The store is located in Hillsdell, five miles away. The anonymous caller did not provide details, but stated that she was an employee, and that there was widespread abuse in the collection and reporting of sales tax by the store. The agency has had a series of crank calls regarding sales tax abuse in Hillsdell.

For this investigation, David has been instructed not to work undercover, but to go in, identify himself, and discuss the situation with the owner and some employees without divulging the reason for the visit. On Wednesday, David drives to the store in a government car, a 2004 Plymouth.

David arrives at the store and buys a magazine for which he is properly not charged sales tax. He speaks to the employee whose name tag says Susan.

Hello, Susan, my name is David Owens, and I'm from the State Tax Department. Here's my identification. We're doing a routine check-up to see if things are in order with regard to sales tax collection and reporting. Is the owner around?

No, Bob is out of town today. He'll be back tomorrow. You seem surprised that his name is Bob. Some people think he must not exist, sort of like a Betty Crocker or something. Can I help you with anything? I'm the Assistant Manager.

Well, it would be helpful if you could answer a few questions for me.

As long as it doesn't get me in trouble with my boss, I'd be glad to, Susan replied.

Don't worry, I won't ask you anything that could, get you in trouble.

OK, then.

Did someone tell employees how to go about collecting sales tax on items?

Bob has a list of items we're not allowed to collect tax on. It's right next to the cash register. Would you like to see it?

If you don't mind. Thanks. It says here not to collect tax on magazines, but there's no mention of newspapers.

I guess that's because he probably assumes we know better than that. I'll ask him to add it to the list.

This is a pretty good list, but what's this written on the bottom here about toilet paper? That's a taxable item.

Oh, I know. Henry who works nights put that in as a joke because he says toilet paper is a necessity, not a luxury, and shouldn't be taxed. I agree. So does Bob. But don't worry, we collect sales tax on it. Nine percent, right?

No, the rate is eight percent.

Just kidding, David. We know that. I guess I shouldn't joke about something like that; I don't want to end up in jail. What else do you need to know?

Who keeps the records and submits the sales tax money to Metro City every quarter?

Bob does that himself, but I'd rather you come back tomorrow to talk with him about that end of it....I think that would be best. I don't know much about it, except that he yells if I don't have everything - the records and stuff - ready for him when he wants it.

What time do you think Bob will be in tomorrow?

I think the morning would be best, you'll be sure to catch him then.

OK, I'll drop by tomorrow around nine. See you then. Thanks again.

The next day, David drives back to the store to meet with Bob at the time stated earlier. When he arrives, Susan immediately introduces him to Bob.

It's nice to meet you, Bob. Nice store you have here. How long have you been in business?

We've been open for five years. Time really flies, doesn't it?

It sure does. As Susan probably mentioned, I'm here on a routine type check-up about sales tax collection.

Sure thing.

Well, I just noticed you're not displaying the Sales Tax Certificate of Authority, that you need to show in order to collect sales tax.

That's strange; it was there yesterday. Here it is. It fell under the counter. We're off to a great start. Let me tape this thing back up.

How many employees work here. Bob?

We have six full-time and three part-time employees, plus myself. I understand you'd like to see our books. Come on in to my office. Stay in here as long as you need. I've got it all laid out for you.

Thanks.

Several hours later, David finishes looking through the books.

Well, Bob, things look in order. The only question I have is why your receipts for 2004 were so much lower than in other years?

A chain store moved in about eight blocks away, and we initially lost a lot of business. But eventually our customers started coming back. We do the little things - save them the Boston papers, things like that. The chain moved downtown in early 2005.

Well, listen, thanks very much for all of your time. I really appreciate it.

No problem. Anytime. Well, I wouldn't go that far, but it's been nice meeting you.

1. What was the name of the Tax Investigator in the above passage?

    A. David Allen
    B. Bob Williams
    C. Derwin Williams
    D. David Owens

    1.____

2. What was the name of the city the investigator visited?

    A. Hillsville
    B. Hillsdale
    C. Hicksville
    D. Hillsdell

    2.____

3. The store under investigation is a

    A. department store
    B. 24-hour massage parlor
    C. newsstand and variety store
    D. sporting goods store

    3.____

4. The phone call received by the agency was

    A. placed by an anonymous employee of the store being accused of sales tax fraud
    B. received by the investigator handling the case
    C. placed by an anonymous caller
    D. received by the investigator's supervisor

    4.____

5. The investigator on this case

    A. did not work undercover
    B. was instructed to work undercover, but refused because of the nature of the case
    C. worked undercover
    D. pretended to his supervisor that he worked undercover

    5.____

6. According to the above passage, it is

    A. not correct to charge sales tax for a magazine
    B. correct to charge sales tax for pet food

    6.____

C. correct to charge sales tax for a newspaper
D. correct to charge sales tax for a magazine

7. The Assistant Manager of the store is
   A. Susan
   B. David
   C. Bob
   D. Betty Crocker

8. What day was the initial investigation conducted?
   A. Monday
   B. Wednesday
   C. Tuesday
   D. Thursday

9. The list the investigator was shown contained
   A. a list of sales taxable items
   B. a list of non-taxable items
   C. a list of products on which sales tax was mistakenly charged
   D. the Certificate of Authority

10. According to the above passage, sales tax was to be charged on
    A. pet food
    B. cigarettes
    C. gasoline
    D. toilet paper

11. According to the above passage, the sales tax was _____%.
    A. seven
    B. nine
    C. eight
    D. ten

12. According to the passage, how often was the sales tax submitted?
    A. Every month
    B. Quarterly
    C. Twice a year
    D. Once every six months

13. According to the passage, where are the sales tax monies sent?
    A. River City
    B. Metro City
    C. Metropolis
    D. Hillswood

14. According to the passage, which of the following is TRUE? Bob's business, called Bob's
    A. News and Variety, has been open for five years
    B. Department Store, has been open for six years
    C. Variety, has been open for six years
    D. News, has been open for five years

15. The only question the investigator had about Bob's books was why receipts for _____ than in other years.
    A. 2005 were so much lower
    B. 2004 were so much lower
    C. 2005 were so much higher
    D. 2004 were so much higher

KEY (CORRECT ANSWERS)

1. D
2. D
3. C
4. C
5. A

6. A
7. A
8. B
9. B
10. D

11. C
12. B
13. B
14. D
15. B

PHILOSOPHY, PRINCIPLES, PRACTICES, AND TECHNICS OF SUPERVISION, ADMINISTRATION, MANAGEMENT, AND ORGANIZATION

TABLE OF CONTENTS

	Page
MEANING OF SUPERVISION	1
THE OLD AND THE NEW SUPERVISION	1
THE EIGHT (8) BASIC PRINCIPLES OF THE NEW SUPERVISION	1
I. Principle of Responsibility	1
II. Principle of Authority	2
III. Principle of Self-Growth	2
IV. Principle of Individual Worth	2
V. Principle of Creative Leadership	2
VI. Principle of Success and Failure	2
VII. Principle of Science	3
VIII. Principle of Cooperation	3
WHAT IS ADMINISTRATION?	3
I. Practices Commonly Classed as "Supervisory"	3
II. Practices Commonly Classed as "Administrative"	3
III. Practices Commonly Classed as Both "Supervisory" and "Administrative"	4
RESPONSIBILITIES OF THE SUPERVISOR	4
COMPETENCIES OF THE SUPERVISOR	4
THE PROFESSIONAL SUPERVISOR-EMPLOYEE RELATIONSHIP	4
MINI-TEXT IN SUPERVISION, ADMINISTRATION, MANAGEMENT, AND ORGANIZATION	5
I. Brief Highlights	5
A. Levels of Management	6
B. What the Supervisor Must Learn	6
C. A Definition of Supervision	6
D. Elements of the Team Concept	6
E. Principles of Organization	6
F. The Four Important Parts of Every Job	7
G. Principles of Delegation	7
H. Principles of Effective Communications	7
I. Principles of Work Improvement	7
J. Areas of Job Improvement	7
K. Seven Key Points in Making Improvements	8

	L.	Corrective Techniques for Job Improvement	8
	M.	A Planning Checklist	8
	N.	Five Characteristics of Good Directions	9
	O.	Types of Directions	9
	P.	Controls	9
	Q.	Orienting the New Employee	9
	R.	Checklist for Orienting New Employees	9
	S.	Principles of Learning	10
	T.	Causes of Poor Performance	10
	U.	Four Major Steps in On-the-Job Instructions	10
	V.	Employees Want Five Things	10
	W.	Some Don'ts in Regard to Praise	11
	X.	How to Gain Your Workers' Confidence	11
	Y.	Sources of Employee Problems	11
	Z.	The Supervisor's Key to Discipline	11
	AA.	Five Important Processes of Management	12
	BB.	When the Supervisor Fails to Plan	12
	CC.	Fourteen General Principles of Management	12
	DD.	Change	12
II.	Brief Topical Summaries		13
	A.	Who/What is the Supervisor?	13
	B.	The Sociology of Work	13
	C.	Principles and Practices of Supervision	14
	D.	Dynamic Leadership	14
	E.	Processes for Solving Problems	15
	F.	Training for Results	15
	G.	Health, Safety, and Accident Prevention	16
	H.	Equal Employment Opportunity	16
	I.	Improving Communications	16
	J.	Self-Development	17
	K.	Teaching and Training	17
		1. The Teaching Process	17
		a. Preparation	17
		b. Presentation	18
		c. Summary	18
		d. Application	18
		e. Evaluation	18
		2. Teaching Methods	18
		a. Lecture	18
		b. Discussion	18
		c. Demonstration	19
		d. Performance	19
		e. Which Method to Use	19

PHILOSOPHY, PRINCIPLES, PRACTICES, AND TECHNICS
OF
SUPERVISION, ADMINISTRATION, MANAGEMENT, AND ORGANIZATION

MEANING OF SUPERVISION

The extension of the democratic philosophy has been accompanied by an extension in the scope of supervision. Modern leaders and supervisors no longer think of supervision in the narrow sense of being confined chiefly to visiting employees, supplying materials, or rating the staff. They regard supervision as being intimately related to all the concerned agencies of society, they speak of the supervisor's function in terms of "growth," rather than the "improvement" of employees.

This modern concept of supervision may be defined as follows: Supervision is leadership and the development of leadership within groups which are cooperatively engaged in inspection, research, training, guidance, and evaluation.

THE OLD AND THE NEW SUPERVISION

TRADITIONAL
1. Inspection
2. Focused on the employee
3. Visitation
4. Random and haphazard
5. Imposed and authoritarian
6. One person usually

MODERN
1. Study and analysis
2. Focused on aims, materials, methods, supervisors, employees, environment
3. Demonstrations, intervisitation, workshops, directed reading, bulletins, etc.
4. Definitely organized and planned (scientific)
5. Cooperative and democratic
6. Many persons involved (creative)

THE EIGHT (8) BASIC PRINCIPLES OF THE NEW SUPERVISION

I. Principle of Responsibility
   Authority to act and responsibility for acting must be joined.
   A. If you give responsibility, give authority.
   B. Define employee duties clearly.
   C. Protect employees from criticism by others.
   D. Recognize the rights as well as obligations of employees.
   E. Achieve the aims of a democratic society insofar as it is possible within the area of your work.
   F. Establish a situation favorable to training and learning.
   G. Accept ultimate responsibility for everything done in your section, unit, office, division, department.
   H. Good administration and good supervision are inseparable.

II. Principle of Authority
The success of the supervisor is measured by the extent to which the power of authority is not used.
   A. Exercise simplicity and informality in supervision
   B. Use the simplest machinery of supervision
   C. If it is good for the organization as a whole, it is probably justified.
   D. Seldom be arbitrary or authoritative.
   E. Do not base your work on the power of position or of personality.
   F. Permit and encourage the free expression of opinions.

III. Principle of Self-Growth
The success of the supervisor is measured by the extent to which, and the speed with which, he is no longer needed.
   A. Base criticism on principles, not on specifics.
   B. Point out higher activities to employees.
   C. Train for self-thinking by employees to meet new situations.
   D. Stimulate initiative, self-reliance, and individual responsibility
   E. Concentrate on stimulating the growth of employees rather than on removing defects.

IV. Principle of Individual Worth
Respect for the individual is a paramount consideration in supervision.
   A. Be human and sympathetic in dealing with employees.
   B. Don't nag about things to be done.
   C. Recognize the individual differences among employees and seek opportunities to permit best expression of each personality.

V. Principle of Creative Leadership
The best supervision is that which is not apparent to the employee.
   A. Stimulate, don't drive employees to creative action.
   B. Emphasize doing good things.
   C. Encourage employees to do what they do best.
   D. Do not be too greatly concerned with details of subject or method.
   E. Do not be concerned exclusively with immediate problems and activities.
   F. Reveal higher activities and make them both desired and maximally possible.
   G. Determine procedures in the light of each situation but see that these are derived from a sound basic philosophy.
   H. Aid, inspire, and lead so as to liberate the creative spirit latent in all good employees.

VI. Principle of Success and Failure
There are no unsuccessful employees, only unsuccessful supervisors who have failed to give proper leadership.
   A. Adapt suggestions to the capacities, attitudes, and prejudices of employees.
   B. Be gradual, be progressive, be persistent.
   C. Help the employee find the general principle; have the employee apply his own problem to the general principle.
   D. Give adequate appreciation for good work and honest effort.
   E. Anticipate employee difficulties and help to prevent them.
   F. Encourage employees to do the desirable things they will do anyway.
   G. Judge your supervision by the results it secures.

VII. Principle of Science
Successful supervision is scientific, objective, and experimental. It is based on facts, not on prejudices.
   A. Be cumulative in results.
   B. Never divorce your suggestions from the goals of training.
   C. Don't be impatient of results.
   D. Keep all matters on a professional, not a personal, level.
   E. Do not be concerned exclusively with immediate problems and activities.
   F. Use objective means of determining achievement and rating where possible.

VIII. Principle of Cooperation
Supervision is a cooperative enterprise between supervisor and employee.
   A. Begin with conditions as they are.
   B. Ask opinions of all involved when formulating policies.
   C. Organization is as good as its weakest link.
   D. Let employees help to determine policies and department programs.
   E. Be approachable and accessible—physically and mentally.
   F. Develop pleasant social relationships.

WHAT IS ADMINISTRATION

Administration is concerned with providing the environment, the material facilities, and the operational procedures that will promote the maximum growth and development of supervisors and employees. (Organization is an aspect and a concomitant of administration.)

There is no sharp line of demarcation between supervision and administration; these functions are intimately interrelated and, often, overlapping. They are complementary activities.

I. Practices Commonly Classed as "Supervisory"
   A. Conducting employees' conferences
   B. Visiting sections, units, offices, divisions, departments
   C. Arranging for demonstrations
   D. Examining plans
   E. Suggesting professional reading
   F. Interpreting bulletins
   G. Recommending in-service training courses
   H. Encouraging experimentation
   I. Appraising employee morale
   J. Providing for intervisitation

II. Practices Commonly Classified as "Administrative"
   A. Management of the office
   B. Arrangement of schedules for extra duties
   C. Assignment of rooms or areas
   D. Distribution of supplies
   E. Keeping records and reports
   F. Care of audio-visual materials
   G. Keeping inventory records
   H. Checking record cards and books

    I.   Programming special activities
    J.   Checking on the attendance and punctuality of employees

III.   Practices Commonly Classified as Both "Supervisory" and "Administrative"
    A.   Program construction
    B.   Testing or evaluating outcomes
    C.   Personnel accounting
    D.   Ordering instructional materials

RESPONSIBILITIES OF THE SUPERVISOR

A person employed in a supervisory capacity must constantly be able to improve his own efficiency and ability. He represent the employer to the employees and only continuous self-examination can make him a capable supervisor.

Leadership and training are the supervisor's responsibility. An efficient working unit is one in which the employees work with the supervisor. It is his job to bring out the best in his employees. He must always be relaxed, courteous, and calm in his association with his employees. Their feelings are important, and a harsh attitude does not develop the most efficient employees.

COMPETENCES OF THE SUPERVISOR

I.   Complete knowledge of the duties and responsibilities of his position.
II.   To be able to organize a job, plan ahead, and carry through.
III.   To have self-confidence and initiative.
IV.   To be able to handle the unexpected situation and make quick decisions.
V.   To be able to properly train subordinates in the positions they are best suited for.
VI.   To be able to keep good human relations among his subordinates.
VII.   To be able to keep good human relations between his subordinates and himself and to earn their respect and trust.

THE PROFESSIONAL SUPERVISOR-EMPLOYEE RELATIONSHIP

There are two kinds of efficiency: one kind is only apparent and is produced in organizations through the exercise of mere discipline; this is but a simulation of the second, or true, efficiency which springs from spontaneous cooperation. If you are a manager, no matter how great or small your responsibility, it is your job, in the final analysis, to create and develop this involuntary cooperation among the people whom you supervise. For, no matter how powerful a combination of money, machines, and materials a company may have, this is a dead and sterile thing without a team of willing, thinking, and articulate people to guide it.

The following 21 points are presented as indicative of the exemplary basic relationship that should exist between supervisor and employee:

1. Each person wants to be liked and respected by his fellow employee and wants to be treated with consideration and respect by his superior.
2. The most competent employee will make an error. However, in a unit where good relations exist between the supervisor and his employees, tenseness and fear do not exist. Thus, errors are not hidden or covered up, and the efficiency of a unit is not impaired.

3. Subordinates resent rules, regulations, or orders that are unreasonable or unexplained.
4. Subordinates are quick to resent unfairness, harshness, injustices, and favoritism.
5. An employee will accept responsibility if he knows that he will be complimented for a job well done, and not too harshly chastised for failure; that his supervisor will check the cause of the failure, and, if it was the supervisor's fault, he will assume the blame therefore. If it was the employee's fault, his supervisor will explain the correct method or means of handling the responsibility.
6. An employee wants to receive credit for a suggestion he has made, that is used. If a suggestion cannot be used, the employee is entitled to an explanation. The supervisor should not say "no" and close the subject.
7. Fear and worry slow up a worker's ability. Poor working environment can impair his physical and mental health. A good supervisor avoids forceful methods, threats, and arguments to get a job done.
8. A forceful supervisor is able to train his employees individually and as a team, and is able to motivate them in the proper channels.
9. A mature supervisor is able to properly evaluate his subordinates and to keep them happy and satisfied.
10. A sensitive supervisor will never patronize his subordinates.
11. A worthy supervisor will respect his employees' confidences.
12. Definite and clear-cut responsibilities should be assigned to each executive.
13. Responsibility should always be coupled with corresponding authority.
14. No change should be made in the scope or responsibilities of a position without a definite understanding to that effect on the part of all persons concerned.
15. No executive or employee, occupying a single position in the organization, should be subject to definite orders from more than one source.
16. Orders should never be given to subordinates over the head of a responsible executive. Rather than do this, the officer in question should be supplanted.
17. Criticisms of subordinates should, whoever possible, be made privately, and in no case should a subordinate be criticized in the presence of executives or employees of equal or lower rank.
18. No dispute or difference between executives or employees as to authority or responsibilities should be considered too trivial for prompt and careful adjudication.
19. Promotions, wage changes, and disciplinary action should always be approved by the executive immediately superior to the one directly responsible.
20. No executive or employee should ever be required, or expected, to be at the same time an assistant to, and critic of, another.
21. Any executive whose work is subject to regular inspection should, wherever practicable, be given the assistance and facilities necessary to enable him to maintain an independent check of the quality of his work.

MINI-TEXT IN SUPERVISION, ADMINISTRATION, MANAGEMENT, AND ORGANIZATION

I. Brief Highlights

Listed concisely and sequentially are major headings and important data in the field for quick recall and review.

A. Levels of Management
Any organization of some size has several levels of management. In terms of a ladder, the levels are:

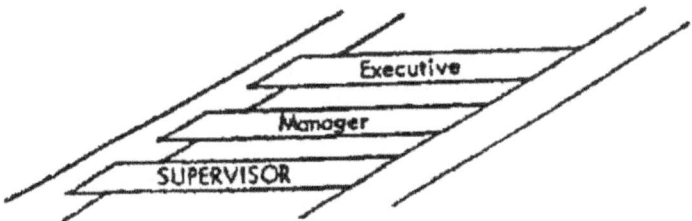

The first level is very important because it is the beginning point of management leadership.

B. What the Supervisor Must Learn
A supervisor must learn to:
1. Deal with people and their differences
2. Get the job done through people
3. Recognize the problems when they exist
4. Overcome obstacles to good performance
5. Evaluate the performance of people
6. Check his own performance in terms of accomplishment

C. A Definition of Supervisor
The term supervisor means any individual having authority, in the interests of the employer, to hire, transfer, suspend, lay-off, recall, promote, discharge, assign, reward, or discipline other employees or responsibility to direct them, or to adjust their grievances, or effectively to recommend such action, if, in connection with the foregoing, exercise of such authority is not of a merely routine or clerical nature but requires the use of independent judgment.

D. Elements of the Team Concept
What is involved in teamwork? The component parts are:
1. Members
2. A leader
3. Goals
4. Plans
5. Cooperation
6. Spirit

E. Principles of Organization
1. A team member must know what his job is.
2. Be sure that the nature and scope of a job are understood.
3. Authority and responsibility should be carefully spelled out.
4. A supervisor should be permitted to make the maximum number of decisions affecting his employees.
5. Employees should report to only one supervisor.
6. A supervisor should direct only as many employees as he can handle effectively.
7. An organization plan should be flexible.

8. Inspection and performance of work should be separate.
9. Organizational problems should receive immediate attention.
10. Assign work in line with ability and experience.

F. The Four Important Parts of Every Job
1. Inherent in every job is the *accountability* for results.
2. A second set of factors in every job is *responsibilities*.
3. Along with duties and responsibilities one must have the *authority* to act within certain limits without obtaining permission to proceed.
4. No job exists in a vacuum. The supervisor is surrounded by key *relationships*.

G. Principles of Delegation
Where work is delegated for the first time, the supervisor should think in terms of these questions:
1. Who is best qualified to do this?
2. Can an employee improve his abilities by doing this?
3. How long should an employee spend on this?
4. Are there any special problems for which he will need guidance?
5. How broad a delegation can I make?

H. Principles of Effective Communications
1. Determine the media.
2. To whom directed?
3. Identification and source authority.
4. Is communication understood?

I. Principles of Work Improvement
1. Most people usually do only the work which is assigned to them.
2. Workers are likely to fit assigned work into the time available to perform it.
3. A good workload usually stimulates output.
4. People usually do their best work when they know that results will be reviewed or inspected.
5. Employees usually feel that someone else is responsible for conditions of work, workplace layout, job methods, type of tools/equipment, and other such factors.
6. Employees are usually defensive about their job security.
7. Employees have natural resistance to change.
8. Employees can support or destroy a supervisor.
9. A supervisor usually earns the respect of his people through his personal example of diligence and efficiency.

J. Areas of Job Improvement
The areas of job improvement are quite numerous, but the most common ones which a supervisor can identify and utilize are:
1. Departmental layout
2. Flow of work
3. Workplace layout
4. Utilization of manpower
5. Work methods
6. Materials handling

7. Utilization
8. Motion economy

K. Seven Key Points in Making Improvements
1. Select the job to be improved
2. Study how it is being done now
3. Question the present method
4. Determine actions to be taken
5. Chart proposed method
6. Get approval and apply
7. Solicit worker participation

l. Corrective Techniques of Job Improvement
Specific Problems
1. Size of workload
2. Inability to meet schedules
3. Strain and fatigue
4. Improper use of men and skills
5. Waste, poor quality, unsafe conditions
6. Bottleneck conditions that hinder output
7. Poor utilization of equipment and machine
8. Efficiency and productivity of labor

General Improvement
1. Departmental layout
2. Flow of work
3. Work plan layout
4. Utilization of manpower
5. Work methods
6. Materials handling
7. Utilization of equipment
8. Motion economy

Corrective Techniques
1. Study with scale model
2. Flow chart study
3. Motion analysis
4. Comparison of units produced to standard allowance
5. Methods analysis
6. Flow chart and equipment study
7. Down time vs. running time
8. Motion analysis

M. A Planning Checklist
1. Objectives
2. Controls
3. Delegations
4. Communications
5. Resources
6. Manpower

7. Equipment
8. Supplies and materials
9. Utilization of time
10. Safety
11. Money
12. Work
13. Timing of improvements

N. Five Characteristics of Good Directions
In order to get results, directions must be:
1. Possible of accomplishment
2. Agreeable with worker interests
3. Related to mission
4. Planned and complete
5. Unmistakably clear

O. Types of Directions
1. Demands or direct orders
2. Requests
3. Suggestion or implication
4. volunteering

P. Controls
A typical listing of the overall areas in which the supervisor should establish controls might be:
1. Manpower
2. Materials
3. Quality of work
4. Quantity of work
5. Time
6. Space
7. Money
8. Methods

Q. Orienting the New Employee
1. Prepare for him
2. Welcome the new employee
3. Orientation for the job
4. Follow-up

R. Checklist for Orienting New Employees   Yes   No
1. Do you appreciate the feelings of new employees
   when they first report for work?   ___   ___
2. Are you aware of the fact that the new employee must
   make a big adjustment to his job?   ___   ___
3. Have you given him good reasons for liking the job and
   the organization?   ___   ___
4. Have you prepared for his first day on the job?   ___   ___
5. Did you welcome him cordially and make him feel needed? ___   ___

	Yes	No

6. Did you establish rapport with him so that he feels free to talk and discuss matters with you? ___ ___
7. Did you explain his job to him and his relationship to you? ___ ___
8. Does he know that his work will be evaluated periodically on a basis that is fair and objective? ___ ___
9. Did you introduce him to his fellow workers in such a way that they are likely to accept him? ___ ___
10. Does he know what employee benefits he will receive? ___ ___
11. Does he understand the importance of being on the job and what to do if he must leave his duty station? ___ ___
12. Has he been impressed with the importance of accident prevention and safe practice? ___ ___
13. Does he generally know his way around the department? ___ ___
14. Is he under the guidance of a sponsor who will teach the right way of doing things? ___ ___
15. Do you plan to follow-up so that he will continue to adjust successfully to his job? ___ ___

S. Principles of Learning
  1. Motivation
  2. Demonstration or explanation
  3. Practice

T. Causes of Poor Performance
  1. Improper training for job
  2. Wrong tools
  3. Inadequate directions
  4. Lack of supervisory follow-up
  5. Poor communications
  6. Lack of standards of performance
  7. Wrong work habits
  8. Low morale
  9. Other

U. Four Major Steps in On-The-Job Instruction
  1. Prepare the worker
  2. Present the operation
  3. Tryout performance
  4. Follow-up

V. Employees Want Five Things
  1. Security
  2. Opportunity
  3. Recognition
  4. Inclusion
  5. Expression

W. Some Don'ts in Regard to Praise
1. Don't praise a person for something he hasn't done.
2. Don't praise a person unless you can be sincere.
3. Don't be sparing in praise just because your superior withholds it from you.
4. Don't let too much time elapse between good performance and recognition of it

X. How to Gain Your Workers' Confidence
Methods of developing confidence include such things as:
1. Knowing the interests, habits, hobbies of employees
2. Admitting your own inadequacies
3. Sharing and telling of confidence in others
4. Supporting people when they are in trouble
5. Delegating matters that can be well handled
6. Being frank and straightforward about problems and working conditions
7. Encouraging others to bring their problems to you
8. Taking action on problems which impede worker progress

Y. Sources of Employee Problems
On-the-job causes might be such things as:
1. A feeling that favoritism is exercised in assignments
2. Assignment of overtime
3. An undue amount of supervision
4. Changing methods or systems
5. Stealing of ideas or trade secrets
6. Lack of interest in job
7. Threat of reduction in force
8. Ignorance or lack of communications
9. Poor equipment
10. Lack of knowing how supervisor feels toward employee
11. Shift assignments

Off-the-job problems might have to do with:
1. Health
2. Finances
3. Housing
4. Family

Z. The Supervisor's Key to Discipline
There are several key points about discipline which the supervisor should keep in mind:
1. Job discipline is one of the disciplines of life and is directed by the supervisor.
2. It is more important to correct an employee fault than to fix blame for it.
3. Employee performance is affected by problems both on the job and off.
4. Sudden or abrupt changes in behavior can be indications of important employee problems.
5. Problems should be dealt with as soon as possible after they are identified.
6. The attitude of the supervisor may have more to do with solving problems than the techniques of problem solving.
7. Correction of employee behavior should be resorted to only after the supervisor is sure that training or counseling will not be helpful.

8. Be sure to document your disciplinary actions.
9. Make sure that you are disciplining on the basis of facts rather than personal feelings.
10. Take each disciplinary step in order, being careful not to make snap judgments, or decisions based on impatience.

AA. Five Important Processes of Management
1. Planning
2. Organizing
3. Scheduling
4. Controlling
5. Motivating

BB. When the Supervisor Fails to Plan
1. Supervisor creates impression of not knowing his job
2. May lead to excessive overtime
3. Job runs itself—supervisor lacks control
4. Deadlines and appointments missed
5. Parts of the work go undone
6. Work interrupted by emergencies
7. Sets a bad example
8. Uneven workload creates peaks and valleys
9. Too much time on minor details at expense of more important tasks

CC. Fourteen General Principles of Management
1. Division of work
2. Authority and responsibility
3. Discipline
4. Unity of command
5. Unity of direction
6. Subordination of individual interest to general interest
7. Remuneration of personnel
8. Centralization
9. Scalar chain
10. Order
11. Equity
12. Stability of tenure of personnel
13. Initiative
14. Esprit de corps

DD. Change

Bringing about change is perhaps attempted more often, and yet less well understood, than anything else the supervisor does. How do people generally react to change? (People tend to resist change that is imposed upon them by other individuals or circumstances.

Change is characteristic of every situation. It is a part of every real endeavor where the efforts of people are concerned.

1. Why do people resist change?
   People may resist change because of:
   a. Fear of the unknown
   b. Implied criticism
   c. Unpleasant experiences in the past
   d. Fear of loss of status
   e. Threat to the ego
   f. Fear of loss of economic stability

2. How can we best overcome the resistance to change?
   In initiating change, take these steps:
   a. Get ready to sell
   b. Identify sources of help
   c. Anticipate objections
   d. Sell benefits
   e. Listen in depth
   f. Follow up

II. Brief Topical Summaries

   A. Who/What is the Supervisor?
      1. The supervisor is often called the "highest level employee and the lowest level manager."
      2. A supervisor is a member of both management and the work group. He acts as a bridge between the two.
      3. Most problems in supervision are in the area of human relations, or people problems.
      4. Employees expect: Respect, opportunity to learn and to advance, and a sense of belonging, and so forth.
      5. Supervisors are responsible for directing people and organizing work. Planning is of paramount importance.
      6. A position description is a set of duties and responsibilities inherent to a given position.
      7. It is important to keep the position description up-to-date and to provide each employee with his own copy.

   B. The Sociology of Work
      1. People are alike in many ways; however, each individual is unique.
      2. The supervisor is challenged in getting to know employee differences. Acquiring skills in evaluating individuals is an asset.
      3. Maintaining meaningful working relationships in the organization is of great importance.
      4. The supervisor has an obligation to help individuals to develop to their fullest potential.
      5. Job rotation on a planned basis helps to build versatility and to maintain interest and enthusiasm in work groups.
      6. Cross training (job rotation) provides backup skills.

7. The supervisor can help reduce tension by maintaining a sense of humor, providing guidance to employees, and by making reasonable and timely decisions. Employees respond favorably to working under reasonably predictable circumstances.
8. Change is characteristic of all managerial behavior. The supervisor must adjust to changes in procedures, new methods, technological changes, and to a number of new and sometimes challenging situations.
9. To overcome the natural tendency for people to resist change, the supervisor should become more skillful in initiating change.

C. Principles and Practices of Supervision
1. Employees should be required to answer to only one superior.
2. A supervisor can effectively direct only a limited number of employees, depending upon the complexity, variety, and proximity of the jobs involved.
3. The organizational chart presents the organization in graphic form. It reflects lines of authority and responsibility as well as interrelationships of units within the organization.
4. Distribution of work can be improved through an analysis using the "Work Distribution Chart."
5. The "Work Distribution Chart" reflects the division of work within a unit in understandable form.
6. When related tasks are given to an employee, he has a better chance of increasing his skills through training.
7. The individual who is given the responsibility for tasks must also be given the appropriate authority to insure adequate results.
8. The supervisor should delegate repetitive, routine work. Preparation of recurring reports, maintaining leave and attendance records are some examples.
9. Good discipline is essential to good task performance. Discipline is reflected in the actions of employees on the job in the absence of supervision.
10. Disciplinary action may have to be taken when the positive aspects of discipline have failed. Reprimand, warning, and suspension are examples of disciplinary action.
11. If a situation calls for a reprimand, be sure it is deserved and remember it is to be done in private.

D. Dynamic Leadership
1. A style is a personal method or manner of exerting influence.
2. Authoritarian leaders often see themselves as the source of power and authority.
3. The democratic leader often perceives the group as the source of authority and power.
4. Supervisors tend to do better when using the pattern of leadership that is most natural for them.
5. Social scientists suggest that the effective supervisor use the leadership style that best fits the problem or circumstances involved.
6. All four styles—telling, selling, consulting, joining—have their place. Using one does not preclude using the other at another time.

7. The theory X point of view assumes that the average person dislikes work, will avoid it whenever possible, and must be coerced to achieve organizational objectives.
8. The theory Y point of view assumes that the average person considers work to be a natural as play, and, when the individual is committed, he requires little supervision or direction to accomplish desired objectives.
9. The leader's basic assumptions concerning human behavior and human nature affect his actions, decisions, and other managerial practices.
10. Dissatisfaction among employees is often present, but difficult to isolate. The supervisor should seek to weaken dissatisfaction by keeping promises, being sincere and considerate, keeping employees informed, and so forth.
11. Constructive suggestions should be encouraged during the natural progress of the work.

E. Processes for Solving Problems
1. People find their daily tasks more meaningful and satisfying when they can improve them.
2. The causes of problems, or the key factors, are often hidden in the background. Ability to solve problems often involves the ability to isolate them from their backgrounds. There is some substance to the cliché that some persons "can't see the forest for the trees."
3. New procedures are often developed from old ones. Problems should be broken down into manageable parts. New ideas can be adapted from old one.
4. People think differently in problem-solving situations. Using a logical, patterned approach is often useful. One approach found to be useful includes these steps:
   a. Define the problem
   b. Establish objectives
   c. Get the facts
   d. Weigh and decide
   e. Take action
   f. Evaluate action

F. Training for Results
1. Participants respond best when they feel training is important to them.
2. The supervisor has responsibility for the training and development of those who report to him.
3. When training is delegated to others, great care must be exercised to insure the trainer has knowledge, aptitude, and interest for his work as a trainer.
4. Training (learning) of some type goes on continually. The most successful supervisor makes certain the learning contributes in a productive manner to operational goals.
5. New employees are particularly susceptible to training. Older employees facing new job situations require specific training, as well as having need for development and growth opportunities.
6. Training needs require continuous monitoring.
7. The training officer of an agency is a professional with a responsibility to assist supervisors in solving training problems.

8. Many of the self-development steps important to the supervisor's own growth are equally important to the development of peers and subordinates. Knowledge of these is important when the supervisor consults with others on development and growth opportunities.

G. Health, Safety, and Accident Prevention
1. Management-minded supervisors take appropriate measures to assist employees in maintaining health and in assuring safe practices in the work environment.
2. Effective safety training and practices help to avoid injury and accidents.
3. Safety should be a management goal. All infractions of safety which are observed should be corrected without exception.
4. Employees' safety attitude, training and instruction, provision of safe tools and equipment, supervision, and leadership are considered highly important factors which contribute to safety and which can be influenced directly by supervisors.
5. When accidents do occur, they should be investigated promptly for very important reasons, including the fact that information which is gained can be used to prevent accidents in the future.

H. Equal Employment Opportunity
1. The supervisor should endeavor to treat all employees fairly, without regard to religion, race, sex, or national origin.
2. Groups tend to reflect the attitude of the leader. Prejudice can be detected even in very subtle form. Supervisors must strive to create a feeling of mutual respect and confidence in every employee.
3. Complete utilization of all human resources is a national goal. Equitable consideration should be accorded women in the work force, minority-group members, the physically and mentally handicapped, and the older employee. The important question is: "Who can do the job?"
4. Training opportunities, recognition for performance, overtime assignments, promotional opportunities, and all other personnel actions are to be handled on an equitable basis.

I. Improving Communications
1. Communications is achieving understanding between the sender and the receiver of a message. It also means sharing information—the creation of understanding.
2. Communication is basic to all human activity. Words are means of conveying meanings; however, real meanings are in people.
3. There are very practical differences in the effectiveness of one-way, impersonal, and two-way communications. Words spoken face-to-face are better understood. Telephone conversations are effective, but lack the rapport of person-to-person exchanges. The whole person communicates.
4. Cooperation and communication in an organization go hand in hand. When there is a mutual respect between people, spelling out rules and procedures for communicating is unnecessary.
5. There are several barriers to effective communications. These include failure to listen with respect and understanding, lack of skill in feedback, and misinterpreting the meanings of words used by the speaker. It is also common

practice to listen to what we want to hear, and tune out things we do not want to hear.
    6. Communication is management's chief problem. The supervisor should accept the challenge to communicate more effectively and to improve interagency and intra-agency communications.
    7. The supervisor may often plan for and conduct meetings. The planning phase is critical and may determine the success or the failure of a meeting.
    8. Speaking before groups usually requires extra effort. Stage fright may never disappear completely, but it can be controlled.

J. Self-Development
    1. Every employee is responsible for his own self-development.
    2. Toastmaster and toastmistress clubs offer opportunities to improve skills in oral communications.
    3. Planning for one's own self-development is of vital importance. Supervisors know their own strengths and limitations better than anyone else.
    4. Many opportunities are open to aid the supervisor in his developmental efforts, including job assignments; training opportunities, both governmental and non-governmental—to include universities and professional conferences and seminars.
    5. Programmed instruction offers a means of studying at one's own rate.
    6. Where difficulties may arise from a supervisor's being away from his work for training, he may participate in televised home study or correspondence courses to meet his self-development needs.

K. Teaching and Training
    1. The Teaching Process
    Teaching is encouraging and guiding the learning activities of students toward established goals. In most cases this process consists of five steps: preparation, presentation, summarization, evaluation, and application.

        a. Preparation
        Preparation is two-fold in nature; that of the supervisor and the employee. Preparation by the supervisor is absolutely essential to success. He must know what, when, where, how, and whom he will teach. Some of the factors that should be considered are:
        1) The objectives
        2) The materials needed
        3) The methods to be used
        4) Employee participation
        5) Employee interest
        6) Training aids
        7) Evaluation
        8) Summarization

        Employee preparation consists in preparing the employee to receive the material. Probably the most important single factor in the preparation of the employee is arousing and maintaining his interest. He must know the objectives of the training, why he is there, how the material can be used, and its importance to him.

b. Presentation
In presentation, have a carefully designed plan and follow it. The plan should be accurate and complete, yet flexible enough to meet situations as they arise. The method of presentation will be determined by the particular situation and objectives.

c. Summary
A summary should be made at the end of every training unit and program. In addition, there may be internal summaries depending on the nature of the material being taught. The important thing is that the trainee must always be able to understand how each part of the new material relates to the whole.

d. Application
The supervisor must arrange work so the employee will be given a chance to apply new knowledge or skills while the material is still clear in his mind and interest is high. The trainee does not really know whether he has learned the material until he has been given a chance to apply it. If the material is not applied, it loses most of its value.

e. Evaluation
The purpose of all training is to promote learning. To determine whether the training has been a success or failure, the supervisor must evaluate this learning.
In the broadest sense, evaluation includes all the devices, methods, skills, and techniques used by the supervisor to keep himself and the employees informed as to their progress toward the objectives they are pursuing. The extent to which the employee has mastered the knowledge, skills, and abilities, or changed his attitudes, as determined by the program objectives, is the extent to which instruction has succeeded or failed.
Evaluation should not be confined to the end of the lesson, day, or program but should be used continuously. We shall note later the way this relates to the rest of the teaching process.

2. Teaching Methods
A teaching method is a pattern of identifiable student and instructor activity used in presenting training material.
All supervisors are faced with the problem of deciding which method should be used at a given time.

a. Lecture
The lecture is direct oral presentation of material by the supervisor. The present trend is to place less emphasis on the trainer's activity and more on that of the trainee.

b. Discussion
Teaching by discussion or conference involves using questions and other techniques to arouse interest and focus attention upon certain areas, and by doing so creating a learning situation. This can be one of the most

valuable methods because it gives the employees an opportunity to express their ideas and pool their knowledge.

    c. Demonstration
The demonstration is used to teach how something works or how to do something. It can be used to show a principle or what the results of a series of actions will be. A well-staged demonstration is particularly effective because it shows proper methods of performance in a realistic manner.

    d. Performance
Performance is one of the most fundamental of all learning techniques or teaching methods. The trainee may be able to tell how a specific operation should be performed but he cannot be sure he knows how to perform the operation until he has done so.
As with all methods, there are certain advantages and disadvantages to each method.

    e. Which Method to Use
Moreover, there are other methods and techniques of teaching. It is difficult to use any method without other methods entering into it. In any learning situation, a combination of methods is usually more effective than any one method alone.

Finally, evaluation must be integrated into the other aspects of the teaching-learning process.

It must be used in the motivation of the trainees; it must be used to assist in developing understanding during the training; and it must be related to employee application of the results of training.

This is distinctly the role of the supervisor.

GLOSSARY OF LEGAL TERMS

TABLE OF CONTENTS

	Page
Action ... Affiant	1
Affidavit ... At Bar	2
At Issue ... Burden of Proof	3
Business ... Commute	4
Complainant ... Conviction	5
Cooperative ... Demur (v.)	6
Demurrage ... Endorsement	7
Enjoin ... Facsimile	8
Factor ... Guilty	9
Habeas Corpus ... Incumbrance	10
Indemnify ... Laches	11
Landlord and Tenant ... Malice	12
Mandamus ... Obiter Dictum	13
Object (v.) ... Perjury	14
Perpetuity ... Proclamation	15
Proffered Evidence ... Referee	16
Referendum ... Stare Decisis	17
State ... Term	18
Testamentary ... Warrant (Warranty) (v.)	19
Warrant (n.) ... Zoning	20

GLOSSARY OF LEGAL TERMS

A

ACTION - "Action" includes a civil action and a criminal action.

A FORTIORI - A term meaning you can reason one thing from the existence of certain facts.

A POSTERIORI - From what goes after; from effect to cause.

A PRIORI - From what goes before; from cause to effect.

AB INITIO - From the beginning.

ABATE - To diminish or put an end to.

ABET - To encourage the commission of a crime.

ABEYANCE - Suspension, temporary suppression.

ABIDE - To accept the consequences of.

ABJURE - To renounce; give up.

ABRIDGE - To reduce; contract; diminish.

ABROGATE - To annul, repeal, or destroy.

ABSCOND - To hide or absent oneself to avoid legal action.

ABSTRACT - A summary.

ABUT - To border on, to touch.

ACCESS - Approach; in real property law it means the right of the owner of property to the use of the highway or road next to his land, without obstruction by intervening property owners.

ACCESSORY - In criminal law, it means the person who contributes or aids in the commission of a crime.

ACCOMMODATED PARTY - One to whom credit is extended on the strength of another person signing a commercial paper.

ACCOMMODATION PAPER - A commercial paper to which the accommodating party has put his name.

ACCOMPLICE - In criminal law, it means a person who together with the principal offender commits a crime.

ACCORD - An agreement to accept something different or less than that to which one is entitled, which extinguishes the entire obligation.

ACCOUNT - A statement of mutual demands in the nature of debt and credit between parties.

ACCRETION - The act of adding to a thing; in real property law, it means gradual accumulation of land by natural causes.

ACCRUE - To grow to; to be added to.

ACKNOWLEDGMENT - The act of going before an official authorized to take acknowledgments, and acknowledging an act as one's own.

ACQUIESCENCE - A silent appearance of consent.

ACQUIT - To legally determine the innocence of one charged with a crime.

AD INFINITUM - Indefinitely.

AD LITEM - For the suit.

AD VALOREM - According to value.

ADJECTIVE LAW - Rules of procedure.

ADJUDICATION - The judgment given in a case.

ADMIRALTY - Court having jurisdiction over maritime cases.

ADULT - Sixteen years old or over (in criminal law).

ADVANCE - In commercial law, it means to pay money or render other value before it is due.

ADVERSE - Opposed; contrary.

ADVOCATE - (v.) To speak in favor of;
(n.) One who assists, defends, or pleads for another.

AFFIANT - A person who makes and signs an affidavit.

AFFIDAVIT - A written and sworn to declaration of facts, voluntarily made.
AFFINITY- The relationship between persons through marriage with the kindred of each other; distinguished from consanguinity, which is the relationship by blood.
AFFIRM - To ratify; also when an appellate court affirms a judgment, decree, or order, it means that it is valid and right and must stand as rendered in the lower court.
AFOREMENTIONED; AFORESAID - Before or already said.
AGENT - One who represents and acts for another.
AID AND COMFORT - To help; encourage.
ALIAS - A name not one's true name.
ALIBI - A claim of not being present at a certain place at a certain time.
ALLEGE - To assert.
ALLOTMENT - A share or portion.
AMBIGUITY - Uncertainty; capable of being understood in more than one way.
AMENDMENT - Any language made or proposed as a change in some principal writing.
AMICUS CURIAE - A friend of the court; one who has an interest in a case, although not a party in the case, who volunteers advice upon matters of law to the judge. For example, a brief amicus curiae.
AMORTIZATION - To provide for a gradual extinction of (a future obligation) in advance of maturity, especially, by periodical contributions to a sinking fund which will be adequate to discharge a debt or make a replacement when it becomes necessary.
ANCILLARY - Aiding, auxiliary.
ANNOTATION - A note added by way of comment or explanation.
ANSWER - A written statement made by a defendant setting forth the grounds of his defense.
ANTE - Before.
ANTE MORTEM - Before death.
APPEAL - The removal of a case from a lower court to one of superior jurisdiction for the purpose of obtaining a review.
APPEARANCE - Coming into court as a party to a suit.
APPELLANT - The party who takes an appeal from one court or jurisdiction to another (appellate) court for review.
APPELLEE - The party against whom an appeal is taken.
APPROPRIATE - To make a thing one's own.
APPROPRIATION - Prescribing the destination of a thing; the act of the legislature designating a particular fund, to be applied to some object of government expenditure.
APPURTENANT - Belonging to; accessory or incident to.
ARBITER - One who decides a dispute; a referee.
ARBITRARY - Unreasoned; not governed by any fixed rules or standard.
ARGUENDO - By way of argument.
ARRAIGN - To call the prisoner before the court to answer to a charge.
ASSENT - A declaration of willingness to do something in compliance with a request.
ASSERT - Declare.
ASSESS - To fix the rate or amount.
ASSIGN - To transfer; to appoint; to select for a particular purpose.
ASSIGNEE - One who receives an assignment.
ASSIGNOR - One who makes an assignment.
AT BAR - Before the court.

AT ISSUE - When parties in an action come to a point where one asserts something and the other denies it.
ATTACH - Seize property by court order and sometimes arrest a person.
ATTEST - To witness a will, etc.; act of attestation.
AVERMENT - A positive statement of facts.

B

BAIL - To obtain the release of a person from legal custody by giving security and promising that he shall appear in court; to deliver (goods, etc.) in trust to a person for a special purpose.
BAILEE - One to whom personal property is delivered under a contract of bailment.
BAILMENT - Delivery of personal property to another to be held for a certain purpose and to be returned when the purpose is accomplished.
BAILOR - The party who delivers goods to another, under a contract of bailment.
BANC (OR BANK) - Bench; the place where a court sits permanently or regularly; also the assembly of all the judges of a court.
BANKRUPT - An insolvent person, technically, one declared to be bankrupt after a bankruptcy proceeding.
BAR - The legal profession.
BARRATRY - Exciting groundless judicial proceedings.
BARTER - A contract by which parties exchange goods for other goods.
BATTERY - Illegal interfering with another's person.
BEARER - In commercial law, it means the person in possession of a commercial paper which is payable to the bearer.
BENCH - The court itself or the judge.
BENEFICIARY - A person benefiting under a will, trust, or agreement.
BEST EVIDENCE RULE, THE - Except as otherwise provided by statute, no evidence other than the writing itself is admissible to prove the content of a writing. This section shall be known and may be cited as the best evidence rule.
BEQUEST - A gift of personal property under a will.
BILL - A formal written statement of complaint to a court of justice; also, a draft of an act of the legislature before it becomes a law; also, accounts for goods sold, services rendered, or work done.
BONA FIDE - In or with good faith; honestly.
BOND - An instrument by which the maker promises to pay a sum of money to another, usually providing that upon performances of a certain condition the obligation shall be void.
BOYCOTT - A plan to prevent the carrying on of a business by wrongful means.
BREACH - The breaking or violating of a law, or the failure to carry out a duty.
BRIEF - A written document, prepared by a lawyer to serve as the basis of an argument upon a case in court, usually an appellate court.
BURDEN OF PRODUCING EVIDENCE - The obligation of a party to introduce evidence sufficient to avoid a ruling against him on the issue.
BURDEN OF PROOF - The obligation of a party to establish by evidence a requisite degree of belief concerning a fact in the mind of the trier of fact or the court. The burden of proof may require a party to raise a reasonable doubt concerning the existence of nonexistence of a fact or that he establish the existence or nonexistence of a fact by a preponderance of the evidence, by clear and convincing proof, or by proof beyond a reasonable doubt.

Except as otherwise provided by law, the burden of proof requires proof by a preponderance of the evidence.

BUSINESS, A - Shall include every kind of business, profession, occupation, calling or operation of institutions, whether carried on for profit or not.

BY-LAWS - Regulations, ordinances, or rules enacted by a corporation, association, etc., for its own government.

C

CANON - A doctrine; also, a law or rule, of a church or association in particular.

CAPIAS - An order to arrest.

CAPTION - In a pleading, deposition or other paper connected with a case in court, it is the heading or introductory clause which shows the names of the parties, name of the court, number of the case on the docket or calendar, etc.

CARRIER - A person or corporation undertaking to transport persons or property.

CASE - A general term for an action, cause, suit, or controversy before a judicial body.

CAUSE - A suit, litigation or action before a court.

CAVEAT EMPTOR - Let the buyer beware. This term expresses the rule that the purchaser of an article must examine, judge, and test it for himself, being bound to discover any obvious defects or imperfections.

CERTIFICATE - A written representation that some legal formality has been complied with.

CERTIORARI - To be informed of; the name of a writ issued by a superior court directing the lower court to send up to the former the record and proceedings of a case.

CHANGE OF VENUE - To remove place of trial from one place to another.

CHARGE - An obligation or duty; a formal complaint; an instruction of the court to the jury upon a case.

CHARTER - (n.) The authority by virtue of which an organized body acts;
    (v.) in mercantile law, it means to hire or lease a vehicle or vessel for transportation.

CHATTEL - An article of personal property.

CHATTEL MORTGAGE - A mortgage on personal property.

CIRCUIT - A division of the country, for the administration of justice; a geographical area served by a court.

CITATION - The act of the court by which a person is summoned or cited; also, a reference to legal authority.

CIVIL (ACTIONS)- It indicates the private rights and remedies of individuals in contrast to the word "criminal" (actions) which relates to prosecution for violation of laws.

CLAIM (n.) - Any demand held or asserted as of right.

CODICIL - An addition to a will.

CODIFY - To arrange the laws of a country into a code.

COGNIZANCE - Notice or knowledge.

COLLATERAL - By the side; accompanying; an article or thing given to secure performance of a promise.

COMITY - Courtesy; the practice by which one court follows the decision of another court on the same question.

COMMIT - To perform, as an act; to perpetrate, as a crime; to send a person to prison.

COMMON LAW - As distinguished from law created by the enactment of the legislature (called statutory law), it relates to those principles and rules of action which derive their authority solely from usages and customs of immemorial antiquity, particularly with reference to the ancient unwritten law of England. The written pronouncements of the common law are found in court decisions.

COMMUTE - Change punishment to one less severe.

COMPLAINANT - One who applies to the court for legal redress.
COMPLAINT - The pleading of a plaintiff in a civil action; or a charge that a person has committed a specified offense.
COMPROMISE - An arrangement for settling a dispute by agreement.
CONCUR - To agree, consent.
CONCURRENT - Running together, at the same time.
CONDEMNATION - Taking private property for public use on payment therefor.
CONDITION - Mode or state of being; a qualification or restriction.
CONDUCT - Active and passive behavior; both verbal and nonverbal.
CONFESSION - Voluntary statement of guilt of crime.
CONFIDENTIAL COMMUNICATION BETWEEN CLIENT AND LAWYER - Information transmitted between a client and his lawyer in the course of that relationship and in confidence by a means which, so far as the client is aware, discloses the information to no third persons other than those who are present to further the interest of the client in the consultation or those to whom disclosure is reasonably necessary for the transmission of the information or the accomplishment of the purpose for which the lawyer is consulted, and includes a legal opinion formed and the advice given by the lawyer in the course of that relationship.
CONFRONTATION - Witness testifying in presence of defendant.
CONSANGUINITY - Blood relationship.
CONSIGN - To give in charge; commit; entrust; to send or transmit goods to a merchant, factor, or agent for sale.
CONSIGNEE - One to whom a consignment is made.
CONSIGNOR - One who sends or makes a consignment.
CONSPIRACY - In criminal law, it means an agreement between two or more persons to commit an unlawful act.
CONSPIRATORS - Persons involved in a conspiracy.
CONSTITUTION - The fundamental law of a nation or state.
CONSTRUCTION OF GENDERS - The masculine gender includes the feminine and neuter.
CONSTRUCTION OF SINGULAR AND PLURAL - The singular number includes the plural; and the plural, the singular.
CONSTRUCTION OF TENSES - The present tense includes the past and future tenses; and the future, the present.
CONSTRUCTIVE - An act or condition assumed from other parts or conditions.
CONSTRUE - To ascertain the meaning of language.
CONSUMMATE - To complete.
CONTIGUOUS - Adjoining; touching; bounded by.
CONTINGENT - Possible, but not assured; dependent upon some condition.
CONTINUANCE - The adjournment or postponement of an action pending in a court.
CONTRA - Against, opposed to; contrary.
CONTRACT - An agreement between two or more persons to do or not to do a particular thing.
CONTROVERT - To dispute, deny.
CONVERSION - Dealing with the personal property of another as if it were one's own, without right.
CONVEYANCE - An instrument transferring title to land.
CONVICTION - Generally, the result of a criminal trial which ends in a judgment or sentence that the defendant is guilty as charged.

COOPERATIVE - A cooperative is a voluntary organization of persons with a common interest, formed and operated along democratic lines for the purpose of supplying services at cost to its members and other patrons, who contribute both capital and business.

CORPUS DELICTI - The body of a crime; the crime itself.

CORROBORATE - To strengthen; to add weight by additional evidence.

COUNTERCLAIM - A claim presented by a defendant in opposition to or deduction from the claim of the plaintiff.

COUNTY - Political subdivision of a state.

COVENANT - Agreement.

CREDIBLE - Worthy of belief.

CREDITOR - A person to whom a debt is owing by another person, called the "debtor."

CRIMINAL ACTION - Includes criminal proceedings.

CRIMINAL INFORMATION - Same as complaint.

CRITERION (sing.)

CRITERIA (plural) - A means or tests for judging; a standard or standards.

CROSS-EXAMINATION - Examination of a witness by a party other than the direct examiner upon a matter that is within the scope of the direct examination of the witness.

CULPABLE - Blamable.

CY-PRES - As near as (possible). The rule of *cy-pres* is a rule for the construction of instruments in equity by which the intention of the party is carried out *as near as may be*, when it would be impossible or illegal to give it literal effect.

D

DAMAGES - A monetary compensation, which may be recovered in the courts by any person who has suffered loss, or injury, whether to his person, property or rights through the unlawful act or omission or negligence of another.

DECLARANT - A person who makes a statement.

DE FACTO - In fact; actually but without legal authority.

DE JURE - Of right; legitimate; lawful.

DE MINIMIS - Very small or trifling.

DE NOVO - Anew; afresh; a second time.

DEBT - A specified sum of money owing to one person from another, including not only the obligation of the debtor to pay, but the right of the creditor to receive and enforce payment.

DECEDENT - A dead person.

DECISION - A judgment or decree pronounced by a court in determination of a case.

DECREE - An order of the court, determining the rights of all parties to a suit.

DEED - A writing containing a contract sealed and delivered; particularly to convey real property.

DEFALCATION - Misappropriation of funds.

DEFAMATION - Injuring one's reputation by false statements.

DEFAULT - The failure to fulfill a duty, observe a promise, discharge an obligation, or perform an agreement.

DEFENDANT - The person defending or denying; the party against whom relief or recovery is sought in an action or suit.

DEFRAUD - To practice fraud; to cheat or trick.

DELEGATE (v.)- To entrust to the care or management of another.

DELICTUS - A crime.

DEMUR (v.) - To dispute the sufficiency in law of the pleading of the other side.

DEMURRAGE - In maritime law, it means, the sum fixed or allowed as remuneration to the owners of a ship for the detention of their vessel beyond the number of days allowed for loading and unloading or for sailing; also used in railroad terminology.

DENIAL - A form of pleading; refusing to admit the truth of a statement, charge, etc.

DEPONENT - One who gives testimony under oath reduced to writing.

DEPOSITION - Testimony given under oath outside of court for use in court or for the purpose of obtaining information in preparation for trial of a case.

DETERIORATION - A degeneration such as from decay, corrosion or disintegration.

DETRIMENT - Any loss or harm to person or property.

DEVIATION - A turning aside.

DEVISE - A gift of real property by the last will and testament of the donor.

DICTUM (sing.)

DICTA (plural) - Any statements made by the court in an opinion concerning some rule of law not necessarily involved nor essential to the determination of the case.

DIRECT EVIDENCE - Evidence that directly proves a fact, without an inference or presumption, and which in itself if true, conclusively establishes that fact.

DIRECT EXAMINATION - The first examination of a witness upon a matter that is not within the scope of a previous examination of the witness.

DISAFFIRM - To repudiate.

DISMISS - In an action or suit, it means to dispose of the case without any further consideration or hearing.

DISSENT - To denote disagreement of one or more judges of a court with the decision passed by the majority upon a case before them.

DOCKET (n.) - A formal record, entered in brief, of the proceedings in a court.

DOCTRINE - A rule, principle, theory of law.

DOMICILE - That place where a man has his true, fixed and permanent home to which whenever he is absent he has the intention of returning.

DRAFT (n.) - A commercial paper ordering payment of money drawn by one person on another.

DRAWEE - The person who is requested to pay the money.

DRAWER - The person who draws the commercial paper and addresses it to the drawee.

DUPLICATE - A counterpart produced by the same impression as the original enlargements and miniatures, or by mechanical or electronic re-recording, or by chemical reproduction, or by other equivalent technique which accurately reproduces the original.

DURESS - Use of force to compel performance or non-performance of an act.

E

EASEMENT - A liberty, privilege, or advantage without profit, in the lands of another.

EGRESS - Act or right of going out or leaving; emergence.

EIUSDEM GENERIS - Of the same kind, class or nature. A rule used in the construction of language in a legal document.

EMBEZZLEMENT - To steal; to appropriate fraudulently to one's own use property entrusted to one's care.

EMBRACERY - Unlawful attempt to influence jurors, etc., but not by offering value.

EMINENT DOMAIN - The right of a state to take private property for public use.

ENACT - To make into a law.

ENDORSEMENT - Act of writing one's name on the back of a note, bill or similar written instrument.

ENJOIN - To require a person, by writ of injunction from a court of equity, to perform or to abstain or desist from some act.
ENTIRETY - The whole; that which the law considers as one whole, and not capable of being divided into parts.
ENTRAPMENT - Inducing one to commit a crime so as to arrest him.
ENUMERATED - Mentioned specifically; designated.
ENURE - To operate or take effect.
EQUITY - In its broadest sense, this term denotes the spirit and the habit of fairness, justness, and right dealing which regulate the conduct of men.
ERROR - A mistake of law, or the false or irregular application of law as will nullify the judicial proceedings.
ESCROW - A deed, bond or other written engagement, delivered to a third person, to be delivered by him only upon the performance or fulfillment of some condition.
ESTATE - The interest which any one has in lands, or in any other subject of property.
ESTOP - To stop, bar, or impede.
ESTOPPEL - A rule of law which prevents a man from alleging or denying a fact, because of his own previous act.
ET AL. (alii) - And others.
ET SEQ. (sequential) - And the following.
ET UX. (uxor) - And wife.
EVIDENCE - Testimony, writings, material objects, or other things presented to the senses that are offered to prove the existence or non-existence of a fact.
    Means from which inferences may be drawn as a basis of proof in duly constituted judicial or fact finding tribunals, and includes testimony in the form of opinion and hearsay.
EX CONTRACTU
EX DELICTO - In law, rights and causes of action are divided into two classes, those arising *ex contractu* (from a contract) and those arising *ex delicto* (from a delict or tort).
EX OFFICIO - From office; by virtue of the office.
EX PARTE - On one side only; by or for one.
EX POST FACTO - After the fact.
EX POST FACTO LAW - A law passed after an act was done which retroactively makes such act a crime.
EX REL. (relations) - Upon relation or information.
EXCEPTION - An objection upon a matter of law to a decision made, either before or after judgment by a court.
EXECUTOR (male)
EXECUTRIX (female) - A person who has been appointed by will to execute the will.
EXECUTORY - That which is yet to be executed or performed.
EXEMPT - To release from some liability to which others are subject.
EXONERATION - The removal of a burden, charge or duty.
EXTRADITION - Surrender of a fugitive from one nation to another.

F

F.A.S.- "Free alongside ship"; delivery at dock for ship named.
F.O.B.- "Free on board"; seller will deliver to car, truck, vessel, or other conveyance by which goods are to be transported, without expense or risk of loss to the buyer or consignee.
FABRICATE - To construct; to invent a false story.
FACSIMILE - An exact or accurate copy of an original instrument.

FACTOR - A commercial agent.
FEASANCE - The doing of an act.
FELONIOUS - Criminal, malicious.
FELONY - Generally, a criminal offense that may be punished by death or imprisonment for more than one year as differentiated from a misdemeanor.
FEME SOLE - A single woman.
FIDUCIARY - A person who is invested with rights and powers to be exercised for the benefit of another person.
FIERI FACIAS - A writ of execution commanding the sheriff to levy and collect the amount of a judgment from the goods and chattels of the judgment debtor.
FINDING OF FACT - Determination from proof or judicial notice of the existence of a fact. A ruling implies a supporting finding of fact; no separate or formal finding is required unless required by a statute of this state.
FISCAL - Relating to accounts or the management of revenue.
FORECLOSURE (sale) - A sale of mortgaged property to obtain satisfaction of the mortgage out of the sale proceeds.
FORFEITURE - A penalty, a fine.
FORGERY - Fabricating or producing falsely, counterfeited.
FORTUITOUS - Accidental.
FORUM - A court of justice; a place of jurisdiction.
FRAUD - Deception; trickery.
FREEHOLDER - One who owns real property.
FUNGIBLE - Of such kind or nature that one specimen or part may be used in the place of another.

G

GARNISHEE - Person garnished.
GARNISHMENT - A legal process to reach the money or effects of a defendant, in the possession or control of a third person.
GRAND JURY - Not less than 16, not more than 23 citizens of a county sworn to inquire into crimes committed or triable in the county.
GRANT - To agree to; convey, especially real property.
GRANTEE - The person to whom a grant is made.
GRANTOR - The person by whom a grant is made.
GRATUITOUS - Given without a return, compensation or consideration.
GRAVAMEN - The grievance complained of or the substantial cause of a criminal action.
GUARANTY (n.) - A promise to answer for the payment of some debt, or the performance of some duty, in case of the failure of another person, who, in the first instance, is liable for such payment or performance.
GUARDIAN - The person, committee, or other representative authorized by law to protect the person or estate or both of an incompetent (or of a *sui juris* person having a guardian) and to act for him in matters affecting his person or property or both. An incompetent is a person under disability imposed by law.
GUILTY - Establishment of the fact that one has committed a breach of conduct; especially, a violation of law.

H

HABEAS CORPUS - You have the body; the name given to a variety of writs, having for their object to bring a party before a court or judge for decision as to whether such person is being lawfully held prisoner.

HABENDUM - In conveyancing; it is the clause in a deed conveying land which defines the extent of ownership to be held by the grantee.

HEARING - A proceeding whereby the arguments of the interested parties are heared.

HEARSAY - A type of testimony given by a witness who relates, not what he knows personally, but what others have told hi, or what he has heard said by others.

HEARSAY RULE, THE - (a) "Hearsay evidence" is evidence of a statement that was made other than by a witness while testifying at the hearing and that is offered to prove the truth of the matter stated; (b) Except as provided by law, hearsay evidence is inadmissible; (c) This section shall be known and may be cited as the hearsay rule.

HEIR - Generally, one who inherits property, real or personal.

HOLDER OF THE PRIVILEGE - (a) The client when he has no guardian or conservator; (b) A guardian or conservator of the client when the client has a guardian or conservator; (c) The personal representative of the client if the client is dead; (d) A successor, assign, trustee in dissolution, or any similar representative of a firm, association, organization, partnership, business trust, corporation, or public entity that is no longer in existence.

HUNG JURY - One so divided that they can't agree on a verdict.

HUSBAND-WIFE PRIVILEGE - An accused in a criminal proceeding has a privilege to prevent his spouse from testifying against him.

HYPOTHECATE - To pledge a thing without delivering it to the pledgee.

HYPOTHESIS - A supposition, assumption, or toehry.

I

I.E. (id est) - That is.

IB., OR IBID.(ibidem) - In the same place; used to refer to a legal reference previously cited to avoid repeating the entire citation.

ILLICIT - Prohibited; unlawful.

ILLUSORY - Deceiving by false appearance.

IMMUNITY - Exemption.

IMPEACH - To accuse, to dispute.

IMPEDIMENTS - Disabilities, or hindrances.

IMPLEAD - To sue or prosecute by due course of law.

IMPUTED - Attributed or charged to.

IN LOCO PARENTIS - In place of parent, a guardian.

IN TOTO - In the whole; completely.

INCHOATE - Imperfect; unfinished.

INCOMMUNICADO - Denial of the right of a prisoner to communicate with friends or relatives.

INCOMPETENT - One who is incapable of caring for his own affairs because he is mentally deficient or undeveloped.

INCRIMINATION - A matter will incriminate a person if it constitutes, or forms an essential part of, or, taken in connection with other matters disclosed, is a basis for a reasonable inference of such a violation of the laws of this State as to subject him to liability to punishment therefor, unless he has become for any reason permanently immune from punishment for such violation.

INCUMBRANCE - Generally a claim, lien, charge or liability attached to and binding real property.

INDEMNIFY - To secure against loss or damage; also, to make reimbursement to one for a loss already incurred by him.
INDEMNITY - An agreement to reimburse another person in case of an anticipated loss falling upon him.
INDICIA - Signs; indications.
INDICTMENT - An accusation in writing found and presented by a grand jury charging that a person has committed a crime.
INDORSE - To write a name on the back of a legal paper or document, generally, a negotiable instrument
INDUCEMENT - Cause or reason why a thing is done or that which incites the person to do the act or commit a crime; the motive for the criminal act.
INFANT - In civil cases one under 21 years of age.
INFORMATION - A formal accusation of crime made by a prosecuting attorney.
INFRA - Below, under; this word occurring by itself in a publication refers the reader to a future part of the publication.
INGRESS - The act of going into.
INJUNCTION - A writ or order by the court requiring a person, generally, to do or to refrain from doing an act.
INSOLVENT - The condition of a person who is unable to pay his debts.
INSTRUCTION - A direction given by the judge to the jury concerning the law of the case.
INTERIM - In the meantime; time intervening.
INTERLOCUTORY - Temporary, not final; something intervening between the commencement and the end of a suit which decides some point or matter, but is not a final decision of the whole controversy.
INTERROGATORIES - A series of formal written questions used in the examination of a party or a witness usually prior to a trial.
INTESTATE - A person who dies without a will.
INURE - To result, to take effect.
IPSO FACTO - By the fact iself; by the mere fact.
ISSUE (n.) The disputed point or question in a case,

J

JEOPARDY - Danger, hazard, peril.
JOINDER - Joining; uniting with another person in some legal steps or proceeding.
JOINT - United; combined.
JUDGE - Member or members or representative or representatives of a court conducting a trial or hearing at which evidence is introduced.
JUDGMENT - The official decision of a court of justice.
JUDICIAL OR JUDICIARY - Relating to or connected with the administration of justice.
JURAT - The clause written at the foot of an affidavit, stating when, where and before whom such affidavit was sworn.
JURISDICTION - The authority to hear and determine controversies between parties.
JURISPRUDENCE - The philosophy of law.
JURY - A body of persons legally selected to inquire into any matter of fact, and to render their verdict according to the evidence.

L

LACHES - The failure to diligently assert a right, which results in a refusal to allow relief.

LANDLORD AND TENANT - A phrase used to denote the legal relation existing between the owner and occupant of real estate.
LARCENY - Stealing personal property belonging to another.
LATENT - Hidden; that which does not appear on the face of a thing.
LAW - Includes constitutional, statutory, and decisional law.
LAWYER-CLIENT PRIVILEGE - (1) A "client" is a person, public officer, or corporation, association, or other organization or entity, either public or private, who is rendered professional legal services by a lawyer, or who consults a lawyer with a view to obtaining professional legal services from him; (2) A "lawyer" is a person authorized, or reasonably believed by the client to be authorized, to practice law in any state or nation; (3) A "representative of the lawyer" is one employed to assist the lawyer in the rendition of professional legal services; (4) A communication is "confidential" if not intended to be disclosed to third persons other than those to whom disclosure is in furtherance of the rendition of professional legal services to the client or those reasonably necessary for the transmission of the communication.

General rule of privilege - A client has a privilege to refuse to disclose and to prevent any other person from disclosing confidential communications made for the purpose of facilitating the rendition of professional legal services to the client, (1) between himself or his representative and his lawyer or his lawyer's representative, or (2) between his lawyer and the lawyer's representative, or (3) by him or his lawyer to a lawyer representing another in a matter of common interest, or (4) between representatives of the client or between the client and a representative of the client, or (5) between lawyers representing the client.

LEADING QUESTION - Question that suggests to the witness the answer that the examining party desires.
LEASE - A contract by which one conveys real estate for a limited time usually for a specified rent; personal property also may be leased.
LEGISLATION - The act of enacting laws.
LEGITIMATE - Lawful.
LESSEE - One to whom a lease is given.
LESSOR - One who grants a lease
LEVY - A collecting or exacting by authority.
LIABLE - Responsible; bound or obligated in law or equity.
LIBEL (v.) - To defame or injure a person's reputation by a published writing.
(n.) - The initial pleading on the part of the plaintiff in an admiralty proceeding.
LIEN - A hold or claim which one person has upon the property of another as a security for some debt or charge.
LIQUIDATED - Fixed; settled.
LIS PENDENS - A pending civil or criminal action.
LITERAL - According to the language.
LITIGANT - A party to a lawsuit.
LITATION - A judicial controversy.
LOCUS - A place.
LOCUS DELICTI - Place of the crime.
LOCUS POENITENTIAE - The abandoning or giving up of one's intention to commit some crime before it is fully completed or abandoning a conspiracy before its purpose is accomplished.

M

MALFEASANCE - To do a wrongful act.
MALICE - The doing of a wrongful act Intentionally without just cause or excuse.

MANDAMUS - The name of a writ issued by a court to enforce the performance of some public duty.
MANDATORY (adj.) Containing a command.
MARITIME - Pertaining to the sea or to commerce thereon.
MARSHALING - Arranging or disposing of in order.
MAXIM - An established principle or proposition.
MINISTERIAL - That which involves obedience to instruction, but demands no special discretion, judgment or skill.
MISAPPROPRIATE - Dealing fraudulently with property entrusted to one.
MISDEMEANOR - A crime less than a felony and punishable by a fine or imprisonment for less than one year.
MISFEASANCE - Improper performance of a lawful act.
MISREPRESENTATION - An untrue representation of facts.
MITIGATE - To make or become less severe, harsh.
MITTIMUS - A warrant of commitment to prison.
MOOT (adj.) Unsettled, undecided, not necessary to be decided.
MORTGAGE - A conveyance of property upon condition, as security for the payment of a debt or the performance of a duty, and to become void upon payment or performance according to the stipulated terms.
MORTGAGEE - A person to whom property is mortgaged.
MORTGAGOR - One who gives a mortgage.
MOTION - In legal proceedings, a "motion" is an application, either written or oral, addressed to the court by a party to an action or a suit requesting the ruling of the court on a matter of law.
MUTUALITY - Reciprocation.

N

NEGLIGENCE - The failure to exercise that degree of care which an ordinarily prudent person would exercise under like circumstances.
NEGOTIABLE (instrument) - Any instrument obligating the payment of money which is transferable from one person to another by endorsement and delivery or by delivery only.
NEGOTIATE - To transact business; to transfer a negotiable instrument; to seek agreement for the amicable disposition of a controversy or case.
NOLLE PROSEQUI - A formal entry upon the record, by the plaintiff in a civil suit or the prosecuting officer in a criminal action, by which he declares that he "will no further prosecute" the case.
NOLO CONTENDERE - The name of a plea in a criminal action, having the same effect as a plea of guilty; but not constituting a direct admission of guilt.
NOMINAL - Not real or substantial.
NOMINAL DAMAGES - Award of a trifling sum where no substantial injury is proved to have been sustained.
NONFEASANCE - Neglect of duty.
NOVATION - The substitution of a new debt or obligation for an existing one.
NUNC PRO TUNC - A phrase applied to acts allowed to be done after the time when they should be done, with a retroactive effect.("Now for then.")

O

OATH - Oath includes affirmation or declaration under penalty of perjury.
OBITER DICTUM - Opinion expressed by a court on a matter not essentially involved in a case and hence not a decision; also called dicta, if plural.

OBJECT (v.) - To oppose as improper or illegal and referring the question of its propriety or legality to the court.
OBLIGATION - A legal duty, by which a person is bound to do or not to do a certain thing.
OBLIGEE - The person to whom an obligation is owed.
OBLIGOR - The person who is to perform the obligation.
OFFER (v.) - To present for acceptance or rejection.
    (n.) - A proposal to do a thing, usually a proposal to make a contract.
OFFICIAL INFORMATION - Information within the custody or control of a department or agency of the government the disclosure of which is shown to be contrary to the public interest.
OFFSET - A deduction.
ONUS PROBANDI - Burden of proof.
OPINION - The statement by a judge of the decision reached in a case, giving the law as applied to the case and giving reasons for the judgment; also a belief or view.
OPTION - The exercise of the power of choice; also a privilege existing in one person, for which he has paid money, which gives him the right to buy or sell real or personal property at a given price within a specified time.
ORDER - A rule or regulation; every direction of a court or judge made or entered in writing but not including a judgment.
ORDINANCE - Generally, a rule established by authority; also commonly used to designate the legislative acts of a municipal corporation.
ORIGINAL - Writing or recording itself or any counterpart intended to have the same effect by a person executing or issuing it. An "original" of a photograph includes the negative or any print therefrom. If data are stored in a computer or similar device, any printout or other output readable by sight, shown to reflect the data accurately, is an "original."
OVERT - Open, manifest.

P

PANEL - A group of jurors selected to serve during a term of the court.
PARENS PATRIAE - Sovereign power of a state to protect or be a guardian over children and incompetents.
PAROL - Oral or verbal.
PAROLE - To release one in prison before the expiration of his sentence, conditionally.
PARITY - Equality in purchasing power between the farmer and other segments of the economy.
PARTITION - A legal division of real or personal property between one or more owners.
PARTNERSHIP - An association of two or more persons to carry on as co-owners a business for profit.
PATENT (adj.) - Evident.
    (n.) - A grant of some privilege, property, or authority, made by the government or sovereign of a country to one or more individuals.
PECULATION - Stealing.
PECUNIARY - Monetary.
PENULTIMATE - Next to the last.
PER CURIAM - A phrase used in the report of a decision to distinguish an opinion of the whole court from an opinion written by any one judge.
PER SE - In itself; taken alone.
PERCEIVE - To acquire knowledge through one's senses.
PEREMPTORY - Imperative; absolute.
PERJURY - To lie or state falsely under oath.

PERPETUITY - Perpetual existence; also the quality or condition of an estate limited so that it will not take effect or vest within the period fixed by law.
PERSON - Includes a natural person, firm, association, organization, partnership, business trust, corporation, or public entity.
PERSONAL PROPERTY - Includes money, goods, chattels, things in action, and evidences of debt.
PERSONALTY - Short term for personal property.
PETITION - An application in writing for an order of the court, stating the circumstances upon which it is founded and requesting any order or other relief from a court.
PLAINTIFF - A person who brings a court action.
PLEA - A pleading in a suit or action.
PLEADINGS - Formal allegations made by the parties of their respective claims and defenses, for the judgment of the court.
PLEDGE - A deposit of personal property as a security for the performance of an act.
PLEDGEE - The party to whom goods are delivered in pledge.
PLEDGOR - The party delivering goods in pledge.
PLENARY - Full; complete.
POLICE POWER - Inherent power of the state or its political subdivisions to enact laws within constitutional limits to promote the general welfare of society or the community.
POLLING THE JURY - Call the names of persons on a jury and requiring each juror to declare what his verdict is before it is legally recorded.
POST MORTEM - After death.
POWER OF ATTORNEY - A writing authorizing one to act for another.
PRECEPT - An order, warrant, or writ issued to an officer or body of officers, commanding him or them to do some act within the scope of his or their powers.
PRELIMINARY FACT - Fact upon the existence or nonexistence of which depends the admissibility or inadmissibility of evidence. The phrase "the admissibility or inadmissibility of evidence" includes the qualification or disqualification of a person to be a witness and the existence or nonexistence of a privilege.
PREPONDERANCE - Outweighing.
PRESENTMENT - A report by a grand jury on something they have investigated on their own knowledge.
PRESUMPTION - An assumption of fact resulting from a rule of law which requires such fact to be assumed from another fact or group of facts found or otherwise established in the action.
PRIMA FACUE - At first sight.
PRIMA FACIE CASE - A case where the evidence is very patent against the defendant.
PRINCIPAL - The source of authority or rights; a person primarily liable as differentiated from "principle" as a primary or basic doctrine.
PRO AND CON - For and against.
PRO RATA - Proportionally.
PROBATE - Relating to proof, especially to the proof of wills.
PROBATIVE - Tending to prove.
PROCEDURE - In law, this term generally denotes rules which are established by the Federal, State, or local Governments regarding the types of pleading and courtroom practice which must be followed by the parties involved in a criminal or civil case.
PROCLAMATION - A public notice by an official of some order, intended action, or state of facts.

PROFFERED EVIDENCE - The admissibility or inadmissibility of which is dependent upon the existence or nonexistence of a preliminary fact.
PROMISSORY (NOTE) - A promise in writing to pay a specified sum at an expressed time, or on demand, or at sight, to a named person, or to his order, or bearer.
PROOF - The establishment by evidence of a requisite degree of belief concerning a fact in the mind of the trier of fact or the court.
PROPERTY - Includes both real and personal property.
PROPRIETARY (adj.) - Relating or pertaining to ownership; usually a single owner.
PROSECUTE - To carry on an action or other judicial proceeding; to proceed against a person criminally.
PROVISO - A limitation or condition in a legal instrument.
PROXIMATE - Immediate; nearest
PUBLIC EMPLOYEE - An officer, agent, or employee of a public entity.
PUBLIC ENTITY - Includes a national, state, county, city and county, city, district, public authority, public agency, or any other political subdivision or public corporation, whether foreign or domestic.
PUBLIC OFFICIAL - Includes an official of a political dubdivision of such state or territory and of a municipality.
PUNITIVE - Relating to punishment.

Q

QUASH - To make void.
QUASI - As if; as it were.
QUID PRO QUO - Something for something; the giving of one valuable thing for another.
QUITCLAIM (v.) - To release or relinquish claim or title to, especially in deeds to realty.
QUO WARRANTO - A legal procedure to test an official's right to a public office or the right to hold a franchise, or to hold an office in a domestic corporation.

R

RATIFY - To approve and sanction.
REAL PROPERTY - Includes lands, tenements, and hereditaments.
REALTY - A brief term for real property.
REBUT - To contradict; to refute, especially by evidence and arguments.
RECEIVER - A person who is appointed by the court to receive, and hold in trust property in litigation.
RECIDIVIST - Habitual criminal.
RECIPROCAL - Mutual.
RECOUPMENT - To keep back or get something which is due; also, it is the right of a defendant to have a deduction from the amount of the plaintiff's damages because the plaintiff has not fulfilled his part of the same contract.
RECROSS EXAMINATION - Examination of a witness by a cross-examiner subsequent to a redirect examination of the witness.
REDEEM - To release an estate or article from mortgage or pledge by paying the debt for which it stood as security.
REDIRECT EXAMINATION - Examination of a witness by the direct examiner subsequent to the cross-examination of the witness.
REFEREE - A person to whom a cause pending in a court is referred by the court, to take testimony, hear the parties, and report thereon to the court.

REFERENDUM - A method of submitting an important legislative or administrative matter to a direct vote of the people.
RELEVANT EVIDENCE - Evidence including evidence relevant to the credulity of a witness or hearsay declarant, having any tendency in reason to prove or disprove any disputed fact that is of consequence to the determination of the action.
REMAND - To send a case back to the lower court from which it came, for further proceedings.
REPLEVIN - An action to recover goods or chattels wrongfully taken or detained.
REPLY (REPLICATION) - Generally, a reply is what the plaintiff or other person who has instituted proceedings says in answer to the defendant's case.
RE JUDICATA - A thing judicially acted upon or decided.
RES ADJUDICATA - Doctrine that an issue or dispute litigated and determined in a case between the opposing parties is deemed permanently decided between these parties.
RESCIND (RECISSION) - To avoid or cancel a contract.
RESPONDENT - A defendant in a proceeding in chancery or admiralty; also, the person who contends against the appeal in a case.
RESTITUTION - In equity, it is the restoration of both parties to their original condition (when practicable), upon the rescission of a contract for fraud or similar cause.
RETROACTIVE (RETROSPECTIVE) - Looking back; effective as of a prior time.
REVERSED - A term used by appellate courts to indicate that the decision of the lower court in the case before it has been set aside.
REVOKE - To recall or cancel.
RIPARIAN (RIGHTS) - The rights of a person owning land containing or bordering on a water course or other body of water, such as lakes and rivers.

S

SALE - A contract whereby the ownership of property is transferred from one person to another for a sum of money or for any consideration.
SANCTION - A penalty or punishment provided as a means of enforcing obedience to a law; also, an authorization.
SATISFACTION - The discharge of an obligation by paying a party what is due to him; or what is awarded to him by the judgment of a court or otherwise.
SCIENTER - Knowingly; also, it is used in pleading to denote the defendant's guilty knowledge.
SCINTILLA - A spark; also the least particle.
SECRET OF STATE - Governmental secret relating to the national defense or the international relations of the United States.
SECURITY - Indemnification; the term is applied to an obligation, such as a mortgage or deed of trust, given by a debtor to insure the payment or performance of his debt, by furnishing the creditor with a resource to be used in case of the debtor's failure to fulfill the principal obligation.
SENTENCE - The judgment formally pronounced by the court or judge upon the defendant after his conviction in a criminal prosecution.
SET-OFF - A claim or demand which one party in an action credits against the claim of the opposing party.
SHALL and MAY - "Shall" is mandatory and "may" is permissive.
SITUS - Location.
SOVEREIGN - A person, body or state in which independent and supreme authority is vested.
STARE DECISIS - To follow decided cases.

STATE - "State" means this State, unless applied to the different parts of the United States. In the latter case, it includes any state, district, commonwealth, territory or insular possession of the United States, including the District of Columbia.
STATEMENT - (a) Oral or written verbal expression or (b) nonverbal conduct of a person intended by him as a substitute for oral or written verbal expression.
STATUTE - An act of the legislature. Includes a treaty.
STATUTE OF LIMITATION - A statute limiting the time to bring an action after the right of action has arisen.
STAY - To hold in abeyance an order of a court.
STIPULATION - Any agreement made by opposing attorneys regulating any matter incidental to the proceedings or trial.
SUBORDINATION (AGREEMENT) - An agreement making one's rights inferior to or of a lower rank than another's.
SUBORNATION - The crime of procuring a person to lie or to make false statements to a court.
SUBPOENA - A writ or order directed to a person, and requiring his attendance at a particular time and place to testify as a witness.
SUBPOENA DUCES TECUM - A subpoena used, not only for the purpose of compelling witnesses to attend in court, but also requiring them to bring with them books or documents which may be in their possession, and which may tend to elucidate the subject matter of the trial.
SUBROGATION - The substituting of one for another as a creditor, the new creditor succeeding to the former's rights.
SUBSIDY - A government grant to assist a private enterprise deemed advantageous to the public.
SUI GENERIS - Of the same kind.
SUIT - Any civil proceeding by a person or persons against another or others in a court of justice by which the plaintiff pursues the remedies afforded him by law.
SUMMONS - A notice to a defendant that an action against him has been commenced and requiring him to appear in court and answer the complaint.
SUPRA - Above; this word occurring by itself in a book refers the reader to a previous part of the book.
SURETY - A person who binds himself for the payment of a sum of money, or for the performance of something else, for another.
SURPLUSAGE - Extraneous or unnecessary matter.
SURVIVORSHIP - A term used when a person becomes entitled to property by reason of his having survived another person who had an interest in the property.
SUSPEND SENTENCE - Hold back a sentence pending good behavior of prisoner.
SYLLABUS - A note prefixed to a report, especially a case, giving a brief statement of the court's ruling on different issues of the case.

T

TALESMAN - Person summoned to fill a panel of jurors.
TENANT - One who holds or possesses lands by any kind of right or title; also, one who has the temporary use and occupation of real property owned by another person (landlord), the duration and terms of his tenancy being usually fixed by an instrument called "a lease."
TENDER - An offer of money; an expression of willingness to perform a contract according to its terms.
TERM - When used with reference to a court, it signifies the period of time during which the court holds a session, usually of several weeks or months duration.

TESTAMENTARY - Pertaining to a will or the administration of a will.
TESTATOR (male)
TESTATRIX (female) - One who makes or has made a testament or will.
TESTIFY (TESTIMONY) - To give evidence under oath as a witness.
TO WIT - That is to say; namely.
TORT - Wrong; injury to the person.
TRANSITORY - Passing from place to place.
TRESPASS - Entry into another's ground, illegally.
TRIAL - The examination of a cause, civil or criminal, before a judge who has jurisdiction over it, according to the laws of the land.
TRIER OF FACT - Includes (a) the jury and (b) the court when the court is trying an issue of fact other than one relating to the admissibility of evidence.
TRUST - A right of property, real or personal, held by one party for the benefit of another.
TRUSTEE - One who lawfully holds property in custody for the benefit of another.

U

UNAVAILABLE AS A WITNESS - The declarant is (1) Exempted or precluded on the ground of privilege from testifying concerning the matter to which his statement is relevant; (2) Disqualified from testifying to the matter; (3) Dead or unable to attend or to testify at the hearing because of then existing physical or mental illness or infirmity; (4) Absent from the hearing and the court is unable to compel his attendance by its process; or (5) Absent from the hearing and the proponent of his statement has exercised reasonable diligence but has been unable to procure his attendance by the court's process.
ULTRA VIRES - Acts beyond the scope and power of a corporation, association, etc.
UNILATERAL - One-sided; obligation upon, or act of one party.
USURY - Unlawful interest on a loan.

V

VACATE - To set aside; to move out.
VARIANCE - A discrepancy or disagreement between two instruments or two aspects of the same case, which by law should be consistent.
VENDEE - A purchaser or buyer.
VENDOR - The person who transfers property by sale, particularly real estate; the term "seller" is used more commonly for one who sells personal property.
VENIREMEN - Persons ordered to appear to serve on a jury or composing a panel of jurors.
VENUE - The place at which an action is tried, generally based on locality or judicial district in which an injury occurred or a material fact happened.
VERDICT - The formal decision or finding of a jury.
VERIFY - To confirm or substantiate by oath.
VEST - To accrue to.
VOID - Having no legal force or binding effect.
VOIR DIRE - Preliminary examination of a witness or a juror to test competence, interest, prejudice, etc.

W

WAIVE - To give up a right.
WAIVER - The intentional or voluntary relinquishment of a known right.
WARRANT (WARRANTY) (v.) - To promise that a certain fact or state of facts, in relation to the subject matter, is, or shall be, as it is represented to be.

WARRANT (n.) - A writ issued by a judge, or other competent authority, addressed to a sheriff, or other officer, requiring him to arrest the person therein named, and bring him before the judge or court to answer or be examined regarding the offense with which he is charged.

WRIT - An order or process issued in the name of the sovereign or in the name of a court or judicial officer, commanding the performance or nonperformance of some act.

WRITING - Handwriting, typewriting, printing, photostating, photographing and every other means of recording upon any tangible thing any form of communication or representation, including letters, words, pictures, sounds, or symbols, or combinations thereof.

WRITINGS AND RECORDINGS - Consists of letters, words, or numbers, or their equivalent, set down by handwriting, typewriting, printing, photostating, photographing, magnetic impulse, mechanical or electronic recording, or other form of data compilation.

Y

YEA AND NAY - Yes and no.

YELLOW DOG CONTRACT - A contract by which employer requires employee to sign an instrument promising as condition that he will not join a union during its continuance, and will be discharged if he does join.

Z

ZONING - The division of a city by legislative regulation into districts and the prescription and application in each district of regulations having to do with structural and architectural designs of buildings and of regulations prescribing use to which buildings within designated districts may be put.

www.ingramcontent.com/pod-product-compliance
Lightning Source LLC
Chambersburg PA
CBHW081809300426
44116CB00014B/2290